Papers of the Fiftieth Algonquian Conference

Actes du cinquantième Congrès des Algonquinistes

PAPERS OF THE ALGONQUIAN CONFERENCES
ACTES DU CONGRÈS DES ALGONQUINISTES

50

Papers of the Fiftieth Algonquian Conference

Actes du cinquantième Congrès des Algonquinistes

EDITED BY Monica Macaulay and Margaret Noodin

MICHIGAN STATE UNIVERSITY PRESS | EAST LANSING

∞ The paper used in this publication meets the minimum requirements of ANSI/NISO Z39.48-1992 (R 1997) (Permanence of Paper).

Michigan State University Press
East Lansing, Michigan 48823-5245

Library of Congress Cataloging-in-Publication Data is available
ISBN 978-1-61186-383-3 (paper)
ISBN 978-1-60917-658-7 (PDF)

Book design by Charlie Sharp, Sharp Designs, East Lansing, Michigan
Cover design by Erin Kirk New
Cover detail of a quill box is used courtesy of Julie L. Loehr

Michigan State University Press is a member of the Green Press Initiative and is committed to developing and encouraging ecologically responsible publishing practices. For more information about the Green Press Initiative and the use of recycled paper in book publishing, please visit *www.greenpressinitiative.org*.

Visit Michigan State University Press at *www.msupress.org*

CONTENTS

PREFACE

The Fiftieth Algonquian Conference was held at the North Campus of the University of Alberta, in Edmonton, Alberta, from October 25 through 28, 2018. While located in Edmonton, this conference was a joint effort of several organizations and individuals on the Western Canadian Plains, co-hosted by Antti Arppe (University of Alberta), Inge Genee (University of Lethbridge, Alberta), and Arok Wolvengrey (First Nations University of Canada, Regina, Saskatchewan), as well as the Maskwacîs Education Schools Commission (MESC, Maskwacîs, Alberta). Based on the list of the locations and hosts of the 49 previous Algonquian Conferences, compiled by Amy Dahlstrom for the 50-Year Retrospective, this appeared to have been the first time that this conference took place anywhere east of the Rocky Mountains and west of Manitoba, where many Algonquian peoples such as the Cree, Blackfoot, and Ojibwe, as well as the Métis, continue to live.

Among all the things to pay attention to in organizing such a conference, the one thing that one has little control over, but still frets about in advance, is the weather, which in Alberta tends to be quite fickle. There have been years when students have been greeted for their first day of classes in September with sleet and subzero temperatures, and one could then not have avoided recalling Mordecai Richler's blunt characterization of Edmonton—at this point playing host to the conference for the first time. Indeed, the fall preceding the conference had been even more persistently cold, rainy, and overcast than usual, without the quite regular intervention of one or two weeks of summery warmth before or around Canadian Thanksgiving, to ease everyone into accepting the inevitable coming of winter. However, for once we were most fortunate in that the weather warmed up and the skies cleared just in time for the duration of the conference, presenting the city in the best possible light—maybe we will not have to wait another 50 years for the Algonquian Conference to be organized in these parts of Canada?

To mark this 50th occasion, we decided to organize a retrospective, with both established characters and fresher faces in the domain of Algonquian studies, on the topic: *Algonquian studies: Where did we come from and where we are going*? This retrospective took place on Saturday afternoon in advance of the conference dinner, and was chaired by Inge Genee, with speakers Antti Arppe, Amy Dahlstrom, Chris Wolfart, Rich Rhodes, Richard Preston (read by Arden Ogg), David Pentland, David Costa, Monica Macaulay, Margaret Noodin and some of her students (BillyJack Parent, Cynid Bergloff, and Nathon Breu), Mary Ann Corbiere (read by Inge Genee), Janine Metallic, Bernie Francis, and Dorothy Thunder. While one never knows how such a potpourri will end up playing out overall, with so many speakers, each having only a short allocation of time but full liberty to choose what to say, with a few speakers recruited literally at the last minute, in the end the retrospective both as a whole and in terms of the individual well-chosen anecdotes, personal recollections, and thoughtful observations worked out as well as we could have hoped for, and was very well received by the conference participants. We are glad that two presentations from the retrospective have been included as written contributions in these proceedings, and sincerely hope that the rest will also eventually find their way into print.

This 50th edition would not have been possible without the help and goodwill of many individuals and organizations. We were grateful to previous organizers, Jimena Terraza, Meg Noodin, Nicole Rosen, and Monica Macaulay, who shared their experiences (and budgets) with us, greatly facilitating our own planning. In recognizing the long local Algonquian history in Edmonton and beyond on the Plains, we were glad that Bruce Cutknife from MESC had the opportunity to welcome the conference participants on their behalf, as well as deliver an opening plenary on Cree place names in Alberta. We also want to recognize the significant efforts and initiative that our two local student organizers, Atticus Harrigan and Katherine Schmirler, put into making sure that the conference was realized in good order, in particular when the organizing faculty members were at times preoccupied writing a major funding proposal. Likewise, we are grateful to the current and former student and other local volunteers, in particular Maeghan Jerry, Taylor Casavant, and Eddie Santos, who ensured, for instance, that the classroom technology worked without a hitch, presentations kept to schedule, and coffee and tea remained plentiful, among many other small but important things. Also, we appreciated that the brand-new Royal Alberta Museum was able and willing to host us for the conference dinner. Finally, we want to thank the Department of Linguistics and the Faculty of Arts (at the University of Alberta) as well as the Social Sciences and Humanities Research Council of Canada (SSHRC) for the generous funding and practical support that they provided to make possible the organization of this conference.

Additional Conference Papers

In addition to the papers published in this volume, the following papers were presented at the conference:

Anti Arppe and Claudia Heinrich (University of Alberta): An Exploratory Corpus-Based Investigation of the Nominal Diminutive in Plains Cree.

Cynthia Bergloff, Nathon Breu, and BillyJack Parent (University of Wisconsin–Milwaukee): Contemporary Topics in Anishinaabemowin.

Jerome Biedny, Matthew Burner, Andrea Cudworth, and Monica Macaulay (University of Wisconsin–Madison): Classifier Medials Across Algonquian: A First Look.

Melissa Bishop and Allyson Eamer (University of Ontario Institute of Technology): Leveraging Digital Technologies for Language Revitalization: Elders' Perspective.

Heather Bliss (Simon Fraser University) and Martina Wiltschko (University of British Columbia): Blackfoot Demonstratives in Discourse.

Diane Campeau (Université de Sherbrooke): Indigenous Perspectives and Knowledges in the Public School: Challenging the Curriculum.

Vincent Collette (First Nations University of Canada): Aspects of the Morphosyntax of Creenglish in Eastern James Bay.

David J. Costa (Miami University): Verb Negation in Indiana Miami.

Christopher Cox (Carleton University), Olivia N. Sammons (University of Alberta/ Carleton University), Katie Thompson (Sauk Language Department, Sac and Fox Nation of Oklahoma), and Oliver Adams (Johns Hopkins University): Exploring Automatic Speech Recognition for Algonquian Languages.

Beverly Crier (Samson Cree Nation, Inter-Governmental Office), Brian Lightning (Samson Cree Nation), Bruce Cutknife (Samson Cree Nation, MESC), Ida Bull (Louis Bull Cree Nation, MESC), Betty Simon (Samson Cree Nation, MESC), and Jolene Rain (Samson Cree Nation, MESC): Maskwacîs Cree Language APP—Maskosis Goes to School.

Rose-Marie Déchaine (University of British Columbia): The Syntax of the Realis/ Irrealis Contrast in Nêhiyawêwin (Plains Cree).

Rose-Marie Déchaine (University of British Columbia), Monique Dufresne (Queen's University), and Charlotte Reinholtz (Queen's University): (In)Variance in the Cree Dialect Continuum: Evidence from (Ir)Realis Syntax.

Christopher Hammerly and Alex Göbel (University of Massachusetts Amherst): A "Perspective" on Obviation from Attitude Contexts.

Atticus G. Harrigan, Timothy Mills, and Antti Arppe (University of Alberta): Preliminary Speech Synthesis for Plains Cree.

Janine Metallic (McGill University): Indigenous Language Learning and Young Adults: A Look into the Experiences of Young Adult Mi'gmaw Language Learners.

Margaret Noodin (University of Wisconsin–Milwaukee): *Oshki-nagamowinan Abajitooyaang Ji-gikinoamawangidwa* // New Songs We Use to Teach.

Will Oxford (University of Manitoba): Subjecthood and the Algonquian Spurious Passive.

David Pentland (University of Manitoba): The Earliest Records of the Montagnais Language: Further Reassessments.

Sara Potkonjak (York University) Kimberly Cho (University of Toronto—Ontario Institute for Studies in Education (OISE)), Mary Ann Corbiere (University of Sudbury), Enrica Piccardo (University of Toronto), Alan Corbiere (Lakeview School, M'Chigeeng First Nation): Action-Oriented Learning in the Anishinaabemowin Context: Integrating Indigenous and Plurilingual Perspectives to Foster Language Revitalization.

Richard A. Rhodes (University of California, Berkley): Morphological Transitivity in Ojibwe.

Olivia N. Sammons (University of Alberta/Carleton University): Animacy and Gender in Michif.

Katherine Schmirler (University of Alberta) and Anja Arnhold (University of Alberta): Acoustic Correlates of Stress in Maskwacîs Plains Cree.

Lia Morgan Siewert (University of Texas): Scripted Fluency: Memorization and the Future of Anishinaabemowin Preservation.

Lucy Thomason (Smithsonian Institution): "They were taken a little ways off and thrown away next to a black oak on the north side where the sun did not strike."

50th Algonquian Conference Retrospective

Richard Preston

Gordon Day, at the (then) National Museum, launched the series at a motel in Ste Pierre de Wakefield, Quebec. There was a lake there and the motel had a canoe or two for the use of patrons. The idea was to be free of campus and dorm, and to have papers written in plain prose so nonspecialists could have the benefit of knowing what was going on in all fields of anthropology. The first paper was a survey of anthropology in northeastern North America. John Honigmann couldn't make it to the conference and asked me to read it in his place.

We had Bill Fenton there, from the Iroquoian conference group, Nick Smith, librarian at Ogdensburg, who had summered on reserves in the Eastern Algonquian area. Harold Hickerson gave a ramble of casual references to the Northern European fur trade, which we didn't know much about, but had only a few sheets of blank paper, in case he had an idea while on his ramble. Fenton broke in, "Man, where is your data?" HH replied "I don't have any." BF countered, "Well, go get some," so Hickerson sat down and we proceeded. Ives Goddard's paper was a deconstruction of his PhD supervisor's paper, which seemed a bit risky at the time. Ives later explained that he and Karl Teeter had an agreement that this was okay to do. I gave a paper on Cree songs and asked for guidance . . . none came.

Nick and I got out canoeing for an hour or so. We did likewise for the second

Algonquian Conference (AC), at Trent University. The third was a rustic resort at Big Moose, New York, hosted by Charles Bishop, and I believe Nick and I got out there, too. Canoeing is a good cure for conference-paper fatigue.

Already the linguists had forgone making their work comprehensible to nonlinguists . . . theoretical phonetics was simply too exciting to pay any heed to us unwashed. Some of us found this off-putting, and a few gave up on future conferences. Fritz Jennings, a fine historian, was the first to abandon. Others, like me, thought there might be some virtue in this variety of academic self-flagellation.

The ideal was set too high for us motley academics, and our locations dwindled down to universities and intellectual segmentation, and a published proceedings.

We did manage to attract one Algonquian presenter, Mildred Milliea. She described the native language curriculum project she worked on. It used a church-based orthography, and Ives asked her if there had been any linguists around to sell the IPA. She said, "Oh, yes, but we don't buy." Such is the gap between the intelligentsia and the folk.

I tried to revive the Gordon Day recipe by hosting the seventh at a hotel in Niagara-on-the-Lake. But the long view shows that the proceedings have provided a ready archive of hundreds of papers, so the goal that Gordon set was replaced by something of great value. It was also a congenial venue for grad students to dip their conference paper toes.

Bon voyage, wherever the AC takes you,

Dick Preston, still an ethnographer, with a few satirical items in the Algonquian and Iroquoian Linguistics Newsletter as "Old Porcupine's Corner." I recall John Nichols getting flack for it by some who thought he was writing it himself. Some people get quite anxious at being satirized.

Algonquian Studies

Where We Came from and Where We Are Going

Mary Ann Naokwegijig-Corbiere

My words do not speak directly to the topic, as I never thought of my work as engaging in Algonquian studies or even in studies of my own language. I do have a thought about where we—at least those concerned with the revitalization of Algonquian languages—ought to be going. Perhaps outlining briefly the roundabout path by which I happened upon this circle of scholars will explain the basis of my hopes with regard to my own language.

I learned of this distinguished circle by happenstance. I never knew there were scholars studying my language and providing so many marvelous insights into this gift my parents left me and my siblings. When I applied to a university, it was with the aim of contributing to the saving of the natural environment and its creatures. My life took a few unexpected turns, a fateful one being running into a former classmate from Grade 8—in a bar across from the Sudbury arena, the Sunday evening after the championship game in the annual Native Challenge Cup hockey tournament. That was a can't-miss event in Nishnaabe social calendars in the 1980s and we were always slow to make our way back to the rez and our workaday world. The former classmate was then part of a group working to establish the Native Social Work program at Laurentian. They needed a facilitator for community consultation workshops and she urged me to apply. The School of Social Work and the Department of Native Studies were collaborating on that initiative.

At the interview for that one-year contract job, Jim Dumont me asked the fateful question, "What do you think of your language?" It needed virtually no thought for me to answer, and I replied instantly, "I love it. That's why I came back home after university in Toronto, so I could be among speakers again." I had been away from home for high school and university from 1969 until 1979. It turned out that Native Studies was also looking for someone to teach Ojibway part-time that year. The instructor was off to do her master's. So when they offered me the workshop facilitator position, they asked if I could also teach the language one night a week. Though I loved my language, being a teacher of it was not something I believed was within my capabilities. "Well, you speak it so you'll be able to," they assured me, so I reluctantly gave it a try. To my surprise, I discovered I thoroughly enjoyed figuring out its wondrous workings so I could help students make sense in it. After the social work project job ended, I was asked if I wanted to write a correspondence course on introduction to Ojibway. Seeing how much I enjoyed trying to figure out its workings, I was less reluctant to give that a shot. *Sorry, whales. I must leave your saving to others.* The master's student didn't return and I applied for the full-time faculty position that thus opened up in 1989.

For the first few years of teaching, I still did not know of this fabulous circle of scholars. I was trying to figure out, largely on my own, how I could explain the mysterious workings of Ojibwe to learners. An instructional designer was always part of a distance course development team. That person was a vital mentor on general second-language teaching methods. The late, great Lena White—who had also worked on the Native Social Work project and was involved in the Native Language Instructors Program (NLIP)—was another important mentor. She introduced me to the Fiero system and shared workbooks she had developed for NLIP students. It wasn't until Native Studies hired Dr. Roger Spielmann a few years after I was hired that I learned of the work of people like Rand Valentine, John Nichols, and Richard Rhodes, and the knowledge such scholars had to offer. I was, to be honest, initially quite arrogant in my ignorance.

Not to give this as an excuse, but we Nishnaabek are a people proud of how we withstood the onslaught of colonization and retained our language, and who have a firm belief that WE have all the knowledge needed to teach our language. That ethos shaped how I went about trying to explain to learners the ways that eNshinaabemjik express their thoughts. The intermediate- and advanced-level correspondence courses I developed in the 1990s make some sense. But as I gained some knowledge, in bits and pieces, of relevant linguistic concepts—largely through attending Algonquian conferences, and Rand having taken me under his wing in a sense—I am now much better equipped to produce a pedagogical grammar. That I aim to do as my final project before I retire. The need for such is what leads to my suggestion regarding one of the paths Algonquian studies ought to be taking.

At this stage in the life of the Nishnaabemwin speech community, it's highly unlikely that, five or ten years hence, there will be mother-tongue speakers with an interest in making a vocation of teaching the language in a university context or pursuing linguistics studies with that end in mind. Besides, given the turn hiring is taking in universities, it seems unlikely that full-time Nishnaabemwin instructors will ever be hired again. This adds to the urgency of my concern.

It is wonderful to be able to imagine what our ancestors in the distant past might have sounded like, thanks to the research of Ives Goddard. It is great fun to see the morphology and phonology that underlies seeming quirks such as the verb *naa* sounding totally different when my fellow Wiky speakers ask someone, "*Gegoo na gii-ish*?" ('Did you say something to me?'). Now I have a better answer when students ask why that is, rather than saying simply, "That's just the way it's said." I have a better framework for presenting the complex ways our verbs morph as the actor and goal combination varies; as we wonder whether something might be so; and as we unconsciously surmise the reason for something. The challenge now is to figure out how the fruits of the wonderful research you as linguists do can be put to use to enable learners in our classes to make sense in Nishnaabemwin.

Not all universities that offer Nishnaabemwin courses have a linguistics program. Indigenous language courses are often housed in Indigenous Studies departments and are perhaps but one of the several courses required for an Indigenous Studies major. Mother-tongue speakers who get hired to teach come in—as was the case with me—usually with little if any knowledge of relevant linguistics concepts. Moreover, students invariably have a range of aptitudes. Rare are learners like Alan Corbiere, Jessica Shonias, and Monte McGahey, who can readily make use of a systematic approach of the sort I use in the Nishnaabemwin manuals, and who can decode linguistics terminology fairly readily with the aid of a linguistics dictionary. But many are those who see learning their language as absolutely essential to their completeness as Nishnaabek, but whose learning styles differ from that of people like those I've mentioned. Hence the value of projects such as "21st-century tools," and LINCDIRE's development of a task-based learning method. And hence my hope.

That hope is that the branch of Algonquian studies that works with Nishnaabemwin will also focus more on pedagogical tools and strategies that will give our languages a chance to remain living languages. Unless that's done, what will be left of them will be their "fleeting sounds" (Perley 2012:138) that will have been captured by those amazing and endlessly evolving technological tools while the last speakers still had breath. As coming generations of Algonquianists in the academy continue to prod and dissect them, our languages will be out of reach of those for whom they are an integral component of their identity, the thread that keeps them connected to their forebears. They will be saved, but simply as—in the words of Perley—"zombie voices—undead voices that are disembodied and techno-mechanized" (2012:133). Algonquian studies, I fervently hope, will help ensure they remain fully alive even if only among families like the McGaheys, the Treuers, and the Fairbanks.

REFERENCE

Perley, Bernard C. 2012. Zombie Linguistics: Experts, Endangered Languages and the Curse of Undead Voices. *Anthropological Forum: A Journal of Social Anthropology and Comparative Sociology* 22(2):133–149. http://dx.doi.org/10.1080/00664677.2012.694170.

The Importance of Being Not-Obviative

Irene Appelbaum

In this paper, I discuss the notion of obviation in the language isolate Ktunaxa, and in the Central Algonquian language Meskwaki.[1] While there are important differences between these two languages with respect to obviation, my concern in this paper is with a feature of obviation found in both languages—namely, that PROXIMATE SHIFTS ARE OFTEN NOT ACCOMPANIED BY PROXIMATE SWITCHES. That is, while a proximate shift introduces a new proximate, the previous proximate need not, and frequently, does not, become obviative when a new proximate is introduced. Although this fact is well known, I believe it has a consequence that has been underappreciated. I will argue that an implication of proximate shifts not being proximate switches is that PROXIMATE SHIFTS FAIL TO TRACK DISCOURSE PROMINENCE IN A NARRATIVE. By "track discourse prominence," here, I mean, systematically identify the most discourse-prominent referent in the narrative. It is widely assumed that when a proximate shift occurs, the new proximate becomes most discourse prominent at that point in the narrative, and remains so until the next proximate shift. The central aim of this article is to argue that this assumption should be rejected. Specifically, I will argue that when a proximate shift does not include the previous proximate becoming obviative, the previous proximate retains its proximate status and that, therefore, the status of the new proximate is not MORE discourse prominent than the preceding proximate; instead, their relationship is one of DISCOURSE PARITY. Because such proximate shifts without switches are frequent, it will often be the case that a proximate shift does not produce a new most-discourse-prominent referent. Hence, simply tracking the new proximate in successive proximate shifts will not systematically identify the most discourse-prominent referent in a narrative.

This article is organized as follows. After providing a brief overview of morphological and grammatical features of obviation in Ktunaxa and Meskwaki,[2] I discuss the difference between proximate shifts and proximate switches, giving examples from each language and highlighting the fact that when a proximate shift is not also a proximate switch, the proximate-shift sentence usually contains a single third-person NP. In the following section, I further discuss sentences containing a single third-person NP and argue that for such NPs we should distinguish proximate status per se from substantive discourse prominence, and that we should restrict the attribution of the latter to contexts where there are at least two participants. I argue against the claim that the single proximate NP of a sentence is most discourse prominent on the grounds that this claim is either vacuous or false. I then discuss examples of proximate shifts that are not also proximate switches, to support my argument. Most of the examples come from a single story in Ktunaxa, but I also provide some analogous examples in Meskwaki. In the following section, I explain in greater detail how these examples support the argument that in proximate shifts without switches, the new proximate achieves only discourse parity, not most-discourse-prominent status. The final section of the paper contains a summary of the argument and overall conclusion.

Overview of Obviation in Ktunaxa and Meskwaki

In both Ktunaxa and Meskwaki, the proximate is the less marked member. As shown in Table 1, in Ktunaxa, the proximate is unmarked and the obviative is marked with the suffix -*s*. For words ending in [s] or [ts], obviation may be indicated by lengthening. There is no number distinction for third-person forms in Ktunaxa.[3]

In Meskwaki, the proximate singular and plural are distinguished: In the singular, the proximate is marked with -*a* and the obviative with -*ani*. In the plural, the proximate suffix is -*aki*, while the obviative suffix is -*ahi*. See Table 2.[4]

In both languages, third-person possessed nouns are obligatorily obviative

TABLE 1. Ktunaxa obviation

	PROXIMATE	OBVIATIVE	
SG, PL	ka$_a$ke·n-Ø	ka$_a$ke·n-s	‘wolf’
SG, PL	skın·ku·ts-Ø	skın·ku·ts-·	‘coyote’

TABLE 2. Meskwaki obviation

	‘WOMAN’	
	PROXIMATE (ANIMATE)	OBVIATIVE (ANIMATE)
SG	ehkwe·w-a	ehkwe·w-**ani**
PL	ehkwe·w-**aki**	ehwe·w-**ahi**

(and the possessor may be either proximate or obviative). In Ktunaxa, there is no grammatical animacy (or other grammatical gender). Ktunaxa, however, has a semantic animacy hierarchy in which animate human nouns outrank animate nonhuman nouns, which, in turn, outrank inanimate nouns: ANIMATE HUMAN > ANIMATE NONHUMAN > INANIMATE.[5] This hierarchy shows itself in the Ktunaxa obviation system when a sentence contains two third-person NPs that differ in semantic animacy. In such cases, the NP ranked higher in animacy will be proximate. In Meskwaki, only grammatically animate nouns overtly mark the proximate/obviative distinction (Dahlstrom 2017:39). In both languages, then, it is only when two NPs are equally animate, and neither is third-person possessed, that discourse considerations play a role in proximate/obviative assignment.

Proximate Shifts and Proximate Switches

The proximate/obviative distinction applies when there are two or more third-person NPs in a sentence:

(1) Ktunaxa[6]

mıtyaẋ$_a$-ne·	skın·ku·ts-Ø	kławła-s
chase-IND	Coyote-**PROX**	Grizzly.Bear-**OBV**

‘Coyote chased Grizzly Bear.’ (Boas 2005:3, line 10)

(2) Meskwaki[7]

a·kwi wi·to·hkaw-a·čini i·tepi wi·h-a·-niči ow-i·w-**ani**
not allow-3>3'/NEG there FUT-go.thither-3'/AOR his-wife-**OBV.SG**

i·n-**a** neniw-**a**
that-**PROX.SG** man-**PROX.SG**
'That man doesn't allow his wife to go there.' (Goddard 2006:71, cited in Dahlstrom 2017:39)

A PROXIMATE SHIFT occurs whenever there is a change in the proximate NP in successive sentences. In such cases, the new proximate is often a previously obviative NP. In a PROXIMATE SWITCH, in addition to the previous proximate no longer being proximate, the previous proximate appears as obviative (Goddard 1990:334). Example (3) illustrates a proximate switch from Meskwaki. In (3a) the son (referred to here as 'his' and 'him') is the referent of the proximate NP, and 'father' is obviative. In the following sentence, (3b), the father is the referent of the new proximate (and now the father is referred to by 'his' and 'him'). Since the proximate NP has changed from 'son' to 'father', we have a proximate shift. Since the previous proximate, 'son', additionally becomes obviative in the proximate-shift sentence, this is also a proximate switch.

(3) Meskwaki

a. e·h=ikoči o·s-**ani.**
AOR=say.to.3'>3/AOR his.father-**OBV.SG**
'His (P) father (O) told him (P).'

b. e·h=ikoči okwis-**ani,**
AOR=say.to.3'>3 /AOR his.son-**OBV.SG**
'His (P) son (O) told him (P).' (Dahlstrom 1996:131, examples 24–27)

When a sentence contains only a single third-person NP, that NP is considered proximate:

(4) Ktunaxa

ła-wax̣-e· skun·ku·ts-**Ø**
again-arrive-IND Coyote-**PROX**
'Coyote returned.' (Boas 2005:66, line 31)

(5) Meskwaki

peteki	e·h=ihpahoči	mahkw-a.
back	AOR=run.thither.3/AOR	bear-**PROX.SG**

'The bear ran back.' (Dahlstrom 1996:152, line 241)

This point is widely and explicitly acknowledged: Speaking about Meskwaki, Goddard says, "If there is only one third person in a context, it can only be proximate" (1990:317). Dahlstrom, speaking about Plains Cree, states, "In contexts containing only one third person . . . the form used is always the unmarked proximate one" (2014:96). And Dryer says about Ktunaxa: "At most one argument per clause (and most commonly exactly one if the clause contains ONE or more third person arguments) can be proximate" (1996:14, emphasis added).

Because the sole third-person NP in such sentences is proximate, a proximate shift need not involve a proximate switch. That is, since the sentence introducing a new proximate need not contain a second, that is, obviative, argument, it certainly need not contain the previous proximate as obviative. Moreover, the previous proximate not only NEED NOT become obviative when there is a proximate shift, it often DOES NOT become obviative. In other words, proximate shifts are not typically proximate switches. As Goddard notes, "Although such transitions do occur . . . THEY GENERALLY SEEM TO BE AVOIDED" (1990:334, emphasis added).

In still other words, proximate shifts do not typically occur with transitive verbs. As Dahlstrom says of a particular example: "This episode is atypical in [that] the shift . . . coincides with the use of transitive verbs. IT IS MORE COMMON . . . WITH INTRANSITIVE VERBS" (2014:114, emphasis added).

The examples that follow involve proximate shifts that are not proximate switches. In (6a), *skın·ku·ts* 'Coyote' is proximate and *kianuqłumnas* 'Rabbit' is obviative. In (6b), there is a proximate shift in which *kianuqłumna* 'Rabbit' becomes the new proximate. However, since *skın·ku·ts* 'Coyote' does not become obviative in (6b), this is not a proximate switch.

(6) Ktunaxa

a.

qakıł-ne·	[skın·ku·ts-Ø]	[kianuqłumna-s]	qapsin	kın=sıł-ts̓ına·k.
say.to-IND	[Coyote-**PROX**]	[Rabbit-**OBV**]	why	SUB2=CONT-run

'Coyote said to Rabbit, "Why are you running?"'

b. qake$_{i}$-ne· kianuqłumna-Ø, “hu=s-x̣a’mktse·k”
say-IND Rabbit-**PROX**, “1=CONT-running.away”.
‘Rabbit said, “I am running away”.’ (Boas 2005:55, lines 2–3)

Similarly, in (7a), ‘the old woman’ is proximate and ‘Lazybones’, obviative. A proximate shift occurs in (7b) making ‘Lazybones’ proximate. But since ‘the old woman’ does not become obviative in (7b) —she does not appear at all—this is a proximate shift, but not a proximate switch.

(7) Meskwaki
e·h=natoma·či metemo·h-e·h-a i·n-ini pačan-ani.
aor=call.3>3’/aor old.woman-dim-prox.sg that-obv.sg Lazybones-obv.sg
‘The old woman called that Lazybones.’

i·tepi e·h=a·či pačan-a
there aor=go.3/aor Lazybones-prox.sg
‘Lazybones went there.’ (Dahlstrom 1996:155, lines 263–264)

Proximate Shifts and Discourse Prominence

In proximate shifts without switches, a tension arises regarding the status of the single third-person NP in the proximate-shift sentence. While its description as proximate is not problematic, its status as discourse prominent is not as straightforward. On the one hand, in general terms, a proximate NP is typically considered the most discourse prominent. On the other hand, when the attribute of discourse prominence is ascribed to proximates, it is almost always in the context of an opposing obviative. And it is not obvious that proximate morphology per se confers discourse prominence. This is especially true for languages such as Ktunaxa, where the proximate is unmarked. The issue raised by such shifts without switches, then, is whether to say that the single third-person NP in such cases is most discourse prominent simply because it is proximate, or to say that it is neutral with respect to discourse prominence because there is no contrast case.

If we say that the sole third-person NP in such cases is neutral with respect to discourse prominence, then clearly the proximate shift is not identifying a new most-discourse-prominent NP. By hypothesis, it is neutral. Not all proximate shifts in a story are of this sort—that is, sentences with a single third-person NP. However, to the extent that they are (and when there is not a scene change—see later discussion), the new proximate in the proximate-shift sentence will not pick out the most discourse-prominent referent. Since the proximate, on this interpretation, does not consistently identify the most discourse-prominent referent, proximate shifts will fail to track discourse prominence overall throughout the narrative.

If, alternatively, we say that the single third-person NP in such proximate shifts is not only formally proximate, but also identifies the most discourse prominent referent in the narrative at that point, the question naturally arises: In virtue of WHAT is it most discourse prominent?

One possibility is to say that the single third-person NP is the most discourse prominent because it is the ONLY third-person NP in the sentence. But by this logic, we could also say it is the LEAST discourse prominent. (Instead of claiming no other third-person NP in the sentence is more discourse prominent, we would say here that no other third-person NP in the sentence is less discourse prominent.) This way of assigning discourse prominence to the single third-person NP in such proximate shifts without switches is vacuous.

In order to formulate a nonvacuous standard of discourse prominence in such cases, we would have to say something like the following: If there WERE additional third-person NPs, they WOULD be obviative. The reasoning would go something like this: The proximate-shift sentence happens to be intransitive and to have only one third-person NP, but if the semantics or pragmatics of the sentence required additional third-person NPs, they would (likely) be less discourse prominent and hence would (likely) be obviative.

The problem with this notion of discourse prominence is that it appears to be false. That is, in the cases we are considering, an additional third-person NP sometimes IS required by the semantics or pragmatics of the sentence. But in these cases, instead of surfacing as obviative, the NP is syntactically suppressed. My claim is that these NPs are often suppressed precisely to prevent them from becoming obviative. In particular, when this additional NP is the previous proximate, syntactically suppressing it blocks the proximate shift from additionally being a proximate switch. I do not wish to imply that such syntactic strategies are explicit or conscious in the mind of the speaker. Instead, I am simply highlighting the fact that, for example, a derived intransitive construction is often used when the corresponding ordinary transitive would do, or that there is a change to the transitive form of a quotative verb when the ditransitive form is used in surrounding sentences. The suggestion here is that if the new proximate WERE more discourse prominent than this additional third-person NP, there would be no motivation to suppress the latter. In terms of the choice of grammatical construction, it would be simpler to use a transitive clause and allow the previous proximate to surface in the sentence as obviative. But as it is, this regularly fails to occur. This suggests that the new proximate is NOT more discourse prominent than the previous proximate at the point in the narrative when the proximate shift occurs.

We next look at some examples. The examples are all proximate shifts that are not proximate switches; that is, they are proximate shifts in which the previous proximate does not become obviative. My goal here is to illustrate the fact that in most of these cases, the previous proximate does not fail to appear as obviative in the proximate-shift sentence simply because it is not relevant to the event portrayed in the proximate-shift sentence. Rather, the previous proximate often syntactically suppresses what remains a semantic argument.

Examples

The examples that follow come from a Ktunaxa narrative, Story 55 of *Kutenai Tales,* "The People Try to Kill Ya^{u}ke$_{l}$kam" (Boas 2005:121–126), narrated by Barnaby. For example 3, I also cite analogous Meskwaki constructions.

We may summarize the Ktunaxa story as follows: The Water Monster, Yauk^{u}e$_{l}$kam, is killed by the people because they are afraid of him. They then throw him into the water, where he is nursed back to life by the fish. He then goes ashore and, along with his relatives (his younger brother, his wife, and their son, Duck), he takes revenge on the people. Specifically, Yauk^{u}e$_{l}$kam kills Crane and his wife, and Duck kills the chief. In the end, the people are even more afraid of Yauk^{u}e$_{l}$kam.

I identified a total of 35 proximate shifts in this story. To simplify matters, I limit the discussion here to the 15 proximate shifts in which there are only two participants on the scene at the time of the proximate shift. Nine of these 15 proximate shifts are accomplished with a sentence containing a single third-person NP. In other words, nine are proximate shifts but not proximate switches.

Of these nine, four correspond to scene changes. Scene changes are clearly marked with a formulaic phrase such as *tax̣as t̓sɩnax̣e· ne*$_{\iota}$ *tɩtqa·ť* 'Then the man started out' (Boas 2005:124, line 89). Proximate shifts without switches that occur in the context of a scene change are not of interest here because we are considering situations where the previous proximate remains on the scene during a proximate shift. In cases where the proximate shift corresponds to a scene change, the previous proximate may well not be present in the new scene.

Examining the remaining five proximate shifts, we see that in four of them, the previous proximate is prevented from being discourse demoted to obviative by the choice of syntactic construction.

Ktunaxa Example 1

In (8a–c), there are two proximate shifts. In (8b) there is a proximate shift from Yauk^{u}e$_{i}$kam to Crane and, in (8c), another shift back to Yauk^{u}e$_{i}$kam. When Yauk^{u}e$_{i}$kam speaks to Crane in (8a), the former is proximate and the latter is obviative, but when Crane speaks to Yauk^{u}e$_{i}$kam in (8b), Crane becomes proximate, but Yauk^{u}e$_{i}$kam does not become obviative. Preventing Yauk^{u}e$_{i}$kam from becoming obviative is a change from the ditransitive form of the verb *qakɩłne·* 'say something to someone' to the transitive *qake$_{i}$ne·* 'say something.' After Crane finishes speaking, there is a proximate shift back to Yauk^{u}e$_{i}$kam, in (8c), and Crane again appears as obviative.

(8) a. qakɩł-ne· [yauk^{u}e$_{i}$ka·m-Ø] [qaspɩłʼuk-s] qapsin-s
say.to-IND yauk^{u}e$_{i}$ka·m-**PROX** Crane-**OBV** why-OBV

kɩn=ups-ke$_{i}$n na$_{a}$ a$_{a}$'kupɩłupin ?
SUB2=take.one's.own-with.hand this young.tree
'Yauk^{u}e$_{i}$kam said to Crane: "What are you doing with that young tree?".'

b. qake$_{i}$-ne· qaspɩłʼuk-Ø sɩł-'aqsan-miyɩt-s n-'upił-ił-ne·
say-IND Crane-**PROX** CONT-several-day-OBV IND-kill-PASS-IND

yauk^{u}e$_{i}$kam-Ø x̣un-mit-quł-ɩł-'ne·.
yauk^{u}e$_{i}$ka·m·-PROX into.water-throw-into.water-PASS-IND
'Crane said: "Several days ago Yauk^{u}e$_{i}$kam was killed and thrown into the water."'
(Boas 2005:122, lines 34–36)

c. q̓akpakit-x̣o$_{u}$-ne· [yauk^{u}e$_{i}$ka·m-Ø] qaspɩłʼuk-s
kill.by.striking-with.body-IND [yauk^{u}e$_{i}$ka·m-**PROX**] Crane-**OBV**
'He knocked Crane down.' (Boas 2005:122, lines 39–40)

Ktunaxa Example 2

We find the same valency-reduction strategy with the quotative verb in (9a–c). In the exchange between Yauk^{u}e$_{i}$kam and his younger brother, a form of *qake$_{i}$ne·* 'say something' is used in each of the three sentences. There are again two proximate shifts: the first one, (9b), away from Yauk^{u}e$_{i}$kam, and the second, (9c), back to Yauk^{u}e$_{i}$kam. When Yauk^{u}e$_{i}$kam speaks to his younger brother in (9a) and (9c), *qakıɫne·* 'say something to someone' is used, and in these sentences, Yauk^{u}e$_{i}$kam is the proximate speaker and the younger brother is the obviative addressee. In (9b), when the younger brother is the speaker, he becomes proximate. But now the transitive form of the quotative verb is used, eliminating the indirect object, and with it, the need for Yauk^{u}e$_{i}$kam to appear as obviative. Although we know from the context that the younger brother is speaking to Yauk^{u}e$_{i}$kam, syntactically the latter has been excised. But when Yauk^{u}e$_{i}$kam again addresses his brother in (9c), the ditransitive form, *qakıɫne·*, reappears with Yauk^{u}e$_{i}$kam as proximate and the younger brother as obviative.

(9) a.

qakıɫ-ne·	[tsa'-e·s-Ø]	[yauk^{u}e$_{i}$ka·m-Ø]
say.to-IND	[younger.brother-POSS3-**OBV**]	[yauk^{u}e$_{i}$ka·m-**PROX**]

kın='ıɫwa	iyamo?
INT2=shoot	game

'Yauk^{u}e$_{i}$kam said to his younger brother, "Did you shoot any game?"'[8]

b.

qake$_{i}$-ne·	[tsa-Ø]	pıḱa·k-s	ho=n-'iɫ$_{u}$wa-n·e·
say-IND	[younger.brother-**PROX**]	long.ago-OBV	1=shoot-IND

tsuk^{u}at-ıɫ-ne·
take-PASS-IND

'Younger brother said, "Long ago I shot some, but it was taken away".'
(Boas 2005:124, lines 78–80)

c. qakɬ-ne· tsa-'e·s-Ø yauk^{u}e$_{i}$ka·m-Ø taẋa ɬun·u
say.to-IND younger.brother.-POSS3-**OBV** Yauk^{u}e$_{i}$ka·m-**PROX** then go.on

ɬa-e·ťškɬ-en' tsʊpqa.
again-look.for-IMP deer
'Yauk^{u}e$_{i}$kam said to his younger brother: 'Go on; look for deer again!''
(Boas 2005:124, line 83, 84)

Meskwaki Example 1

This valency-reduction strategy with quotative verbs is also found in Meskwaki:

(10) a. e·h=iči wa·natohka mečemo·k-a.
AOR=say.3/AOR unconcernedly old.woman-**PROX**.SG
'The old woman asked unconcernedly.'

b. "nesekokwe·ni=ma·hi·='na mahkw-**ani**,
kill.3'>3/INT=after.all=that.ANIM bear-**OBV**.SG
'"He must have been killed by a bear."'

c. ke·htena," e·h=iči
true AOR=say.3/AOR
'"It was true after all," he said.' (Dahlstrom 1996:140, examples 110–112)

As Dahlstrom says of these examples, "The quoting verbs . . . are intransitive (*e·h=iči* 'he/she (prox.) said'). If the transitive form of the quoting verb had been used instead, either the subject or the object would have been made obviative" (Dahlstrom 1996:123).

Ktunaxa Example 3

In this example, there is a proximate switch between (11a) and (11b) in which *naso$_{u}$ke·n* 'chief' becomes the new proximate. The previous proximate, *ne$_{ɩ}$ťšuq̓* 'Duck', does not appear at all in the proximate switch sentence, and therefore does not appear as obviative. However, while this is a case of a proximate shift without an accompanying proximate switch, it does not provide evidence in favor of the view that the construction was chosen IN ORDER to prevent a proximate switch, because the intransitive verb *qa·wax̣$_{a}$mox̣un·e·* 'fall down' does not have an obvious transitive counterpart for which the argument has been suppressed. (Of course, the choice to portray this event as one of the chiefs falling down, rather than as one of Duck knocking him down, is relevant.) Nevertheless, of the five proximate shifts involving two participants, which are not proximate switches (and which also do not correspond to scene changes), this is the only one that does not provide such evidence.

(11)	a.	qa-tsɩn-k̓apałtułe·k	ne$_{i}$ts̓uq̇-Ø	
		not-hold-listen	Duck-PROX	
		'Duck did not obey.'		
	b.	qa·-wax̣$_{a}$-mox̣u-n·e·	ne$_{i}$-Ø	naso$_{u}$k̓^{u}e·n-Ø
		there-arrive-hit-IND	that.one-PROX	chief-PROX
		'The chief fell down.' (Boas 2005:126, line 108)		

Ktunaxa Example 4

In (12b), there is a proximate switch in which the obviative of (12a), 'Duck', becomes proximate (along with his uncle). The previous proximate, 'chief', does not appear in (12b), but this is not because the semantics of the sentence requires no argument beyond 'Duck and his uncle'. There is a second semantic argument in the sentence. It is 'three of them', one of whom refers to the chief. However, because 'three of them' is incorporated—and because the indefinite human object suffix is also used, even though we know who was killed—'chief' is blocked from appearing as an obviative in the proximate shift.

(12)	a.	pał	sł-'upł-aps-e·	ne$_{i}$ts̓uq̇-s	[ne$_{i}$-Ø	naso$_{u}$k^{u}e·n-Ø]
		EVID	CONT-kill-INV-IND	Duck-OBV	that.one-PROX	chief-PROX
		'Duck had killed the chief.'				

	b.	tax̣ą-s	sɩł-qałsał-'upɩł-ka-n	x̣ą$_{a}$-t$_{i}$mo·	ne$_{i}$ts̓uq̇-Ø
		then-OBV	CONT-three.of.them-kill-IHO-IND	uncle-together.with	Duck-PROX
		'Thus, Duck and his uncle killed three of them.' [Lit: 'three-of-them-killed']			
		(Boas 2005:126, lines 109, 110)			

Ktunaxa Example 5

In both Ktunaxa and Meskwaki narratives, passives are often used as a valency-reducing strategy for discourse purposes (see Goddard 1984; Appelbaum in press). Because the passive suppresses the agent, valency reduction works somewhat differently from the quotative-verb case. While valency reduction in the latter case prevents the previous proximate from becoming obviative, the use of a passive serves to prevent the current proximate—the proximate in the passive sentence—from having been an obviative. The proximate shift with a passive in (13) follows the sentence in (12b). If the corresponding direct, transitive form of the verb had been used, 'the chief' (along with 'Crane and his wife') would have been obviative and 'Duck and his uncle' would have remained proximate. (In such a case, there would be no proximate shift.) So the use of a passive instead of its active counterpart does not directly contribute to preventing the previous proximate from becoming obviative. Nevertheless, the choice of a passive clause, rather an inverse transitive clause, serves precisely this purpose.

(13)	ma	k̓-'upɪł-i·ł	qaspɪł'uk-Ø	tɪłnamo'-t$_{i}$mo	a$_{a}$ke·	k̓-upɪł-i·ł
	PAST	SUB-kill-PASS	Crane-**PROX**	wife-together.with	also	SUB-kill-PASS

ne$_{i}$-Ø naso$_{u}$k̓^{u}e·n-Ø
that.one-**PROX** chief-**PROX**
'Crane and his wife were killed, and the chief was killed.'
(Boas 2005:126, lines 110, 111)

Goddard 1984 discusses an analogous example from Meskwaki, presented as (14) below. Although the two sentences are not accompanied by morpheme-by-morpheme glosses, Goddard makes explicit the relevant point: "The use of a passive verb (*e:h=meseneci* 'they were captured') in the second segment is particularly significant . . . since it shows in a concrete way the avoidance of a reversal of obviation status for both third persons" (Goddard 1984:280).

Meskwaki Example 2

(14) a. o:ni=pi e:h=natwe:we:hkawa:či.
'Then he (P) made them [i.e., the Sioux] (O) come by beating the drum.'

b. ma:ne=meko e:h=pya:wa:či aša:haki, kekimesi=mekoho **e:h=mešeneči.**
'Many Sioux (P) came, and all **were captured.**' (Goddard 1984:280, from example 10)

Upshot of Examples

In four of the five proximate shifts that are not also proximate switches (and that also do not correspond to scene changes), it is the particular choice of construction that prevents the proximate shift from being a proximate switch. That is, in these four proximate shifts, the event described in the sentence is semantically transitive (or ditransitive). Nevertheless, it is conveyed in such a way as to prevent the previous proximate from being a syntactic argument, and hence, in such a way as to prevent it from being an obviative syntactic argument. The claim here is that this is not accidental—that it is not a matter of discourse indifference whether the previous proximate loses its proximate status and becomes obviative in the proximate-shift clause. Instead, I have argued that in such cases, the previous proximate is syntactically excluded from the proximate shift sentence IN ORDER to prevent it from becoming obviative. If this is so, the discourse status of this previous proximate must be relevant at the point in the narrative when the proximate shift occurs. If it were not relevant, one would expect a construction in which the previous proximate were allowed to surface as obviative. The importance of being not-obviative in these cases, then, is that it provides evidence that the discourse status of the previous proximate is still relevant. And its discourse status is proximate. Since the new proximate and the previous proximate have the same, that is, proximate, status, the new proximate is not MORE discourse prominent than the previous proximate. Instead, in such cases, the proximate shift yields only discourse parity for the new proximate; it does not become the MOST discourse prominent referent in such cases. To the extent that such proximate shifts without switches occur, the proximate shift will fail to identify the most discourse-prominent referent and hence, overall, proximate shifts will not be a reliable guide to most discourse-prominent status.

Introducing the notion of discourse parity allows us to distinguish cases where a previous proximate is still proximate from cases where it is obviative. In other words, tracking who is proximate on the scene allows us to distinguish discourse shifts from discourse switches. This is because determining whether the previous proximate is still proximate on the scene also tells us whether it is obviative in the proximate-shift sentence. Assuming the previous proximate is still on the scene, if it is not proximate, it is obviative.

By contrast, if we assume that proximate shifts per se track discourse prominence, and that a referent not in the proximate-shift sentence cannot have proximate status, then we will be unable to distinguish when a referent is not proximate because it has been syntactically suppressed, from cases where it is not proximate because it is obviative. This difference is important because it is the latter cases that often correspond to the most significant narrative changes. For example, Yauk^{u}e$_{i}$kam appears in the obviative (in a subordinate clause) in a proximate switch, (15), in the sentence immediately after the sentence reporting that he has been killed. This is NOT a case of discourse parity: Yauk^{u}e$_{i}$kam and the people are both on the scene, but only the people are proximate, and hence, at this point, they are most discourse prominent.

(15)	tax̣a-s	aqłsmak$_{i}$nıḱ-Ø	sukwıłq̓uk$_{u}$-ne·	ḱ-upi·ł	yauk^{u}e$_{i}$ka·m-s
	then-OBV	people-**PROX**	be.happy-IND	SUB-kill	yauk^{u}e$_{i}$ka·m-**OBV**

'The people were glad because they had killed Yauk^{u}e$_{i}$ka·m.'

[Lit: 'The people were glad because of the Yauk^{u}e$_{i}$ka·m killing.']

(Boas 2005:120, lines 9,10)

It would seem to be important to be able to distinguish these narrative reversals from less narratively marked moments such as proximate shifts that occur when Yauk^{u}e$_{i}$kam's interlocutor speaks. Tracking who is proximate on the scene enables us to distinguish these cases, while attending only to who is proximate in the sentence does not. In the latter case, all we can say is that Yauk^{u}e$_{i}$kam fails to be proximate in both.

Summary and Conclusion

Because the single third-person NP of a sentence is proximate, a proximate shift does not require demoting the previous proximate. Because the discourse status of the previous proximate is not altered in such cases, one could argue—as I have—that it remains proximate. If it remains proximate, then there are two proximates on the scene and hence the new proximate is not MOST discourse prominent.

Alternatively, one could argue that since it is not present as a syntactic argument in the proximate-shift sentence, the prior proximate has no status whatsoever in the proximate-shift sentence. As the only proximate in the proximate-shift sentence, the new proximate, on this view, is the only candidate for most discourse-prominent status and hence IS the most discourse prominent. However, against this view, I have argued that this way of understanding discourse prominence is vacuous, and that attempts to treat the new proximate as discourse prominent in a nonvacuous sense often require us to ignore the additional proximates on the scene.

Thus, either the discourse status of the previous proximate is relevant at the point in the narrative when the proximate shift occurs, or it is not. If its discourse status is not relevant, then it should not matter whether this status is proximate or obviative. But the fact that the construction used to accomplish the proximate shift regularly prevents the previous proximate from appearing as obviative suggests that the discourse status of the previous proximate is indeed relevant. And if the status of the previous proximate IS relevant, then not having become obviative, it remains proximate. If it remains proximate, then the new proximate and the previous proximate are equally discourse prominent and so, in these cases, the proximate shift does not tell us who is MOST discourse prominent.

The difficulty is that a proximate shift does not identify who is (or is not) obviative. In particular, a proximate shift does not tell us whether the previous proximate is obviative in the current sentence. But as we have seen, this information is relevant to determining whether a proximate shift produces a new most-discourse-prominent referent or only achieves discourse prominence equal to the previous proximate. I have argued that if we look at who is proximate ON THE SCENE at the time of utterance of the proximate shift sentence, rather than just IN THE SENTENCE, we can capture this distinction and thereby provide a more accurate picture of discourse prominence at that point in the narrative.

Discourse parity also seems an appropriate way to capture the temporarily upgraded status of a secondary character: The main character does not cede discourse prominence; it shares it.

Tracking who is proximate on the scene instead of just in the current sentence also coheres well with the fact that many narratives are structured in terms of acts and scenes (Hymes 1981). A notion of discourse prominence that tracks who is on the scene at each point in the story treats the narrative as just that—a story. In contrast, to actively ignore who remains on the scene and attend only to who is proximate in the current sentence is effectively to treat the story as a list of isolated sentences.

NOTES

1. I gratefully acknowledge support from the NEH-NSF Documenting Endangered Languages Fellowship Program. Any views, findings, conclusions, or recommendations expressed in this paper do not necessarily reflect those of the National Endowment for the Humanities and the National Science Foundation. For helpful questions and comments, I would like to thank Leora Bar-el, Amy Dahlstrom, Kate Hohenstein, Mizuki Miyashita, the University of Montana Linguistics Club, the audience at the 50th Algonquian Conference, and two anonymous reviewers.
2. The term 'Ktunaxa' refers to both the language and the people. The term is sometimes used to refer to the language and people as a whole, and sometimes in contrast to the Montana-based tribe, who are also called 'Ksanka'. I use the term here to refer to the language as a whole. Other terms for the language and the people are 'Kutenai', 'Kootenai', and 'Kootenay.'
3. Forms from Boas (2005:56). Here and throughout, the Ktuanaxa examples are presented, with minor changes, in Boas's orthography.
4. Forms from Dahlstrom (n.d.:3–13, 3–14, 3–16, 3–17).
5. See Comrie 1981 for one of numerous discussions of animacy hierarchies.
6. The following abbreviations are used for interlinear glosses of Ktunaxa examples: 1 = first person, 2 = second person, 3 = third person, CONT = continuative, EVID = evidential, IHO = indefinite human object, IMP = imperative, IND = indicative, INT = interrogative, INV = inverse, OBV = obviative, PASS = passive, PAST = past tense, POSS = possessive, PROX = proximate, SUB = subordinate marker.
7. The Meskwaki examples in this paper come from previously published work by Amy Dahlstrom and Ives Goddard. I have made slight formatting changes in the presentation of these examples (e.g., using small capitals for grammatical categories and labelling the proximate status of an NP as such.) The following abbreviations are used for interlinear glosses of Meskwaki examples: 3 = third-person proximate, 3' = third-person obviative, ANIM = animate, AOR = aorist, DIM = diminutive, FUT = future, INT = interrogative, NEG =

negative, OBV = obviative, PROX = proximate, SG = singular.

8. In this example, 'younger brother' is not overtly marked as obviative because the possessor is proximate.

REFERENCES

Appelbaum, Irene. [In press]. A Discourse Function of the Passive in Kutenai. *Proceedings of the Workshop on Structure and Constituency in the Languages of the Americas 22*, ed. by Anne Bertrand and Heather Burge. Vancouver: University of British Columbia Working Papers in Linguistics (UBCWPL).

Boas, Franz. 2005 [1918]. *Kutenai Tales Together With Texts Collected by Alexander Francis Chamberlain*. Ann Arbor: University of Michigan Library, Digital General Collection. Bureau of American Ethnology Bull. 59. Washington, DC.

Comrie, Bernard. 1981. *Language Universals & Linguistic Typology*. Chicago: University of Chicago Press.

Dahlstrom, Amy. [n.d.] Meskwaki (Fox) Syntax. https://lucian.uchicago.edu/blogs/adahlstrom/publications-2/selected-manuscripts.

Dahlstrom, Amy. 1996. Narrative Structure of a Fox Text. *Nikotwasik Iskwahtem, Paskihtepayih!: Studies in Honour of H.C. Wolfart*, ed. by John D. Nichols and Arden C. Ogg, Memoir 13, pp.113–162. Manitoba: Algonquian and Iroquian Linguistics.

Dahlstrom, Amy. 2014. *Plains Cree Morphosyntax*. London: Routledge.

Dahlstrom, Amy. 2017. Obviation and Information Structure in Meskwaki. *Papers of the Forty-sixth Algonquian Conference 2014*, ed. by Monica Macaulay and Margaret Noodin, pp. 39–54. East Lansing: Michigan State University Press.

Dryer, Matthew. 1996. Grammatical Relations in Ktunaxa (Kutenai): The Belcourt Lecture. Delivered before the University of Manitoba on 24 Februrary 1995. Winnipeg: Voices of Rupert's Land.

Goddard, Ives. 1984. The Obviative in Fox Narrative Discourse. *Papers of the 15th Algonquian Conference*, ed. by William Cowan, pp. 273–286. Ottawa: Carleton University.

Goddard, Ives. 1990. Aspects of the Topic Structure of Fox Narratives: Proximate Shifts and the Use of Overt and Inflectional NPs. *International Journal of American Linguistics* 56(3):317–340.

Hymes, Dell. 1981. *"In Vain I Tried to Tell You": Essays in Native American Ethnopoetics*. Lincoln: University of Nebraska Press.

The Benign Neglect of Language Materials by Historians

A Northeastern Oklahoma Case Study

Amy Dianne Bergseth

As language expresses values and worldviews, the inclusion of language in history is a means of emphasizing, stressing, and valuing Native voices and viewpoints.[1] This is given even more immediacy with the 21st-century potential for a staggering loss of global diversity, including languages and their corresponding cultural knowledge and worldviews (Baldwin 2016; Hinton 2008:351). Although mediated through a Western European filter, Native voices nonetheless have entered into the historical record through the papers of missionaries, ethnologists, "salvage anthropologists," and in recent years both Native and non-Native scholars of indigenous history. In records from the late 19th century in northeastern Oklahoma, Native voices emerge and help create and bring forward other narratives and emphases. These materials indicate a significant period of transition for these smaller Native communities and tribal nations, including many Algonquian-speaking peoples. Despite the challenges of assimilation, with the general assault on Native languages and cultures, many Native people in Northeastern Oklahoma maintained their traditions and languages. Traditional indigenous oral historians gave testimony to linguists of intertribal interactions, cultural and political perseverance, and their own unique voices and opinions of their recent pasts and present communities. The language materials show cultural continuance despite pressures of assimilation that scholars might not perceive in other historical sources (Bergseth 2018:19–21).[2]

Historians recognize the importance of language and culture to the study of history, but this often has not transferred to indigenous America. In 1988 anthropologist and linguist Douglas R. Parks contended that despite the production of 'new Indian histories'—the term used for the 'Cultural Turn' for Native history in the late 20th century—languages were left behind. "The treatment of native language material has suffered a consistent fate among historians: benign neglect," Parks argued. "In contrast to their confreres in other geographical areas, American Indian historians do not ordinarily study the language of the people they chronicle, nor do they master linguistics sufficiently to handle language data competently and insightfully" (Parks 1988:155).[3] The 'language barrier' has often prevented language materials from being incorporated in historical narratives. Language materials can be daunting, intimidating, and even overwhelming for some nonspecialists (nonlinguists) who may themselves be community members. Historians have not included and often still do not include indigenous language materials in historical inquiry. Despite some notable exceptions, such as the strong growth of Anishinaabeg Studies and publications such as the correspondence from prisoners of war after the United States–Dakota War of 1862, this remains quite true (Bergseth 2018:19–21; Bohaker 2006; Canku and Simon 2013; Denetdale 2007; Doerfler, Sinclair, and Stark 2013; Kelsey 2014; Rice 2013; Westerman and Wasicuna 2016; Witgen 2012).

There is, however, a real risk of historians using language as a superficial archival tool without understanding the deep significances behind it. Parks noticed that historians and other writers often include names only briefly in their narratives or they, often erroneously, analyze words only when needed to substantiate their arguments (Parks 1988:155). Concerns of inconsistency and superficiality continue to be echoed even decades later throughout the academy and in Native communities. A 2018 magazine article romanticized first-language Šaawanwa (Shawnee) speaker George Blanchard as a singular hero with the article titled "Meet the Man Who Hopes to Save the Shawnee Language." Despite its sentimentalized heading, the essay detailed the biography of how George Blanchard, an Absentee Shawnee (Šaawanwa) from Little Axe, Oklahoma, ended up working for the Eastern Šaawanwaki in the northeastern corner of the state. The author relayed Blanchard's views and motives. "It is insufficient, George says, to simply glance at words as though they are artifacts or mere novelties. His goal is true comprehension, free from the veil of English. Without it, tribal members cannot access the cultural weight of inherited stories, songs, and ceremonies" (Hansen 2018). Blanchard reminded audiences that the motives and values of Native communities often drastically differed from those of outsiders. Community goals were nothing less than cultural fluency and an unfiltered understanding separate from the Western Euro-American views. But George Blanchard also explicitly cautioned readers against using a language as a remarkable relic devoid and separate from the culture from which it came (Hansen 2018). Incorporation of language materials for historians, however, enters into further debates about source materials and historiography. Historians themselves are indebted to the traditions of antiquarianism, the meticulous collecting and detailing of the past. At the same time, however, historians also criticize and disparage its frequent noninclusion of meaning and relevance. With this mixed view on detail collection and their antiquarian inheritances, then, historians may certainly still plunge into the pitfall of exoticizing indigenous languages (Sweet 2008).

With the intimidating barriers of unfamiliar languages and the dangers of exoticism, consequently historians often approach linguistic documents and indigenous languages with much anxiety. Do the gains ever outweigh the concerns? In my own work, I cannot say that I necessarily avoid the pitfalls. Parks argues for all ethnologists, anthropologists, and historians alike to integrate linguistics into their work. He persuasively illustrates the benefits of linguistics to ethnologists (Parks 1988:154–155).[4] This integration, however, comes with a steep learning curve. A trained historian myself, I do not have any formal training in linguistics. Historians have rarely even looked at the historical linguistic source materials in general. I argue that at least looking at language materials IS an attempt and a step toward giving more credit to a wider range of Native-authored sources as historical records. How can historians contend that their histories gain a "Native perspective" without including Native-made sources that profess indigenous worldviews and values? Other questions concern their omission. What happens when historians come to languages in the archives while glancing through for source materials and pass them over? Ignoring the languages, without any challenge or attempt to even find some usefulness in the materials—what does that do? What do language materials do, and what does their frequent omission mean to the historical record and narration of Native histories? Historians often see language materials as anthropology, and not useful for historical narratives. But the consequence of this is to erase, minimize, and relegate indigenous presence to the past, overlooking the continued vitality or tenuousness of their languages and cultures within the historical narratives. Contemporary concerns over diversity-destroying Pan-Indianism in Oklahoma also rears its ugly head. Oklahoma, having 39 distinct recognized tribal nations residing within its borders, is often seen as an "Indian melting pot" where generic powwow culture often overrides the individual national identity of each community today. Historical sources, however, may break or challenge the stereotypes. These muddied sources that express indigenous values and tribal worldviews, then, often require more work for non-Native scholars to mull over, but provide fulfilling results (Bergseth 2018:12–13, 17–18).

First and foremost, there is also a basic moral and ethical imperative for historians to use tribal self-designations in their narratives. Gerald Taiaiake Alfred (Kahnawà:ke Kanien'ke/Kahnawake Mohawk) in *Peace, Power, and Righteousness* argues: "Today, we recognize the significance and symbolic value of terminology, and the use of our own recovered languages is important not only for the purposes of communication but as a symbol of our survival. In addition, it helps us all avoid insult and injury" (Alfred 2009:23). It is important whenever possible to use indigenous names and terminologies for Native communities and people. For, as Alfred noted, it aids in general communication and helps to prevent more outright offenses and grievances. Parks insists on the need for "linguistically informed standardization" (1988:167). Many self-designations have become normalized today. Diné for Navajo; Anishinaabe or Nishnaabe for the confederacy of the Ojibwe, Odawa, and Potawatomi; and Myaamia for Miami are just three examples. In Canada and the Northeast, Haudenosaunee (alternatively spelled also as Rotinonshonni and Hodinöhsö:ni') has become synonymous with the French and Euro-American term 'Iroquois.' Utilizing indigenous terms and names shows respect and maintains integrity for the Native cultures and communities in historical narratives (Bergseth 2018:22–23).

Indigenous language materials in the historical record also emphasize connections and highlight intertribal interactions. Parks reasons that "the more our understanding of the intricate details of language relationships increases, the deeper our knowledge of the history of tribal interrelationships becomes" (1988:174). Parks describes the association between the Pawnee (South Band), Skidi Pawnee, and Arikara through both language borrowing in social interactions and descendancy from a common ancestral language (Parks 1988:169–178). Language materials also illustrate other interrelationships and interactions between indigenous communities. The importance of relationships to other Algonquian-speaking peoples is reiterated in Myaamia (Miami) stories, both recent histories and origin stories. Waapanaakikaapwa (Gabriel Godfroy) (Myaamia) spoke to the local historian Jacob

Piatt Dunn in the early 20th century about their 'Coming Out Place,' *saakiiweeyonki*, near what is today South Bend, Indiana. In the beginning the Myaamiaki (Miamis) emerged from the earth and pulled themselves up out of the water by tree branches. Near the end of the story the Myaamiaki came across some people who knew and recognized their own language. They gave each other names (Costa 2010:51–53).[5] Kinship and naming served and still serve as indigenous ways of identifying and affiliating oneself with others. Tawaahkwakinanka (George Washington Finley) (Peeyankihšia/Piankashaw-Peewaalia/Peoria) shared a story with the Bureau of American Ethnology linguist Albert Samuel Gatschet in the 1890s. He spoke of Ciinkweensa, who left the Peewaaliaki (Peorias) after the American Civil War, sometime around 1866. Ciinkweensa moved in with the Kiikaapoaki (Kickapoos) and he married a Kiikaapoa (Kickapoo) woman. Algonquian-speaking communities often interacted with each other and intermarried. Tawaahkwakinanka's story about Ciinkweensa reiterates the intercultural and intertribal interactions, through individual and personal marriages and family relations. Linguistic and cultural affinities shaped and continue to shape Algonquian relationships in northeastern Oklahoma (Costa 2010:4–7).

Language materials also reinforce the historic documentation of social, political, and religious intertribal gatherings. The linguist John Peabody Harrington briefly noted that the Lenape had a tradition of calling together intertribal council meetings in the early 20th century. When they did so, they would invite their Algonquian-speaking neighbors—the Šaawanwaki, Myaamiaki, Odawas (Ottawas), Bodéwadmi (Potewatmi/Potawatomi), Thakiwaki (Sauks/Sacs), and Meskwaki (Fox). They would also request the presence of the Wa^{n}dat (Wendat/Wyandot(te) s), Aniyunwiya (Cherokees), Wažažes (Osages), Mvskokes (Muscogees (Creeks)), Okáxpas (Quapaws), Ioways (Iowas), and Kansas (Kaws). Lenape women would cook food for these intertribal gatherings. Although Harrington specifically noted that the meetings were not explicitly political, they still inherently had political ramifications (Harrington 1907–57). Great Lakes and Ohio Valley Native nations had a long-established history of intertribal interactions and alliances and they cemented this with their kinship. These continued for centuries, and language sources reiterate that.

Language materials also provide a history of cultural continuance that is not easily identified in the standard written records such as official accounts of the Indian Office and Indian Agency reports. With so many small tribal nations in the northeastern corner of Oklahoma, many Native people were multilingual and learned each other's languages. Intermarriages were commonplace and multiple languages were often spoken in one family. Many people were at least familiar with, or could understand a little bit of, each other's languages. Grant and Costa mention "Ottawa County [Oklahoma], once the county with the most varied native speech in the United States" (1991:411). Bilingualism or multilingualism was the norm in northeastern Oklahoma for a certain period in the late 19th century and into the 20th century (Bergseth 2018:508–513; Grant and Costa 1991:411–430).

Given the similarities and affinities of many of their languages, Ottawa County Native people often were also familiar with, or understood, neighboring tribal languages. Many of the citizens of northeastern Oklahoma nations spoke languages that belonged to the Algonquian or Iroquoian language families. In the 1970s the Kaion'ke (Cayuga) elder Kenneth Oyler described the unique diversity of northeastern Oklahoma. "There's a lot of different tribes. Some of 'em talk Indian," Oyler said. He pointed out: "You can see and hear where the different tribes can understand one another" (Tyner 1970:4). Similarly, Sa'tsi'tsuwa' (Smith Nichols), an 83-year-old Wa^{n}dat-Kaion'ke born in Sandusky, Ohio, explained in the early 20th century to Canadian anthropologist Charles Marius Barbeau, who was documenting Native culture in Oklahoma: "When they each speak their own language, together, they can understand each other" (Barbeau [n.d.]). The speakers of those Iroquoian languages—the Shotinontowane', Kaion'ke, and Wa^{n}dat—very likely understood each other despite linguistic differences. This remains true today as well. Speakers of Algonquian languages like Šaawanwa, Myaamia, Peewaalia (Peoria), and Odawa (Ottawa) understand each other relatively easily. Iroquoian and Algonquian people speak their own separate languages, but they can often recognize or distinguish the similarities and differences in words and phrases (Bergseth 2018:488–513; Dycus 1969; Grant and Costa 1991:426).[6]

Despite the assaults of forced assimilation and allotment, these Native communities continued to speak their languages in the 20th century. Robert Whitebird, an Okáxpa elder, told an interviewer in the 1960s that at the annual powwow his wife "overheard three Indian women carrying on a conversation, yet each speaking in their own, and different tribal language" (Tyner 1969:3). It is not clear exactly who Whitebird's wife heard speaking, but his comment highlighted the linguistic exchanges that continued in the northeastern corner of Oklahoma. Many of the northeastern Oklahoma tribal nations often spoke to each other across linguistic divides (Bergseth 2018:488–513).

The Bureau of American Ethnology linguist Albert Samuel Gatschet provided an overview of the status of indigenous language usage by the end of the 19th century in northeastern Oklahoma. It is unclear where or how he obtained his information, but his data echoed the 1891 Quapaw Agency, now Miami Agency, statistics reported by the Indian Office. One can speculate that Gatschet's estimates were gained through questioning Native oral historians, such as Tawaahkwakinanka (George Washington Finley) (Peeyankihšia/Piankashaw-Peewaalia) or someone else. Gatschet noted that by the 1890s only a couple dozen Myaamia-Peewaalia fluent speakers lived in the area. He estimated that about half of the Wa^{n}dat spoke their language. Gatschet surmised that most Šaawanwaki, Odawas, and Mō´dokni Máḵlaks (Modocs) still knew their languages. Whether these are Gatschet's own estimates, based on authoritative Native oral historians, or collected elsewhere, the numbers reiterate continued indigenous language use at the end of the 19th century. Gatschet's estimates arguably described a relatively stable, albeit strained and/or endangered, group of indigenous languages by the end of the 19th century (Gatschet 1892:238).[7]

John Peabody Harrington's Peewaalia and Šaawanwa materials echoed the endangerment of indigenous language use by the middle of the 20th century. Although detailing the waning use of Peewaalia, Harrington also detailed a very complex web of intertribal interactions and connections. Harrington's two main consultants were Maggie Young Boyd (Wisækwamok) (Peewaalia) and Alice Black Hoof (Šaawanwa). The surname Black Hoof has often been misspelled and altered to Blalock or Blaylock. In the materials she provided to Harrington, Maggie Young Boyd (Wisækwamok) listed her mother as being Nancy Stand, Sŏ^{w}anáfkikwa. In Alice Blalock's materials, however, Maggie is listed as the half-sister of Mrs. Beaver. This material also lists Maggie's husband, Sipíwa (Crossing the River), whose English name was Samuel Boyd, as being a white man. Grant and Costa, however, have noted that Boyd is a common Šaawanwa last name, that Samuel Boyd was Šaawanwa, and that Samuel Boyd knew the Šaawanwa language (Grant and Costa 1991:410; Harrington 1940–49 Maggie Boyd Vocabulary).[8] Wisækwamok (Maggie Young Boyd) was Peewaalia and knew some Šaawanwa, while Alice Black Hoof (Blalock) was Šaawanwa and knew some Peewaalia. Harrington's materials, then, included a variety of Peewaalia and Šaawanwa (Grant and Costa 1991:410–428; Harrington 1940–49 Alice Blalock Vocabulary).[9]

The language materials also portray a lot of intermarriage between members of the northeastern Oklahoma Indian nations. The husband of Wisækwamok (Maggie Young Boyd), Sipíwa (Samuel Boyd), was Šaawanwa. Alice Black Hoof noted that her brother, Silas Tucker, was Kaahkaahkia (Kaskaskia). Silas Tucker's father was Kaahkaahkia and his mother was Šaawanwa. Alice Black Hoof also commented how the famed artist Charles Banks Wilson's wife was not only Okáxpa but also had Šaawanwa, Peewaalia, and Euro-American ancestry (Grant and Costa 1991:427–428; Harrington 1940–49 Alice Blalock Vocabulary; Harrington 1940–49 Maggie Boyd Vocabulary). Stories of intermarriage and genealogical histories can be found intermingled with the language materials in the archival records and illuminate intertribal interactions and community intermixing by the late 19th century in northeastern Oklahoma.

These Native nations and community members also participated in each other's dances and ceremonies by the mid-19th century. They retained their separate sovereign statuses as tribal nations with their own distinct political systems, languages, and cultures, but they also fostered fellowship and alliances with their neighbors by attending each other's events, feasts, and dances. The Iroquoian- and Algonquian-speaking communities were already familiar with each other as they had lived near one another for many generations in the Great Lakes and Ohio Valley regions. Newer pan-Indian practices, such as the development of the Native American Church and the growth of Big Moon Peyotism in northeastern Oklahoma, served as other avenues for intertribal interactions by the end of the 19th century. Wisækwamok (Maggie Young Boyd) (Peewaalia) provided Harrington with the Peoria word for peyote: *piyóti* (Grant and Costa 1991:424–425; Harrington 1940–49 Maggie Boyd Vocabulary; Harrington 1940–49 Maggie Boyd's Vocabulary Reheard with Alice Blalock).[10]

Tawaahkwakinanka (George Washington Finley) (Peeyankihšia/Piankashaw-Peewaalia) was the ideal consultant for Albert Gatschet, and he shared information about Native life and traditions. Gatschet described Tawaahkwakinanka in 1892 as the "best Peoria [Peewaalia] interpr. [interpreter] . . . about 36 years old. —[Lives] Very near Miami town, in Ottawa [Odawa] Nation. His English [is] no good nor fluent" (Gatschet 1892:51).[11] Besides stories and place names, Tawaahkwakinanka also shared terminologies regarding cultural traditions. He provided the word *mishikamikwa*, which Gatschet defined and translated as 'dance ground'. Gatschet added the comment: "Now quit,—but Shawn. [Šaawanwaki] & Quapaws [Okáxpas] still keep this up, also Senecas [Shotinontowane'á:ka]." Gatschet specifically noted Tawaahkwakinanka as being his source for this specific detail. He went on to clarify that Shotinontowane' dance ceremonies occurred in a long house, and that the Shotinontowane'á:ka and Šaawanwaki also still practiced the Bread

Dance. Tawaahkwakinanka also described the *shishikwa'ni* (gourd rattle) used in many different ceremonial and secular Native dances. He said that the Eastern Šaawanwaki maintained a dance grounds near Tom Captain's place and that the Shotinontowane'á:ka had theirs by the Cowskin River at their Bassett Grove Ceremonial Grounds. Native oral historians such as Tawaahkwakinanka (G. W. Finley) provided extra details regarding dance practices, both continued and lost, among the Native communities in northeastern Oklahoma (Bergseth 2018; Gatschet 1892:185, 195; Wallace 2017:177–182).

Language materials such as those archived by Albert Samuel Gatschet, Charles Marius Barbeau, and John Peabody Harrington provide historians with rich, understudied resources, and they also open up discussion regarding historical narrative perspectives and translations. Whose voices and stories are privileged and shared when discussing Native histories? What other sources besides government documents and agency reports detail Native northeastern Oklahoma pasts, and what content is emphasized? Without linguistic training, the use of language materials can (and often did) exoticize and tokenize peoples and their cultures. But by ignoring them altogether, one also ignores indigenous worldviews and Native voices. Oral historians such as Sa'tsi'tsuwa' (Smith Nichols) (Wa^{n}dat-Kaion'ke), Wisækwamok (Maggie Young Boyd) (Peewaalia), Alice Black Hoof (Šaawanwa), and Tawaahkwakinanka (George Washington Finley) (Peeyankihšia/Piankashaw-Peewaalia) shared their own stories and perspectives with ethnologists and linguists. Their testimonies enrich historical narratives by emphasizing the maintenance of Native customs and languages alongside the struggles and loss of traditions. They complicate the stories of post-removal Indian histories in northeastern Oklahoma and describe a significant period of transition and adaptation for these tribal nations by the end of the 19th century. In a recent interview with the *Los Angeles Times* on the publication of his latest book, the Leech Lake Anishinaabe (Ojibwe) author David Treuer declared, "I don't know any other way to tell Indian history than through Indian voices" (Gilio-Whitaker 2019). This, too, can pertain to any history regarding Native peoples. Despite forced removal and assimilationist pressures, many Native peoples persevered and often maintained their traditions and languages. The incorporation of language materials accentuates and honors these Native voices in the historical record and complicates one-sided or simplified assimilationist narratives of complete loss and total demise.

NOTES

1. Many ideas in this paper were also developed from a presentation, "'Several Small Tribes Live in One Community in Oklahoma': Northeastern Oklahoma Native Language and History Testimony," delivered at Native Testimony: The Second Graduate Student Conference of the Princeton American Indian Studies Working Group, Princeton, New Jersey, on 6 May 2016, as well as in my dissertation. I would like to thank the two anonymous reviewers for their comments, compliments, and critiques. This paper is better because of their reviews that pressed me to reevaluate and reconsider some elements. I would also like to thank Monica Macaulay and Margaret Noodin, co-editors, and editorial assistant Sarah Lundquist. Any errors or mistakes remain my own.
2. Languages communicate our thoughts and values and we use them to express ourselves. English speakers may often forget how much meaning is imbedded in the language if one is not familiar with the Greek- and Latin-majority roots and their meanings. Daryl Baldwin (Myaamia/Miami), 2016 'genius grant' recipient, articulated the importance of indigenous languages. He said, "If there's one thing I've learned over the years it's that language is not a thing; it's an expression. So, then the question is 'what is it an expression of?'" Baldwin answered, "What we've learned over the years is that it's an expression of our indigenous knowledge system and we can articulate pieces of that knowledge system as it is expressed through our language" (Baldwin 2016).
3. See also Parks 1988:153–157.
4. Parks does not advocate for required linguistic training, but points out Plains ethnologists' lack of training and illustrates the importance of linguistics to ethnology (Parks 1988:154–155).
5. Another rendition and analysis of this origin story is published in Ironstrack 2014:181–208. See also Ironstrack 2010.
6. Grant and Costa note: "John White told Costa in early 1992 that he heard some old women speaking to each other in Peoria at a Quapaw powwow in the mid-1950s" (Grant and Costa 1991:426).
7. Tribal populations (as of August 1, 1891) listed in the Commissioner of Indian Affairs Report for 1891: 260 Shotinontowane'á:ka, 291 Wa^{n}dat, 79 Eastern Šaawanwaki, 68 Mō′dokni Mák̲laks, 166 Peewaaliaki, 75 Myaamiaki, 155 Odawas, and 206 Okáxpas. See *Annual Report of Commissioner of Indian Affairs, 1891* (U.S. Congress 1891:234). See also Bergseth 2018.
8. Also spelled Wisǽk̲mò'k or Wisækwamo·k (Early Dawn or Early Morning) and Sówanáfhikwa (Tree With Lots of Limbs). The name of Sipí·wa (Samuel Boyd) is also

spelled as θí·pí<u>wa</u>. See Harrington 1940–49 Maggie Boyd's Vocabulary Reheard with Alice Blalock. See also Grant and Costa 1991:426–428; Harrington 1940–49 Alice Blalock Vocabulary.

9. Also spelled as Blaylock.
10. See also Bergseth 2018.
11. See also Costa 2010:xi–xii, 9.

REFERENCES

Alfred, Gerald Taiaiake. 2009 [1999]. *Peace, Power, Righteousness: An Indigenous Manifesto.* Don Mills, ON: Oxford University Press Canada.

Baldwin, Daryl. 2016. eempaapiikinamankwi kineepwaayoneminaani: We Pick Up the Threads of Our Knowledge. Paper read at the Seventh Biennial Myaamiaki Conference, Miami University, Oxford, Ohio.

Barbeau, C. Marius. [n.d.]. Manuscript B-G-132.5, The Huron-Wyandot Files, C. Marius Barbeau Collection (Fonds C. Marius Barbeau). Canadian Museum of History (Musée Canadien de l'Histoire), Gatineau, QC.

Bergseth, Amy Dianne. 2018. Intertribal Interactions, Relationality, and Community Resilience in the Northeastern Oklahoma Indian Nations, 1800–1930. PhD thesis, University of Oklahoma.

Bohaker, Heidi. 2006. Nindoodemag: The Significance of Algonquian Kinship Networks in the Eastern Great Lakes Region, 1600–1701. *The William and Mary Quarterly, Third Series* 63(1): 23–52.

Canku, Clifford, and Michael Simon (eds.). 2013. *The Dakota Prisoner of War Letters / Dakota Kaŝkapi Okicize Wowapi.* Saint Paul: Minnesota Historical Society Press.

Costa, David J. (ed.). 2010. *myaamia neehi peewaalia aacimoona neehi aalhsoohkaana / Myaamia and Peoria Narratives and Winter Stories.* Oxford, OH, and Miami, OK: Miami Tribe of Oklahoma and Peoria Tribe of Oklahoma. Developed through the Myaamia Project at Miami University.

Denetdale, Jennifer. 2007. *Reclaiming Diné History: The Legacies of Navajo Chief Manuelito and Juanita.* Tucson: University of Arizona Press.

Doerfler, Jill, Niigaanwewidam James Sinclair, and Heidi Kiiwetinepinesiik Stark (eds.). 2013. *Centering Anishinaabeg Studies: Understanding the World through Stories.* East Lansing and Winnipeg: Michigan State University Press and University of Manitoba Press.

Dycus, Peggy. 1969. Interview with Clarence King. Vol. 49, Tape No. T-443–1, Side A, Part I (16

May 1969). Manuscript, The Duke Collection of American Indian Oral History, Western History Collections, University of Oklahoma Libraries, University of Oklahoma, Norman, Oklahoma.

Gatschet, Albert Samuel. 1892. Vocabulary and Text, Notebook No. 1. Manuscript No. 236, National Anthropological Archives, National Museum of Natural History, Smithsonian Institution, Smithsonian Museum Support Center, Suitland, Maryland.

Gilio-Whitaker, Dina. 2019. Q&A: David Treuer on Uncovering the Untold Native American histories of 'Heartbeat of Wounded Knee.' *Los Angeles Times*, 22 January. https://www.latimes.com/books/la-ca-jc-david-treuer-interview-20190122-htmlstory.html.

Grant, Anthony P., and David J. Costa. 1991. Some Observations on John P. Harrington's Peoria Vocabulary. *Anthropological Linguistics* 33(4):406–436.

Hansen, Rose. 2018. Meet the Man Who Hopes to Save the Shawnee Language. *Missouri Life: The Spirit of Discovery*. 23 October. https://www.missourilife.com/saving-shawnee-language.

Harrington, John Peabody. 1907–57. Supplemental Material on the Northeast/Southeast. Manuscript, Supplemental Material on the Northeast/Southeast, National Anthropological Archives, National Museum of Natural History, Smithsonian Institution, Smithsonian Museum Support Center, Suitland, Maryland.

Harrington, John Peabody. 1940–49. Alice Blalock Vocabulary. Manuscript, Shawnee/Peoria Subseries, Northeast/Southeast Series, John Peabody Harrington Papers, National Anthropological Archives, National Museum of Natural History, Smithsonian Institution, Smithsonian Museum Support Center, Suitland, Maryland.

Harrington, John Peabody. 1940–49. Maggie Boyd Vocabulary. Manuscript, Shawnee/Peoria Subseries, Northeast/Southeast Series, John Peabody Harrington Papers, National Anthropological Archives, National Museum of Natural History, Smithsonian Institution, Smithsonian Museum Support Center, Suitland, Maryland.

Harrington, John Peabody. 1940–49. Maggie Boyd's Vocabulary Reheard with Alice Blalock. Manuscript, Shawnee/Peoria Subseries, Northeast/Southeast Series, John Peabody Harrington Papers, National Anthropological Archives, National Museum of Natural History, Smithsonian Institution, Smithsonian Museum Support Center, Suitland, Maryland.

Hinton, Leanne. 2008. Languages and Language Programs. *Handbook of North American Indians, vol. 2: Indians in Contemporary Society*, ed. by Garrick A. Bailey, pp. 351–364. Washington, DC: Smithsonian Institution.

Ironstrack, George Michael. 2010. A Myaamia Beginning. Aacimotaatiiyankwi: A Myaamia Community Blog. 13 August. https://myaamiahistory.wordpress.

com/2010/08/13/a-myaamia-beginning/#_ednref.

Ironstrack, George Michael. 2014. nahi meehtohseeniwinki: iilinweeyankwi neehi iši meehtohseeniwiyankwi aatotamankwi: To Live Well: Our Language and Our Lives. *Beyond Two Worlds: Critical Conversations on Language and Power in Native North America*, ed. by James Joseph Buss and C. Joseph Genetin-Pilawa, pp. 181–208. Albany: State University of New York Press.

Kelsey, Penelope Myrtle. 2014. *Reading the Wampum: Essays on Hodinöhsö:ni' Visual Code and Epistemological Recovery*. Syracuse: Syracuse University Press.

Parks, Douglas R. 1988. The Importance of Language Study for the Writing of Plains Indian History. *New Directions in American Indian History*, ed. by Colin G. Calloway, pp. 153–197. Norman: University of Oklahoma Press.

Rice, Brian. 2013. *The Rotinonshonni: A Traditional Iroquoian History Through the Eyes of Teharonhia:wako and Sawiskera*. Syracuse, NY: Syracuse University Press.

Sweet, Rosemary. 2008. Antiquarianism and History. *Making History: The Changing Face of the Profession in Britain*, ed. by The Institute of Historical Research. https://www.history.ac.uk/makinghistory/resources/articles/antiquarianism.html.

Tyner, J. W. 1969. Interview with Robert Whitebird. Vol. 51, Tape No. T-546–3, Index Side B (23 December 1969). Manuscript, The Duke Collection of American Indian Oral History, Western History Collections, University of Oklahoma Libraries, University of Oklahoma, Norman, Oklahoma.

Tyner, J. W. 1970. Interview with Kenneth Oyler. Vol. 10, Tape No. T-572–3 (13 April 1970). Manuscript, The Duke Collection of American Indian Oral History, Western History Collections, University of Oklahoma Libraries, University of Oklahoma, Norman, Oklahoma.

U. S. Congress, House, 52nd Congress, 1st Session. 1891. Annual Report of Commissioner of Indian Affairs, 1891 [enclosed with 2920 H.exdoc.1] (H.ExDoc.1). Serial Set 2934. 1 October 1891. (I1.1:891/v.2; I20.1:891).

Wallace, Glenna J. 2017. Chiefs of the Eastern Shawnee Tribe. *The Eastern Shawnee Tribe of Oklahoma: Resilience Through Adversity*, ed. by Stephen A. Warren, in collaboration with the Eastern Shawnee Tribe of Oklahoma, pp. 171–213. Norman: University of Oklahoma Press.

Westerman, Gwen N., and Glenn M. Wasicuna. 2016. Letters from the Dakota, 1838–1878. Paper read at Translating Across Time and Space: Endangered Languages, Cultural Revitalization, and the Work of History Conference, American Philosophical Society.

Witgen, Michael J. 2012. *An Infinity of Nations: How the Native New World Shaped Early North America*. Philadelphia: University of Pennsylvania Press.

A Meskwaki Construction in Narrative Texts

Independent Pronoun + Full NP

Amy Dahlstrom

This paper investigates the discourse functions of a construction found in Meskwaki narrative texts in which an independent third-person pronoun co-occurs with a coreferential full NP.[1] An example may be seen in the underlined portions of (1)[2]:

(1) wi·nake·hwi·sahke·ha ayemeko e·hki·ši–nepe·hka·noči.
wi·na=ke·hi=wi·sahke·h-a aye=meko e·h-ki·ši–nepe·hka·no-či
he=moreover=W-SG early=EMPH AOR-PERF–pretend.to.sleep-3/AOR
'Wisahkeha himself was already pretending to sleep.' W1210

The corpus for this article is drawn mostly from the first half of a long (1,110-page) text written in 1913 by Alfred Kiyana, consisting of 550 manuscript pages, with approximately 10 clauses per page. In this corpus 52 tokens of the pronoun + NP construction are found, so it occurs roughly once every 100 clauses. The construction is therefore clearly a marked one. It is, however, found elsewhere in Meskwaki texts from the early 20th century and is a construction with cognate forms in sister languages:

(2) a. Menominee *we·nah oke·ma·w* 'the chief himself'
(Bloomfield 1962:465)

b. Potawatomi *win gé o nene* 'that man also'
(Lewis (in prep.))

c. Miami *neehi wiila amehkwa* . . . 'and then Beaver . . .'
(David J. Costa, personal communication)

d. Plains Cree êwako wiyawâw ocipwêwak . . . 'it was the Ojibwa . . .'
(H. C. Wolfart, personal communication)

e. Nishnaabemwin *wiinwaa go eta nishnaabeg* 'only they, the Indians'
(Valentine 2001:612)

Given the range of sister languages exhibiting cognates to this construction, it appears to be part of the stylistic repertoire of Algonquian narrative discourse.

The independent pronoun in the construction under investigation is part of a series of emphatic independent personal pronouns, primarily used on their own for expressing topic or focus:

(3) a. ni·na 'I'
b. ki·na 'you (singular)'
c. wi·na 'he/she (proximate)'
d. ni·na·na 'we (exclusive)'
e. ki·na·na 'we (inclusive)'
f. ki·nwa·wa 'you (plural)'
g. wi·nwa·wa 'they (proximate)'

For the definitions of topic and focus, see Lambrecht (1994) and Dahlstrom (1993, 1995, 2003, 2017).[3] The topic relation expresses aboutness: the material following an overt topic is a comment about the topic. Example (4) illustrates the use of an independent pronoun to announce a new topic:

(4) **ni·na a·kwi ke·ko·hi tepe·netama·nini**
ni·na a·kwi ke·ko·hi tepe·net-ama·nini
I not something own-1>0/NEG
'**Me**, I don't own anything' W502H

In (4), notice that the first-person topic precedes the negative *a·kwi* 'not'; this is the typical word order for topics in relation to negative elements in Meskwaki (Dahlstrom 1993, 1995).

The term 'focus' as used here corresponds to Lambrecht's sense of argument focus: It expresses the unpredictable element that fills the variable of a presupposed open proposition. For example, consider the independent pronoun in (5), where the third-person object of the verb refers to the culture hero Wisahkeha as a baby and the second-person addressee is Wisahkeha's grandmother:

(5) **ki·na**meko ki·hka·kike·wi–pemena·wa,
ki·na=meko ke-i·h-ka·kike·wi–pemen-a·wa,
you=EMPH 2-FUT-forever–take.care.of-2>3/IND
'**You** [are the one who] will take care of him forever' W22E

The presupposition in (5) is that someone will take care of Wisahkeha forever; the unpredictable information, which is expressed by the pronoun in focus position, is that the addressee is that person. If a focused element is used in a clause containing a negative element, the negative precedes the focused element (Dahlstrom 1993, 1995).

The question investigated in this article is: What is the function of using an independent pronoun in conjunction with a coreferential full NP? In the discussion that follows I first describe the distribution and form of the pronoun + NP construction, and then illustrate some of the construction's functions within narrative texts. Although a single discourse function that accounts for all collected instances of the pronoun + NP cannot be identified, it will be shown that this construction may be employed for expressing something unexpected, for indicating reciprocal action, or for marking episode boundaries within a narrative.

Distribution and Form of the Pronoun + NP Construction

To begin with, it must be emphasized that the independent pronoun seen in the construction under investigation here is not the contrastive enclitic *=wi·na*. In Meskwaki (as in other Algonquian languages) the third-person singular independent pronoun *wi·na* 'he/she (proximate)' has been grammaticalized as an enclitic expressing something like 'but; however.' The form of the enclitic is invariable—always *=wi·na*—and in texts written in the Meskwaki syllabary, which indicates phonological word boundaries, there is never a word boundary symbol written before the contrastive enclitic.

(6) ni·nake·h**wi·na** ana·kowe neki·ši–owi·wi,
ni·na=ke·hi=**wi·na** ana·kowe ne-ki·ši–owi·wi-Ø,
I=moreover=**CONTR** yesterday 1-PERF–have.a.wife-1/IND
'As for me, I got married yesterday' W99N

(7) wi·na**wi·na** e·hki·wi–kečihka·hke·piči.
wi·na=**wi·na** e·h-ki·wi–kečihka·hke·pi-či.
he=**CONTR** AOR-around–sit.with.chest.out-3/AOR
'But he, on the other hand, was just sitting with his chest out.' W365R

Example (6) shows that the enclitic *=wi·na* may be used in a clause where there is no third-person participant at all, here attaching to an independent first-person pronoun. (7) shows that the enclitic *=wi·na* may even attach to the homophonous independent third-person pronoun. The enclitic *=wi·na* is clearly performing a different function from that of the independent pronoun that is its host in (7).

Example (8) shows that the contrastive enclitic can also be used with the pronoun + NP construction under investigation here:

(8) wi·na**wi·na** no·hkomesa pa·pekwa·nahi e·htaši–mayake·nemiči
wi·na=**wi·na** ne-o·hkomes-a
she=**CONTR** 1-grandmother-SG

pa·pekwa=i·nahi e·h-taši–mayake·nem-iči
immediately=after.that AOR-be.engaged.in–think.O.strange-3>1/AOR
'But my grandmother, on the other hand, immediately thinks I'm strange . . . ' W517D

The initial portion of the Meskwaki pronoun + NP construction is clearly not the contrastive enclitic =*wi·na*.

Turning now to the pronoun + NP construction itself, we may make a number of observations regarding the way in which it appears in texts. First, this construction is obviously only possible with third-person referents, since it involves a lexical NP. Less obvious is the fact that the construction is only found with PROXIMATE third-person referents: This follows from the nature of the emphatic series of independent pronouns, which lacks an obviative third person form. In most of the examples in the corpus the pronoun + NP construction expresses a syntactic subject; this is not surprising, since subjects are frequently proximate.[4] Moreover, all examples collected of this constuction involve a third person who is human, a spirit, or an anthropomorphized animal—in every case, a fairly significant character in the narrative text. We may also note that the NP in this construction is never the first mention of a new character.

The pronoun always precedes the NP, as seen in (1) and (8); (1) and (8) also demonstrate that this construction is available both in the narrative portion of texts and in the representation of quotes by the text's characters. A final observation is that the pronoun + NP phrase may be either singular or plural; (9) is an example of a plural pronoun followed by a plural NP.

(9) wi·nwa·wa kemehtose·neni·me·hena·naki mešemeko wi·hki·wi–inose·wa·či,
    wi·nwa·wa ke-mehtose·neni·me·h-ena·n-aki
    they 2-person.DIM-21-PL

    meše=meko wi·h-ki·wi–inose·-wa·či,
    freely=EMPH FUT-around–walk.thither-3P/AOR
    'Our (inclusive) people will walk around just anywhere,' W442

The majority of the examples in the corpus appear at the very beginning of the sentence, or preceded only by a conjunction such as *o·ni* 'and then':

(10) o·ni wi·nameko kehči–maneto·wa e·hašiha·či wi·hanohka·na·čihi neniwahi.
o·ni wi·na=meko kehči–maneto·w-a e·h-aših-a·či
and.then he=EMPH great–spirit-SG AOR-make-3>3'/AOR

IC-wi·h-anohka·n-a·čihi neniw-ahi.
IC-FUT-commission-3>3'/PART/3'P man-OBV.PL
'And then the Great Spirit himself made men to send on errands.' W319A

The left edge of the clause is the typical position for new/shifted topics or focused elements. (11) is a clear example of a shifted topic that exhibits the pronoun + NP construction:

(11) wi·nake·hi kehči–maneto·wa, kapo·twe ahki·ki e·hina·piči, kotakimeko e·hina·piči.
wi·na=ke·hi kehči–maneto·w-a,
he=moreover great–spirit-SG

kapo·twe ahky-eki e·h-ina·pi-či,
at.some.point earth-LOC AOR-look.thither-3/AOR

kotaki=meko e·h-ina·pi-či.
other=EMPH AOR-look.thus-3/AOR
'As for the Great Spirit, pretty soon when he looked down at the earth, he saw that it looked different.' W312CD

Similarly, the pronoun + NP phrase in (12) functions as focus:

(12) wi·nača·hmeko no·hkomese·hena·na neketema·kihekwa,
wi·na=ča·hi=meko ne-o·hkomese·h-ena·n-a ne-ketema·kih-ekwa,
she=SO=EMPH 1-grandmother.DIM-1P-SG 1-bring.ruin.upon-3>1/IND
'So our grandmother herself is the one bringing ruin upon me,' W284C

It is not the case, however, that all NPs appearing as topic or focus are accompanied by a coreferential independent pronoun, as the following examples demonstrate:

(13) **i·niye·kake·hi mehtose·neniwaki,** i·ya·hmekoni e·hpya·wa·či e·ši–ki·hkapiwa·či.

i·niye·ka=ke·hi **mehtose·neniw-aki,** i·ya·hi=meko=i·ni

those.ABSENT.ANIM=moreover **person-PL** yonder=EMPH=now

e·h-pya·-wa·či IC-iši–ki·hkapi-wa·či.

AOR-come-3P/AOR IC-thither–move.seat.closer-3P/PART/OBL

'**As for those other people,** they arrived at the place for their new village.' W117G

(14) o·ni še·škimeko **kehkeše·wi** i·nahi ahte·wi.

o·ni še·ški=meko **kehkeše·w-i** i·nahi ahte·-wi.

and.then only=EMPH **charcoal-SG** there be.there-0/IND

'And then only **charcoal** remained there.' W62F

The pronoun appearing in examples like (11) and (12) must therefore be performing some other function, not simply marking that the NP is functioning as topic or focus. A variety of functions are explored in the following section.

The pronoun + NP construction nearly always occurs in the matrix clause in my corpus of examples. (15), however, shows that the combination of pronoun + NP may occur in an embedded context as well, here within a relative clause:

(15) mani kene·ta·pwa wi·nwa·wa maneto·waki ki·šepye·hamowa·či.

mani ke-ne·t-a·pwa [wi·nwa·wa maneto·w-aki

this 2-see-2P>0/IND they spirit-PL

IC-ki·šepye·h-amowa·či].

IC-PERF.draw-3P>0/PART/0

'You see this [map] which the spirits themselves drew.' (Michelson 1925:54:41)

Additionally, (16) appears to be an example of the pronoun + NP construction in an embedded complement clause.

(16) we·nahi e·ne·nemiya·ke!
wi·nameko ne·ške·nemiyameta maneto·wa wi·hnešiyamečimeko ketene·nemipena.

we·nahi	IC-ine·nem-iya·ke!	
this.is.it	IC-think.thus.of-2>1P/PART/OBL	
[wi·na=meko	IC-neške·nem-iyameta	maneto·wa
he=EMPH	IC-hate-3>1P/PART/3	spirit-SG

wi·h-nes-iyameči=meko]	ke-ene·nem-ipena.
FUT-kill-3>1P/AOR=EMPH	2-think.thus.of-2>1P/IND

'Now I see what you think about us!
You want the spirit who hates us to kill us.' W549HI
[lit. 'you want (with respect to us) for him to kill us']

(16) requires some explication. The first line is included for context. The matrix verb of the second sentence is in final position: *ketene·nemipena* 'you think thus of us' (here translated as 'you want . . . '). What the second-person subject wants is 'for the spirit who hates us to kill us.' The subject of the complement clause is what is expressed with the pronoun + NP construction of interest here.

All possible forms of NPs may appear in the noun phrase portion of this construction. We have already seen that a personal name may appear (1), as may a common noun (15), a possessed kinship term (12), other possessed nouns (9), or a noun modified by a relative clause (16). The NP may also consist of a demonstrative alone:

(17) "mečihwe·na·na apeno·hiwa!
wi·nama·hi·na owi·yawi we·we·ne·netamwa,"

"meči=ihi=we·na=i·na	apeno·hi-wa!	
quite=not=in.fact=that.ANIM	be.child-3/IND	
wi·na=ma·hi=i·na	owi·yawi	we·we·ne·net-amwa,"
she=as.you.know=that.ANIM	herself	have.control.over-3>0/IND

"'Well, she is hardly a child!
She herself has the say over what she does,'" W129NO

Discontinuous NPs are also found in the pronoun + NP construction:

(18) wi·nakoči·na ki·wiki·wi·hkamwa wi·kiya·pye·ni kemešo·hwa·wa
wi·na=koči=i·na ki·wi-ki·wi·hk-amwa
he=you.know=that.ANIM REDUP-go.around.dealing.with-3>0/IND

wi·kiya·py-ani ke-mešo·h-wa·w-a
house-PL 2-grandfather-2P-SG
'That grandfather of yours (pl.) has always been going around visiting the houses.' W250

The next question to ask is, what material may intervene between the pronoun and NP? We have seen numerous examples in which a single enclitic particle appears between the pronoun and the full NP (e.g., [18]). It is also possible to have more than one enclitic in that position:

(19) e·ha·šowa·ška·niči.
e·h-a·šowa·ška·-niči.
AOR-speed.across-3'/AOR
'[W's younger brother] leapt across [the river].'

wi·na**ke·he·yi·kimeko** wi·sahke·ha e·ha·šowa·ška·či.
wi·na=**ke·hi=e·yi·ki=meko** wi·sahke·h-a e·h-a·šowa·ška·-či.
he=**moreover=also=EMPH** W-SG AOR-speed.across-3/AOR
'Wisahkeha himself also leapt across it.' W79IJ

In (19), three enclitic particles follow the independent pronoun *wi·na*. In all examples in which only enclitics appear between the two halves of the construction, I would argue that the pronoun and NP are not separated syntactically. In other words, in my view the pronoun + NP form a unified syntactic constituent, with the placement of the enclitics sensitive to the right edge of the first phonological word.

In other cases, however, the NP coreferential to the independent pronoun may be separated from the pronoun by syntactic material, such as by the object and verb in (20)[5]:

(20) aše·we·na mana nesi·me·ha nemi·na·wa,
wi·nača·hi ma·hani tepe·netamwa manaha a·ya·pa·hte·ha,"
e·hina·či osi·me·hani wi·sahke·ha.

aše=we·na mana ne-si·me·h-a ne-mi·n-a·wa,
merely=in.fact this.ANIM 1-younger.sibling-SG 1-give-1>3/IND

wi·na=ča·hi ma·hani tepe·net-amwa manaha a·ya·pa·hte·h-a,"
he=so these own-3>0/IND this.ANIM A-SG

e·h-in-a·či o-si·me·h-ani wi·sahke·h-a.
AOR-say.thus.about-3>3'/AOR 3-younger.sibling-OBV W-SG

'But actually I have just given them to my younger brother here, so Ayapahteha owns these things himself," Wisahkeha said about his younger brother.' W259DE

I think it is possible that the discontinuous pronoun and NP construction in (20) may be performing a different function than the syntactically unified examples seen earlier, but I will leave that an open question for now.[6]

A single example in the corpus has both the pronoun and the NP appearing at the end of a clause:

(21) i·ni wi·hiši–ašihtawaki," e·hina·či wi·nameko keše·–maneto·wa.

i·ni IC-wi·h-iši–ašihtaw-aki,"
that IC-FUT-thus–make.O2.for.O-1>3/PART/OBL

e·h-in-a·či wi·na=meko keše·–maneto·w-a.
AOR-say.thus.to-3>3'/AOR he=EMPH gentle–spirit-SG

'"That's how many [future people] I will make for him," the Great Spirit said about him.' W383B

I do not know what the function of postposing the pronoun + NP construction may be in this example. Note that the pronoun + NP in (21) cannot be analyzed as beginning a new clause here; it is immediately followed by *o·ni wi·sahke·ha*, ". . ." 'And then Wisahkeha [said], ". . .", which is the beginning of a new sentence.

Some Functions of the Meskwaki Pronoun + NP Construction

Unexpectedness

Several instances of the Meskwaki pronoun + NP construction seem to indicate that the reported event is unexpected or surprising.[7] The context for (22) is that a young man sees his aunt sitting under a tree in which a mountain lion is perched. Surprisingly, the old woman is unaware of the mountain lion above her.

(22) wi·nake·hi·na metemo·he·ha i·nini e·hpwa·wi–kehke·nema·či.

wi·na=ke·hi=i·na   metemo·he·h-a   i·nini
she=moreover=that.ANIM   old.woman.DIM-SG   that.OBV

e·h-pwa·wi–kehke·nem-a·či.
AOR-not–know-3>3'/AOR
'But that old woman didn't know about that [mountain lion] herself.' W16B

(23) provides another example where the pronoun + NP construction seems to indicate something surprising. The context here is that Wisahkeha's brother and nearly all the other children have been murdered at a dance. Wisahkeha's grandmother comes from the dance, weeping, but Wisahkeha asks her casually, "You're not going over to dance?"

(23) wi·nake·hi·na wi·sahke·ha wa·natohkameko,
"ano·hko, a·kwimeko mawi–ni·miyanini?" e·hina·či.

wi·na=ke·hi=i·na   wi·sahke·h-a   wa·natohka=meko,
he=moreover=that.ANIM   W-SG   unconcernedly=EMPH

"ano·hko,   a·kwi=meko   mawi–ni·mi-yanini?"   e·h-in-a·či.
g.m.VOC   not=EMPH   go.and–dance-2/NEG   AOR-say.thus.to-3>3'/AOR
'But Wisahkeha asked her casually, "Grandma, you're not going over to dance?"' W164H

Parallel/Reciprocal Action

Several examples in the corpus lend themselves to a gloss of 'in turn', describing either parallel action (as in (19) in the preceding, when both brothers leap across a river) or reciprocal action, as in (24)[8]:

(24) e·hnenohtawa·či osi·me·hani,
wi·nana·hkači e·hnenohta·koči wi·sahke·ha osi·me·hani.
e·h-nenohtaw-a·či o-si·me·h-ani,
AOR-understand-3>3'/AOR 3-younger.sibling.DIM-OBV

wi·na=na·hkači e·h-nenohtaw-ekoči wi·sahke·h-a o-si·me·h-ani.
he=again AOR-understand-3'>3/AOR W-SG 3-y.sib.DIM-OBV
'He understood his younger brother, and in turn his younger brother also understood Wisahkeha.' W35IJ

(25) is perhaps another example of the pronoun + NP construction used in the second of two parallel clauses, contrasting Wisahkeha's more wicked nature to that of his brother.

(25) a·kwipi wa·waneška·hiničini osi·me·hani.
wi·napi wi·sahke·ha wa·waneška·ha·tesiwa,
a·kwi=ipi wa·waneška·hi-ničini o-si·me·h-ani.
not=HRSY be.wicked-3'/NEG 3-younger.sibling.DIM-OBV

wi·na=ipi wi·sahke·h-a wa·waneška·ha·tesi-wa,
he=HRSY W-SG be.constitutionally.wicked-3/IND
'His younger brother wasn't a rascal, it's said. Wisahkeha, on the other hand, had a wicked character, it's said.' W34IJ

New Episode

Yet another function of the pronoun + NP construction seems to be to signal the beginning of a significant episode in the text. Consider (26), in which the previous context is included before the appearance of the construction in question. (See (10) and (11) in the preceding for other clear examples of this function.)

(26) e·hča·ki–pi·tike·wa·či maneto·waki, mo·hčimeko keše·–maneto·wa.
i·nina·hpi·tike·či e·hawiči, na·hkači okwise·hani e·hpi·tikana·či.

wi·na keše·–maneto·wa, "nahi, nekwi·hi, wi·sahke·ha osi·me·hani ki·howi·hka·ni,"
e·hina·či okwisani.

e·h-ča·ki–pi·tike·-wa·či	maneto·w-aki,	mo·hči=meko	keše·–maneto·w-a.
AOR-all–enter-3P/AOR	spirit-PL	even=EMPH	gentle–spirit-SG

i·nina·hi=IC-pi·tike·-či	e·h-awi-či,
at.that.time=IC-enter-3/CH.C	AOR-be.there-3/PART/LOC

na·hkači	o-kwise·h-ani	e·h-pi·tikan-a·či.
again	3-son.DIM-OBV	AOR-bring.in-3>3'/AOR

wi·na	keše·–maneto·w-a,	"nahi,	nekwi·hi,	wi·sahke·h-a	o-si·me·h-ani
he	gentle–spirit-SG	well,	son.VOC	W-SG	3-y.sib.DIM-OBV

ke-i·h-owi·hka·ni-Ø,"	e·h-in-a·či	o-kwis-ani.
2-FUT-have.O2.as.friend-2/IND	AOR-say.thus.to-3>3'/AOR	3-son-OBV

'All the spirits went into their homes, even the Great Spirit.
At the time he went into his place, he also brought his son inside.
The Great Spirit said to his son, "Listen, son, you will have Wisahkeha's little brother as your friend."' W73M-74B

The quote in (26) marks the start of a new episode. This is the first instance of the Great Spirit's words being quoted in the story, and indeed, the content of what the Great Spirit says is quite significant for the remainder of the text.

Note that use of the pronoun + NP construction in (26) does not fit the description of the functions illustrated previously. It is not unexpected that the Great Spirit would speak to his son, nor is there parallel or reciprocal action that would accommodate a reading of 'in turn'. There is in fact no shift of topic (or subject) occurring at the point where the pronoun + NP construction is used. Instead, attention is drawn to the beginning of a new, significant episode of the text.

Conclusion

This article has shown that the Meskwaki pronoun + NP construction is primarily found with overt topics and focused phrases in matrix clauses; it occurs both in the narrative portions of texts and within direct quotes. No single function unifying all the instances of the pronoun + NP construction has been found. Instead, there seem to be several contexts in which this construction may be employed, including marking something unexpected, parallel or reciprocal action, or the beginning of a significant episode in the text.

NOTES

1. Thanks to Lucy Thomason, H. C. Wolfart, David J. Costa, and the audience at the 50th Algonquian Conference for helpful comments.
2. Abbreviations: 1P = first person exclusive plural, 21 = first person inclusive plural, 3' = obviative, 0 = inanimate, ABSENT = absentative demonstrative, ANIM = animate, AOR = aorist prefix; aorist conjunct inflection, CH.C = changed conjunct, CONTR = contrastive, DIM = diminutive, EMPH = emphatic, FUT = future, HRSY = hearsay evidential, IC = initial change (ablaut rule), IND = independent indicative, LOC = locative, NEG= negative inflection, O = (first) object, O2 = second object, OBL = oblique head of relative clause, OBV = obviative, PART = conjunct participle, PERF = perfective, PL = plural, REDUP = reduplication, SG = singular, VOC = vocative, X = unspecified subject. Subject and object features in verb inflection are separated by > and are followed by identification of the verbal paradigm. The head of a relative clause is identified following the label PART (participle). Vowel length is marked by a raised dot. Examples cited as W are from Kiyana 1913.
3. For other approaches to information structure in Algonquian languages, see Bliss (2005), Junker (2004), Rhodes (2017), and Wolvengrey (2011), inter alia.
4. See (24) in the following for an example of the pronoun + NP construction expressing a proximate object.
5. See Thomason (2003:200) for a similar discontinuous example.
6. Compare the difference word order can make for English intensifier *-self* forms, which are formally similar to the Meskwaki construction under investigation in pairing an emphatic pronoun with a full NP:

    The queen herself opened the exhibit.
    The queen opened the exhibit herself.

Item (i) presupposes that the queen ranks high on some sort of scale; what is unexpected or remarkable is the fact that the queen made an appearance to open the exhibit. In (ii) the *self* form is contrastive, implying that the queen acted alone, without help.

7. See Edmondson and Plank (1978) and Kemmer (1995), inter alia, for discussion of English intensifier *-self* constructions indicating unexpectedness or remarkability. For Meskwaki, it should be noted that the language also has more grammaticalized methods for indicating surprise or mirativity, including a second position enclitic =či·hi 'it was discovered' and a construction combining a particle *keye·hapa* 'in fact, as it turns out' plus the changed unreal mode of the conjunct order.
8. Compare Edmondson and Plank's identification of a particular subtype of English intensifier *-self*, which can be glossed as 'in turn', often involving the reversal of semantic roles:

   (i) Lucrezia poisoned Lorenzo, and was herself poisoned by Cesare (Edmondson and Plank 1978:386).

REFERENCES

Bliss, Heather. 2005. Topic, Focus, and Point of View in Blackfoot. *Proceedings of WCCFL 24*, ed. by John Alderete, pp. 61–69. Somerville, MA: Cascadilla Proceedings Project.

Bloomfield, Leonard. 1962. *The Menomini Language*. New Haven, CT: Yale University Press.

Dahlstrom, Amy. 1993. The Syntax of Discourse Functions in Fox. *BLS 19 Special Session on the Syntax of Native American Languages*, ed. by David Peterson, pp. 11–21. Berkeley, CA: Berkeley Linguistics Society.

Dahlstrom, Amy. 1995. *Topic, Focus, and Other Word Order Problems in Algonquian. The Belcourt Lecture*. Winnipeg: Voices of Rupert's Land.

Dahlstrom, Amy. 2003. Focus Constructions in Meskwaki (Fox). *Proceedings of the LFG03 Conference*, ed. by Miriam Butt and Tracy Holloway King, pp. 144–163. Stanford, CA: CSLI Publications.

Dahlstrom, Amy. 2017. Obviation and Information Structure in Meskwaki. *Papers of the 46th Algonquian Conference*, ed. by Monica Macaulay and Margaret Noodin, pp. 39–54. East Lansing: Michigan State University Press.

Edmondson, Jerold A., and Frans Plank. 1978. Great Expectations: An Intensive Self Analysis. *Linguistics and Philosophy* 2:373–413.

Junker, Marie-Odile. 2004. Focus, Obviation, and Word Order in East Cree. *Lingua* 114:345–365.

Kemmer, Suzanne. 1995. Emphatic and Reflexive-Self: Expectations, Viewpoint, and

Subjectivity. *Subjectivity and Subjectivisation: Linguistic Perspectives*, ed. by Dieter Stein and Susan Wright, pp. 55–82. Cambridge: Cambridge University Press.

Kiyana, Alfred. 1913. wisakea osani okyeni osimeani okomeseani. [Wisahkeha, His Father, His Mother, His Younger Brother, His Grandmother.] Manuscript 2958-a, National Anthropological Archives, Smithsonian Institution, Washington, DC.

Lambrecht, Knud. 1994. *Information Structure and Sentence Form*. Cambridge: Cambridge University Press.

Lewis, Robert. In preparation. Potawatomi Discourse Markers. PhD thesis, University of Chicago.

Michelson, Truman. 1925. Accompanying Papers. *Annual Report of the Bureau of American Ethnology* 40:23–658. Washington, DC: Government Printing Office.

Rhodes, Richard A. 2017. Obviation, Inversion, and the Notion of Topic in Algonquian. *Papers of the 46th Algonquian Conference*, ed. by Monica Macaulay and Margaret Noodin, pp. 197–212. East Lansing: Michigan State University Press.

Thomason, Lucy Grey. 2003. The Proximate and Obviative Contrast in Meskwaki. PhD thesis, University of Texas.

Valentine, J. Randolph. 2001. *Nishnaabemwin Reference Grammar*. Toronto: University of Toronto Press.

Wolvengrey, Arok Elessar. 2011. *Semantic and Pragmatic Functions in Plains Cree Syntax*. Utrecht: LOT.

The Syntax of (IR)REALIS in Innu

Rose-Marie Déchaine and Monique Dufresne

This article explores the syntax of (IR)REALIS in Innu, where REALIS is zero-marked, and IRREALIS is marked by *ka* or its allomorphs *tshika* or *tshê*.[1] Allomorph selection is conditioned by person and clause-type; we call these "PERSON-splits" and "C-splits." The person-split is found with the independent order: *ka* with first/second person (1); *tshika* with third person (2). The C-split occurs in the conjunct order: Irrealis is possible with the subordinating C for which the exponent is initial change *ka* > *kê* > *tshê* (3), but not with other subordinating Cs such as ê (4).[2]

(1) a. ni uâpamânanat
ni [uâpamâ]-nân-at
1 see.TA=1PL=3PL(IND)
'We see them' [D530]

b. **nika** uâpamânanat
ni-ka [uâpamâ]-nân-at
1-IRR see.TA-1PL-3PL(IND)
'We will see them' [D534]

(2) a. uâpamêu
[uâpamê]-u
see.TA-3SG(IND)
'S/he sees them' [D531]

b. **tshika** uâpamêu
tshika [uâpamê]-u
IR see.TA=3SG(IND)
'S/he will see them' [D535]

TABLE 1. Distribution of Innu irrealis allomorphs

<table>
<tr><th colspan="3">SYNTACTIC CONTEXT</th><th colspan="4">MORPHOLOGICAL REALIZATION</th></tr>
<tr><th rowspan="2">ROOT CP</th><th colspan="2">NONROOT CP</th><th rowspan="2">ORDER</th><th colspan="3" rowspan="2">C_{FORCE}</th></tr>
<tr><th>COMPLEMENT</th><th>ADJUNCT</th></tr>
<tr><td>✓ (ka)</td><td>✗</td><td>✗</td><td rowspan="3">INDEPENDENT</td><td rowspan="3">C_{PERS}</td><td>1</td><td>↔ ni(t)=</td></tr>
<tr><td>✓ (ka)</td><td>✗</td><td>✗</td><td>2</td><td>↔ ki(t)=</td></tr>
<tr><td>✓ (tshi ka)</td><td>✗</td><td>✗</td><td>3</td><td>↔ ∅</td></tr>
<tr><td>✗</td><td>✓ (tshê)</td><td>✓ (tshê)</td><td>CONJUNCT</td><td colspan="2">$C_{SUBORDINATE}$</td><td>↔ IC</td></tr>
</table>

(3) a. . . . uiâpamâtshiht
IC+[uâpamâ]-tshiht
C see.TA-1PL>3PL(CJ)
'. . . that we see them' [D268f]

b. . . . tshê uâpamâtshiht
. . . IC+ka [uâpamâ]-tshiht
C.IRR see.TA-1PL>3PL(CJ)
'. . . (for) us to see them' [D272, 551]

(4) a. . . . ê uâpamâtshiht
ê [uâpamâ]-tshiht
C see.TA-1PL>3PL(CJ)
'. . . whenever we see them' [D272]

b. * . . . ê ka uâpamâtshiht
ê ka [uâpamâ]-tshiht
C IRR see.TA-1PL>3PL(CJ)

The factors that condition the C- and person-split are key to our analysis; see Table 1. For the C-split, (independent order) root CPs select (*tshi*)*ka*, but (conjunct order) nonroot CPs select *tshê*. For the person-split (first/second versus third), the locus is C; this indicates that, in Innu, C selects for a particular value of (ir)realis.

Another puzzle relates to interpretation: In (1b) irrealis *ka* has a future construal, but in (3b) it expresses nonfiniteness; such semantic indeterminacy is a hallmark of irrealis. After introducing relevant background, we survey the correlates of irrealis,[3] and then turn our attention to an Innu-specific feature, namely, the proliferation of realis clause-typing. We assess the consequences of this innovation for ir(realis) syntax, focusing on the (non)root CP partition. Finally, we explore how Innu ir(realis) syntax interacts with the derivation of complex Vforms and the broader implications of our analysis.

TABLE 2. Innu agreement paradigms

	PARADIGM 1: PROCLITIC + ENCLITIC AGR			PARADIGM 2: ENCLITIC AGR
	NOMINAL		VERBAL	VERBAL
	(i) PRONOUN	(ii) POSSESSOR 'X's shoe'	(iii) INDEPENDENT 'X sleep'	(iv) CONJUNCT '. . . that X sleep'
1	n-[iǹ]	ni-[massin]	ni [nipa]-n	ê-[nipâ]-ian
1pl	n-[iǹ]-an	ni-[massin]-nan	ni [nipa]-nan	ê-[nipâ]-iat
2	tsh-[iǹ]	tshi-[massin]	tshi [nipa]-n	ê-[nipâ]-in
21	tsh-[iǹ]-an(nu)	tshi-[massin]-nan	tshi [nipa]-nan	ê-[nipâ]-iak[u]
2pl	tsh-[iǹ]-uau	tshi-[massin]-uau	tshi [nipa]-nau	ê [nipâ]-iêk[u]
3	u-[iǹ]	u-[massin]	∅ [nipa]-u	ê [nipâ]-t
3pl	u-[iǹ]-uau	u-[massin]-uau	∅ [nipa]-uat	ê [nipâ]-ht
3obv	—	u-[massin]-iǹu	∅ [nipa]-ǹiti	ê [nipâ]-ǹiti
	PERS-[PRN]-AGR	PERS-[shoe]-AGR	PERS [sleep]-AGR	C [sleep]-AGR
	[D95]	[D56]	[D498]	[D509]

The Integration of (Ir)Realis into Clause Structure

The status of (ir)realis as a linguistic category is debated, especially by Bybee (1998:269), who concludes that (ir)realis is epiphenomenal. However, Michael (2014)—based on Nanti data (Kampan, Arawakan)—argues that the (ir)realis contrast is the basis of diagnostics relating to temporal reference, negation, modality, clause-linking, voice, and valency. We show that the Innu data are likewise consistent with an (ir)realis partition.[4] We do this in two steps: After establishing the formal basis for the person- and C-split, we argue that the (ir)realis partition is conditioned by C_{FORCE} and $C_{FINITENESS}$ (C_{FIN}) and that it has numerous syntactic, semantic, and morphological correlates.

The Formal Basis for the Person-Split and C-Split

Relevant to our analysis of (ir)realis is the existence of two distinct agreement paradigms; see Table 2. One set—which has pro- and enclitic agreement—is attested with Nstems (columns 1 and 2) as well as independent order Vstems (column 3). The other set—which has only enclitic agreement—is found exclusively with conjunct order Vstems (column 4). The latter, instead of proclitic agreement, deploys prefixal C-typing: In column 5, we illustrate this with the ê complementizer. These two agreement paradigms reflect a structural difference in the left periphery of the CP.

Consider the paradigm that deploys pro- and enclitic agreement in figure 1 (5). With Nstems, proclitic agreement realizes a nominal possessor in Spec,DP (5a) (Déchaine 1999); with Vstems it is associated with Spec,CP (Cook 2008, 2014). With the latter, there is a person-split: First/second person is overt (5b.i), but third person is covert (5b.ii).[5] This person-split reflects discourse restrictions on the use of independent order root CPs, which have indexical force: First/second person in C restricts topic-bound *pro* in Spec,CP to 'speaker' (first person) or 'addressee' (second person); in the absence of proclitic agreement, topic-bound *pro* defaults to third person. Now consider the conjunct order in figure 2 (6), which has a much freer distribution, and is found in root and nonroot CPs. Accordingly, we treat conjunct-mode CPs as the elsewhere case; formally, they are analyzed as null-operator environments (Cook 2008, 2014). Significantly, the prefixal C-position is realized by various Cs, including initial change (IC, a general marker of subordination), null C (specified for realis), and ê and *kâ* (realis Cs that introduce adjunct CPs).

(5) **FIGURE 1.** Person Split with Independent Order

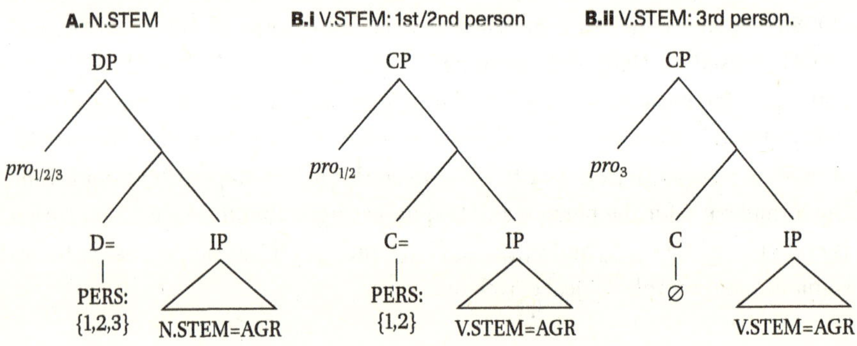

(6) FIGURE 2. C-Split with Conjunct Order

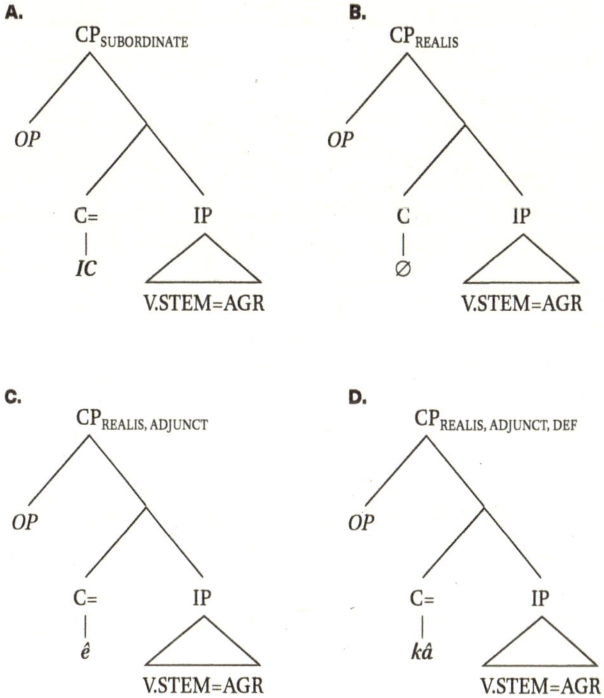

The Layered CP: Detecting the (Ir)Realis Partition

The left periphery of the clause—the set of functional heads associated with the CP domain—can be exploded into several C layers (Rizzi 1997); relevant to our analysis are C_{FORCE} and $C_{FINITENESS}$ (7). C_{FORCE} determines the illocutionary force of the proposition, such as declarative, interrogative, imperative. C_{FIN} imposes finiteness restrictions on the clause, of which (ir)realis is by hypothesis one instantiation. To situate Innu, we introduce Spanish C-stacking in (8), analyzed as the realization of C_{FORCE} and C_{FIN} (Demonte and Fernández-Soriano 2009). Evidence in favor of an exploded C comes from topic XPs, which sandwich between two *que*'s: In (8a) the topic XP is esos árboles 'those trees'; in (8b), it is el dinero 'the money.'

(7) $[_{CP1}\ C_{FORCE}\ [_{CP2}\ C_{FINITENESS}\ [_{IP} \ldots]]]$

(8) a. Ordeno [C que] [TOPIC esos árboles] [C que] les talen.
order.1sg c.force those trees c.fin 3pl cut.sbj
'I order to cut those trees'

b. He dicho [C que] [TOPIC el dinero] [C que] no lo toquen.
I.have said c.force the money c.fin not 3sg touch.sbj
'I said that the money should not be touched'
[Demonte and Fernández-Soriano 2009:40, (33)]

A suggestive link between Innu and the Spanish layered CP is that Spanish C_{FIN} conditions subjunctive marking, as seen in the lower *que* clauses in (8). Since subjunctive reduces to irrealis (Givon 1994; Ilkhanipour 2018), we treat irrealis *ka* (and its allomorphs) as C_{FIN}, and adopt a layered CP analysis, with the top layer C_{FORCE}, and the second layer C_{FIN} qua (ir)realis. For Innu, realis is zero-marked (9a), and irrealis is marked by *ka* or its allomorphs (9b). The layered CP analysis is supported by syntactic, semantic, and morphological evidence; Table 3 lists the diagnostics that support the postulation of an (ir)realis partition in Innu.

(9) a. $[_{CP} \ldots [_{C.FORCE}\ [_{CP}\ [_{C.FIN:REALIS}$ ∅ $[_{IP} \ldots]]]]]$

b. $[_{CP} \ldots [_{C.FORCE}\ [_{CP}\ [_{C.FIN:IRREALIS}$ *ka* $[_{IP} \ldots]]]]]$

Syntactically, C_{FORCE} selects C_{FIN}, the latter the locus of ir(realis); see Table 4. Selection manifests in two ways. First, (independent order) C_{PERS} conditions irrealis allomorph selection: *ka* with first/second person, *tshika* with third person. Second, conjunct order C's associated are conditioned by realis: Zero (∅-), ê, and *kâ* conjunct Cs are realis Cs, and attested only in realis contexts. (See the following for exemplification.)

Semantically, (ir)realis denotes a "(non)-assertion of the actuality of a state or event in the base world at the reference time" (Ilkhanipour 2018:109). Thus, though irrealis (*tshi*)*ka* can have a futurate construal (10a), it is not a dedicated simple future, as confirmed by the possibility of it combining with other operators: with potential *tshi* to express deontic modality (10b); with preterit *-pan* to express a 'weak future' (10c); with dubitative *-kuê* to express epistemic modality (10d),

TABLE 3. Summary of (ir)realis diagnostics in Innu

		VALUE	FORM
SYNTACTIC	1. IRR + AGR	pers-split	IRR ↔ ***ka*** /$C_{PERS:\{1,2\}}$; ***tshika*** /$C_{PERS:3}$
	2. IRR	C-split	$C_{FIN.IRR}$ ↔***ka*** /C_{PERS}; ***tshê*** /C_{IC}
SEMANTIC	3. TEMPORALITY	futurate	{ (***tshi***)***ka***, ***tshê*** }
	4. IRR + POT	deontic	(***tshi***)***ka***-*kî*- . . .
	5. IRR + PRETERIT	weak future	(***tshi***)***ka*** . . . *pan*
	6. IRR + DUB	epistemic	(***tshi***)***ka*** . . . (*a*)*kuê*
MORPHOLOGICAL	7. IRR + NEG	suppletion	*apu*$_{NEG}$ (***tshi***)***ka*** /$C_{\varnothing}$; *êka*$_{NEG}$ ***tshê*** /C_{IC}
	8. IRR + IMVE	suppletion	-*kan* $_{IMVE.IRR.2}$; -*tshêku*$_{IMVE.IRR.2PL}$

TABLE 4. Distribution of Innu (ir)realis

FINITENESS	SYNTACTIC CONTEXT			MORPHOLOGICAL REALIZATION			
	ROOT CP	NONROOT CP: COMPLEMENT	NONROOT CP: ADJUNCT	ORDER	C_{FORCE}		
±REALIS	✓ (***ka***)	✗	✗	INDEPENDENT	C_{PERS}	1	↔ ***ni***(***t***)=
	✓ (***ka***)	✗	✗			2	↔ ***ki***(***t***)=
	✓ (***tshi ka***)	✗	✗			3	↔ ∅
	✗	✓ (***tshê***)	✓ (***tshê***)	CONJUNCT	$C_{SUBORDINATE}$		↔ ***IC***
+REALIS	✓	✓	✗		C_{REALIS}		↔ ∅
	✗	✗	✓		$C_{REALIS,\ ADJUNCT}$		↔ ***ê***
	✗	✗	✓		$C_{REALIS,\ ADJUNCT,\ DEF}$		↔ ***kâ***

which Drapeau (2014:191*ff.*) describes as a 'prophetic future' that announces an imminent event.

(10) a. **nika** pushin
ni-ka pushi-n
1-IRR leave.AI-LCL(IND)
'I <u>will</u> go' ('Je partirai' D176)

b. **nika tshi** nipan
ni-ka tshi nipa-n
1-IRR POT sleep.AI-LCL(IND)
'I <u>could</u> sleep' ('Je pourrais dormir' D205)

c. **Itshêna anitê tshimassina, tshika pitutshêpan tshutaui.**

itshêna	anitê	tshi-massina	tshika	pitutshê-pan	tsh-utaui
remove.TI(IMVE)	there	2-shoes	IRR	enter.AI-PRET(IND)	2-father

'Remove your shoes from there <u>for your father to come in</u>'

('Enlève tes souliers de là pour que ton père entre.' D191)

d. **Mamishkut tshika nipinikuê!**

successively	tshika	nipini-kuê
successively	IRR	summer.II-DUBIT(IND)

'[From now onward], <u>it's going to alternately be summer</u>!'

('[Dorénavant] ce sera l'été en alternance!' D192)

A third argument in support of an (ir)realis partition comes from its interaction with negation and imperatives. This plays out in two ways. On the one hand, some languages mark negative and imperative Vforms with irrealis morphology (e.g., Nanti: Michael 2014). On the other hand, in other languages negative and imperative Vforms, because they are inherently irrealis, trigger blocking effects; this is what we find in Innu. Affirmative realis contexts contrast (independent order) root CPs (11a) with (conjunct order) nonroot CPs (11b). With sentential NEG, independent order root CPs are blocked (12a.i); instead, the conjunct order is used (12a.ii). Moreover, the form of NEG is sensitive to syntactic context: NEG root CPs take *apu* (12a); NEG nonroot CPs take êka (12b).[6] With irrealis, NEG likewise triggers blocking: NEG + irrealis root CPs require the conjunct order (14a) and are negated by *apu . . . ut*; NEG + irrealis nonroot CPs are negated by êka (14b).

(11) a. **nîmu** — b. **. . . nîmit**

a.	b.
[nîm]-u	[nîm]-it
dance.AI-3(IND)	dance.AI-3(CNJ)
'S/he dances/danced' (D311)	'. . . that s/he danced'

(12) a.i ***apu nîmu** — a.ii **apu nîmit** — b. **. . . êka nîmit**

a.i	a.ii	b.
apu [nîm]-u	apu [nîm]-it	êka [nîm]-it
NEG dance.AI-3(IND)	NEG dance.AI-3(CNJ)	NEG dance.AI-3(CNJ)
'S/he does/did not dance'		'. . . that s/he did not dance'

TABLE 5. Innu imperative paradigms (adapted from D514)

	REALIS		IRREALIS
	NEUTRAL (SPEAKER PRESENT)	INDIRECT (SPEAKER ABSENT)	DELAYED (FUTURE)
2	(êka) nîmi!	(êka) nîmi-mê!	(êka) nîmi-kan!
21	(êka) nîmi-tâu!		
2PL	(êka) nîmi-k^u!	(êka) nîmi-mêk!	(êka) nîmi-tshêku!
	(NEG) dance-IMVE	(NEG) dance-IMVE.INDIR	(NEG) dance-IMVE.FUT
	'(don't) X dance!'	'(don't) X dance!'	'X will (not) dance later!'

(13) a. **tshika nîmu.**
tshika [nîm]-u
IRR dance-3(IND)
'S/he will dance'

b. **. . . tshê nîmit.**
IC+ka [nîm]-it
IC.IRR dance-3(CNJ)
'. . . when s/he will dance'

(14) a. ***apu tshika nîmu.**
apu tshika [nîm]-u
NEG IRR dance-3(IND)
'S/he will not dance'

a.ii **apu tshika ut nîmit**
apu tshika ut [nîm]-it
NEG IRR P dance-3(CNJ)

b. **. . . êka tshê nîmit**
êka IC+ka [nîm]-it
NEG IC.IRR dance-3(CNJ)
'. . . when s/he will not dance'

It is sometimes claimed that imperative forms are inherently irrealis. The Innu data in Table 5 suggests a more nuanced view, as there are three distinct imperative paradigms.

Two of the imperative paradigms align with evidentiality (Baraby 2017), contrasting 'neutral' imperatives (speaker present when order is carried out) with 'indirect' imperatives (speaker absent when order is carried out). The third paradigm, the 'delayed' imperative, denotes orders issued for future completion; we take these to be irrealis imperatives.

The Proliferation of Realis Clause-Typing in Innu

An innovative feature of Innu is its large number of realis CPs: Of 13 clause-types, 11 are realis, and only two are irrealis (marked by *ka*). Proliferation of realis clause types is due to realis being further partitioned by the indirect/direct and subjective/indicative modes, giving rise to a six-way realis contrast with root CPs (Table 6).[7] Nonroot CPs (Table 7) present a five-way realis partition; this reflects the fact that the realis + indicative dimension leverages a rich C-paradigm ($C_{\varnothing}$, C_{IC}, $C_{ê}$, $C_{kâ}$). In contrast, irrealis presents a modest two-way split: (*tshi*)*ka* with root CPs; *tshê* with nonroot CPs.

Tables 6 and 7 reveal previously unnoticed features of Innu C-typing: (i) Two Cs (C_{PERS}, $C_{\varnothing}$) cut across the (ir)realis contra st; (ii) C_{PERS} is a hallmark of root CPs, where the one exception is its occurrence with subjective nonroot CPs; and (iii) all other Cs are realis.[8]

Root CPs

As C_{FORCE} and C_{FIN} can be overt or covert, this yields a potential four-way contrast, of which three are attested. While (zero-marked) realis is compatible with overt C_{PERS} and covert $C_{\varnothing}$ (15a-b), irrealis *ka* is only compatible with overt C_{PERS} (16a). This confirms that some Innu C's—here (conjunct order) $C_{\varnothing}$—are specified for realis.

(15)	a.		[CP_{FORCE}	C_{PERS}	[CP_{FIN}	$C_{FIN:REAL}$ ∅	independent
	b.		[$CP_{FORCE:}$	$C_{\varnothing.REALIS}$	[CP_{FIN}	$C_{FIN:REAL}$ ∅	conjunct
(16)	a.		[CP_{FORCE}	C_{PERS}	[CP_{FIN}	$C_{FIN:IRR}$ *ka*	independent
	b.	*	[$CP_{FORCE:}$	$C_{\varnothing.REALIS}$	[CP_{FIN}	$C_{FIN:IRR}$ *ka*	conjunct

Realis Root CPs

Innu root CPs lack overt evidential marking, but nevertheless have evidential force (Drapeau 2014, Ch. 9).[9] This has consequences for the deployment of realis forms, as the felicity conditions for evidentiality require that the speaker have experiential grounds (Waldie 2012)—by definition realis—for the proposition presented. With this in mind, look at the examples in (17) and (18); these root CPs

TABLE 6. Innu (ir)realis root CPs

<table>
<tr><th colspan="6">REALIS</th><th rowspan="3">IRREALIS</th></tr>
<tr><th colspan="3">DIRECT</th><th colspan="3">INDIRECT</th></tr>
<tr><th>INDICATIVE</th><th>SUBJECTIVE</th><th></th><th>INDICATIVE</th><th>SUBJECTIVE</th><th></th></tr>
<tr><td>C_{PERS}-
∅- . . . -∅-∅</td><td>(ka)-C_{PERS}-
∅- . . . - ua-∅</td><td>$C_{\varnothing}$-
∅- . . . -∅</td><td>C_{PERS}-
∅- . . . -∅
-(a)tak</td><td>(ka)-C_{PERS}-
∅- . . .
-(a)tak-ua</td><td>$C_{\varnothing}$-
∅- . . . u
. . . ê</td><td>C_{PERS}-
(tshi)ka . . .</td></tr>
<tr><td>(19a)</td><td>(19b)</td><td>(20)</td><td>(21a)</td><td>(21b)</td><td>(22)</td><td>(23)</td></tr>
</table>

TABLE 7. Innu (ir)realis nonroot CPs

<table>
<tr><th colspan="6">REALIS</th><th rowspan="3">IRREALIS</th></tr>
<tr><th colspan="5">INDICATIVE</th><th rowspan="2">SUBJECTIVE</th></tr>
<tr><th colspan="2">COMPLEMENT</th><th colspan="3">ADJUNCT</th></tr>
<tr><td>$C_{\varnothing}$-∅-</td><td colspan="2">C_{IC}-∅-</td><td>$C_{ê}$-∅-</td><td>$C_{kâ}$-∅-</td><td>(ka)-C_{PERS}-∅-. . .-ua</td><td>C_{IC}-ka (→ tshê)</td></tr>
<tr><td>(25)</td><td>(26a)</td><td>(26b)</td><td>(27a), (28a)</td><td>(27b), (28b)</td><td>(29)</td><td>(31)</td></tr>
</table>

correspond to zero-marked realis clauses, and present propositions that have been directly experienced by the speaker (Cook 2014; Drapeau 2005, 2014). Relative to direct experience, Innu makes a three-way contrast between the narrator's direct experience via publicly accessible participation, (17a) marked by C_{PERS}; privately accessible participation (17b), marked by subjective (*ka*) . . . *ua*; and eyewitness (18), marked by C_{OP} and used to report events where the narrator was present but not participating in the event.

(17) a. <CONTEXT: publicly accessible direct experience>

[. . .] Patshuiantshuapit anitê **nititanan.**

patshuiantshuap-it anitê nit-∅-ita-nan

tent-LOC there 1-REAL-be.AI-1PL(IND)

'We are in the tent.' ('Nous sommes dans une tente.' D138)

b. <CONTEXT: **privately accessible** direct experience, e.g., dream>
ka-nuapatênaua tsêkuan [. . .]
ka-n-∅-[uapatên]-aua   tsêkuan
SBJV-1-REAL-see.TI-SBJV(IND)   thing
'I see something' ('Je vois quelque chose . . . ' D187)

(18) <CONTEXT: publicly accessible eyewitness experience>
êk^u nê Itouaǹ êkuê **uapamat** anitê iǹnua
êk^u   nê   Itouaǹ   êkuê   ∅-∅-uapama-t   anitê   iǹnua
then   DEM   Edouard   then   C-REAL-see.TA-3(CJ)   there   Innu-OBV
'. . . and Edouard saw an Innu there' ('. . . et Édouard a vu un indien là' D193)

Zero-marked direct evidence contrasts with overtly marked indirect evidence: With C_{PERS}, the indirect is realized as *tak* (19); with C_{OP}, it is realized as *-u . . .* -ê (20).[10] That the indirect is conditioned by C indicates that C_{FORCE} (C_{PERS} versus C_{OP}) selects for indirect mode; we return to this in the following. In addition, subjective (*ka*) . . . *-ua*, which presents privately accessible experience, is compatible with indirect. This arises in contexts where the narrator has indirect experience via privately accessible sensory input: In (19b) the narrator cannot see that she is on a hill (because of the snowstorm), but has indirect evidence via propriosensory feedback that she is climbing a hill.

(19) a. <CONTEXT: publicly accessible **indirect evidence**, narrator co-present; e.g., voice heard from afar>
[. . .] uishtaua **tatêuta-miǹitaka** anitê, . . .
u-ishtau-a   ∅-tatêuta-miǹi-tak-a   anitê, . . .
3-brother.in.law-OBV   REAL-make.noise.TI-INDIR-OBV(IND)   there
'[. . .] her brother-in-law makes noise with his voice there, . . . '
('[. . .] son beau-frère au loin fait des bruits de voix là, . . . ' D178)

b. <CONTEXT: **privately accessible indirect evidence**; e.g., narrator is in a snowstorm, and senses that she is climbing a hill>
Tshêk **ka-nit-amatshuênataka**, [. . .]
tshêk   ka-nit-∅-amatshuêna-tak-a, [. . .]
suddenly   SBJV-1-REAL-climb.AI-INDIR-SBJV (IND)
'All of a sudden, I feel that I'm climbing a hill . . . '
('Tout à coup, je sens que je monte une pente . . . ' D178)

(20) <CONTEXT: publicly accessible **indirect evidence**; narrator not co-present>

[. . .] êk[u] *nê Itouaǹ êkuê* **uapamakuê** anitê iǹnua

êk[u]	nê	Itouaǹ	êkuê	∅-∅-uapama-k-uê	anitê	iǹnu-a
then	DEM	Edouard	then	C-REAL-see.TA-3-INDIR(CJ)	there	Innu-OBV

'. . . and apparently Edouard saw an Innu there'

('. . . et Édouard a vu un indien là' D193)

In sum, evidential forms with subjective *-wa* and the indirect evidential *-atak* have (inherent) realis force, and so are (correctly) predicted to be incompatible with irrealis.

Irrealis Root CPs

With root CPs, irrealis *ka* is attested only with (independent order) C_{PERS} (21a). Crucially, (conjunct order) $C_{OP,}$ a realis C, is incompatible with irrealis *ka* (21b).

(21) a. <CONTEXT: committing to a likely future course of action>

Patush **nika mitshishunan** nêtshênat mishakataui.

patush	ni-ka	mitshishu-nan	nêtshênat	mishaka-taui.
later	1-IRR	eat.AI-1PL(IND)	MED.DST.ANIM.3PL	arrive.AI-3PL.SBJV(IND)

'We will eat later when those ones will have arrived.'

('Nous allons manger plus tard quand ceux-là seront arrivés.' D102)

b.* êk[u] nê Itouaǹ êkuê **ka uapamat** anitê iǹnua

êk[u]	nê	Itouaǹ	êkuê	∅-ka	uapama-t	anitê	iǹnu-a
then	DEM	Edouard	then	C-IRR	see.AI-3(CJ)	there	Innu-OBV

[target: '. . . and Edouard will see an Innu there' (adapted from D193)]

Nonroot CPs

Nonroot CPs are introduced by (conjunct order) C_{OP}, with the one exception being subjective (*ka*) . . . *ua*, which recruits C_{PERS}; however, even this apparent exception is a predictable by-product of the interaction of realis with indexical C-typing. We discuss in turn realis and then irrealis nonroot CPs.

Realis Nonroot CPs

With nonroot CPs, in realis contexts, there is a five-way contrast. Realis complement CPs are in the simple conjunct (22a) or condition IC, (22b). Adjunct CPs surface in one of three forms: IC (22b), ê conjunct (22c), or *kâ* conjunct (22d). And Innu has innovated its use of (independent order) C_{PERS} to nonroot contexts, (22e).

(22)						
	a.	$[CP_{FORCE}$	$C_{\varnothing}$	$[CP_{FIN}$	$C_{FIN:REAL}\ \varnothing$	complement CP
	b.	$[CP_{FORCE}$	C_{IC}	$[CP_{FIN}$	$C_{FIN:REAL}\ \varnothing$	complement or adjunct CP
	c.	$[CP_{FORCE:}$	$C_{ê\text{-}}$	$[CP_{FIN}$	$C_{FIN:REAL}\ \varnothing$	adjunct CP
	d.	$[CP_{FORCE:}$	$C_{kâ\text{-}}$	$[CP_{FIN}$	$C_{FIN:REAL}\ \varnothing$	adjunct CP
	e.	$[CP_{FORCE}$	C_{PERS}	$[CP_{FIN}$	$C_{FIN:REAL}\ \varnothing$	complement or adjunct CP

Realis complement CPs with null C (23) are equivalent to untensed clauses (Drapeau 2014:260) and so translate as infinitive, subjunctive, or gerundive.

(23) Ninêkatêǹitên kiê niǹ [**êka** tshêkuan **matshian** anutshish]
ni-nekatêńitê-n kiê niǹ êkâ tshêkuan
1-regret.TI-LCL(IND) also PRN.1 NEG thing.INANIM

∅-∅-matsh-ian anutshish.
C-REAL-eat.AI-1SG(CJ) today
'I also regret not eating anything today'
('Je regrette moi aussi que je ne mange rien aujourd'hui' D260)

Clauses with C_{IC} introduce complement (24a) or adjunct (24b) CPs, and are associated with a temporal restriction: The event-time (*e*-time) of the dependent CP overlaps with that of the root CP (Drapeau 2014:269).

(24) a. <CONTEXT: *e*-time of $CP_{COMPLEMENT}$ and CP_{ROOT} overlap>
tshissêǹimêu [êtaǹiti kashkana]
tshissêńimê-u IC-∅-atań-iti kashkan-a
know.TA-3(IND) IC-REAL-place.II-3PL(CJ) wave-PL
'He knows that there are waves' ('Il sait qu'il y a une vague' D269)

TABLE 8. Innu definiteness effects with realis adjunct clauses

	$C_{ê}$	$C_{kâ}$
EVENT	indefinite event (generic)	definite event (past)
ENTITY	indefinite referent	definite event (presupposed)

b. <CONTEXT: *e*-time time of CP_{ROOT} and $CP_{ADJUNCT}$ overlap>
[patutshêt], tuiêt êkuê nanatuapamat ukauia.

IC-∅-pitutshê-t	tuiêt	êkuê	nanatuapama-t	u-kaui-a
IC-REAL-enter.AI-3(CJ)	immediately	then	find.TA-3(CJ)	3-mother-OBV

As he entered, he immediately went to find his mother'
('En entrant, il alla tout de suite trouver sa mère' D268)

The last two realis Cs to look at are ê and *kâ*, whose selection is sensitive to definiteness writ large; see Table 8. While $C_{ê}$ yields an indefinite (event or entity), $C_{kâ}$ yields a definite (event or entity). These definiteness effects are worthy of their own treatment; for our purposes, it suffices to establish that they are anchored to the C_{REALIS} paradigm.[11]

With "event definiteness," while ê denotes generic event quantification (25a), *kâ* denotes a specific/definite (past) event (25b). Realis adjunct clauses also function as relative clauses, in which case they restrict a nominal, and there is likewise a definiteness contrast: *ê* flags an indefinite referent (26a); *kâ* flags a definite one (26b).

(25) a. <CONTEXT: "generic" event quantification>
Liniment Minard ishnikatakanu [ê mishtikushiu-uitakanit]

Liniment	Minard	ishnikatakanu	[ê	∅	mishtikushiu	uitakanit]
Liniment	Minard	name.AI.3(IND)	C	REAL	French	name-AI.3PL(CJ)

'We call it *Liniment Minard* whenever we name it in French.'
('On appelle ça du Liniment Minard quand on le nomme en français.' D272)

b. <CONTEXT: "definite" (past) event: time of $CP_{ADJUNCT}$ overlaps with CP_{ROOT}>
Êku nana nikaui êka kâ ińniut, apu ut êshku mitshêtuht nitauassimat.

êku	nana	ni-kaui	êka	IC-∅-tshi	ińniu-t,
and	DEM	1-mother	NEG	IC-∅-tshi	alive-3(CJ)

apu	ut	êshku	mitshêtu-ht	nit-auassim-at
NEG	PAST	yet	abundant-3PL(CJ)	1-child-PL

'And when my mother died, my children were not yet numerous.'
('Et quand ma mère est morte, mes enfants n'étaient pas encore nombreux.' D270)

(26) a. <CONTEXT: indefinite (D270), non-restrictive relative (D263)>
Êkuê utinat [akashku-a [$_{CP}$ ê mikushiṅiti]] êkuê pimutakuêt

êkuê	utin-at	akashku-a	ê-∅	mikushi-ṅiti
then	take.TA-3>3'(CJ)	arrow-PL	C-REAL	red.II-3OBV.PL(CJ)

êkuê	pimutakuê-t
and	shoot.arrow.AI-3(CJ)

'And he took an arrow which was red and drew the bow'
('Et il prit une fléche (qui est) rouge et tira' D270)

b. <CONTEXT: definite (D270)>
Êkuê utinat [akashku-a [$_{CP}$ kâ mikushiṅiti]] êkuê pimutakuêt

êkuê	utin-at	akashku-a	IC-∅-tshi	mikushi-ṅiti
then	take.TA-3>3'(CJ)	arrow-PL	IC-∅-tshi	red.II-3OBV.PL(CJ)

êkuê	pimutakuê-t
and	shoot.arrow.AI-3(CJ)

'And he took the arrow which was red and drew the bow'
('Et il prit la fléche (qui est) rouge et tira' D270)

All the examples just shown of nonroot realis CPs involve (conjunct order) C_{OP}. However, there is one context where a nonroot realis CP takes (independent order) C_{PERS}, namely, subjective (*ka*)-... *ua:* (27a) is a complement CP; (27b) is an adjunct (rationale) CP. This noncanonical use of independent order CPs in embedded clauses indirectly confirms our analysis, as it is possible only in contexts where the speaker presents her/his unmediated internal landscape (Aikhenvald 2004;

Peterson 2015). Subjective (*ka*)- . . . *ua*—which anchors the narrator's experience, as it presents dreams, memories, or subjective experience (Drapeau 2014:184)—is indexical, in the sense of Cook (2014), who argues that C_{PERS} is likewise indexical. An indexicality-based analysis predicts the integration of subjective with C_{PERS}. This accords with Drapeau's (2014:261) observation that when a form does not (or here, cannot) exist in the conjunct order, the independent order can (exceptionally) be used for subordination. Our analysis makes a claim about the semantic contexts where this arises, namely, with realis subjective CPs.

(27) a. <CONTEXT: dream>

kiê **ka-pashpapuakani shapanua**, nitishinên

kiê	ka-∅-pashpapuakani-shapan-ua,	nit-ishin-ên
and	SBJV-REAL-window.II-3PL-INDIR-SBJV(IND)	1-see.TI-3(IND)

'. . . and I see that there were windows' ('. . . et je vois qu'il y avait des fenêtres' D187)

b. <CONTEXT: unexpected or astonishing event>

Nanitam uêsh nê uin **ka-natshi-mitshishushapanua**

nanitam	uêsh nê	uin	ka-∅-natshi-mitshishu-shapan-ua
always	because	EMPH	SBJV-REAL-PREV-eat.AI-3SG-INDIR-SBJV(IND)

'Because (it seems to me) he was always eating in a restaurant'

('Car on dirait bien qu'il mangeait toujours dans un restaurant' D185)

Irrealis Nonroot CPs

The final context to consider is irrealis nonroot CPs marked by *tshê*, an allomorph of irrealis *ka* derived from IC, as in (28). This accords with the layered CP analysis that correctly predicts that C_{FIN} will co-occur with and be conditioned by C_{FORCE}. This also correctly accounts for the fact that irrealis *tshê* is compatible with both complement CPs (29a) and adjunct CPs (29b).

(28) a. [C_{FORCE} IC [$C_{FIN.IRR}$ *ka* [$_{vP}$ . . .] . . .

b. [C_{FORCE} IC [$C_{FIN.IRR}$ *tshê* [$_{vP}$ . . .] . . .

(29) a. <CONTEXT: *e*-time of CP_{ROOT} > *e*-time or **irrealis** $CP_{COMPLEMENT}$>
êkue ishit nana Adhémar tshêtutêt [**tshê** pushit]
êkue ishit nana Adhémar tshêtutê-t IC+ka push-it
and then this Adhémar leave.AI-3(CJ) C-IRR go.on.trip.AI-3(CJ)
'and then Adhémar told me when he left that he would go on a trip'
('et alors Adhémar m'a dit en partant qu'il allait partir en voyage' D272)

b. <CONTEXT: *e*-time of CP_{ROOT} > *e*-time of **irrealis** $CP_{ADJUNCT}$>
Êka uiǹ tshika uǹuinau [**tshê** tipishkat]
êka uiǹ tshi-ka uǹui-nau IC+ka tipishkat
NEG EMPH 2-IRR go.outside.AI-2PL(IND) C-IRR be.night.II-0(CJ)
'You will not go out when it will be night'
('Ne sortez pas quand il fera nuit' D271)

What (Ir)Realis Reveals about the Syntactic Derivation of CPs

In Innu, irrealis can be used to adjudicate the syntactic derivation of CPs; we illustrate this by examining the interaction of irrealis *ka* with (Mode) suffixes and (C) prefixes.

Integrating Suffixes via X⁰- versus XP-Movement

For reasons that will become obvious, we focus on how indirect *-tak* and subjective (*ka*) . . . *-ua* (which occur only with C_{REAL}) integrate into the Vcomplex. We look at three cases: realis-indirect *-tak* (30a), realis-subjective (*ka*) . . . *-ua* (30b), and their combination (*ka*) . . . *-tak-ua* (30c).

(30)					
a.		**Pers**	[Vstem]	$\mathbf{Agr}_{1/2}$	***-tak***$_{INDIR}$	$\mathbf{Agr}_{3/3PL/3OBV}$
b.	(*ka*$_{SUBJECTIVE}$)	**Pers**	[Vstem]	$\mathbf{Agr}_{1/2}$	***-ua***$_{SUBJV}$	$\mathbf{Agr}_{3/3PL/3OBV}$
c.	(*ka*$_{SUBJECTIVE}$)	**Pers**	[Vstem]	$\mathbf{Agr}_{1/2}$	***-tak***$_{INDIR}$-***ua***$_{SUBJV}$	$\mathbf{Agr}_{3/3PL/3OBV}$

Relative to the neo-Bloomfieldian position class analysis (Goddard 1979a, 1979b; Oxford 2017), indirect *-tak* and subjective (*ka*) . . . *-ua* show two remarkable properties. First, they occur between the two pronominal agreement positions associated with Person ($Agr_{1/2}$) and Number/Obviation ($Agr_{3/3PL/3OBV}$). Second, they co-occur. This raises two questions relative to Innu realis syntax: (i) How do propositional operators such as indirect *-tak* and subjective (*ka*)... *ua* interact with right-edge pronominal agreement? (ii) Given that indirect and subjective co-occur, in which order are these two evidentials introduced? With this in mind, consider (31), which illustrates 1pl>3pl for the realis-indirect (31a), the realis-subjective (31b), and the realis-subjective-indirect (31c).

(31) a. <CONTEXT: public **indirect evidence**>
nipêtuananatakat
ni-[pêtu-a] -nan-atak -at
1- hear-DIR-1pl -INDIR -3PL(IND)
'We heard them' (REAL.INDIRECT)

b. <CONTEXT: **private** direct evidence>
(ka) nipêtuananuati
ka ni-[pêtu-a] -nan-ua -ti
SBJV 1-hear-DIR-1pl -SBJV-3PL(IND)
'We heard them' (REAL.SUBJV)

c. <CONTEXT: **private indirect evidence**>
(ka) nipêtuananatakuati
ka i-[pêtu-a] -nan-atak -ua -ti
SBJV 1- hear-DIR-1pl -INDIR-SBJV-3PL(IND)
'We heard them' (REAL.SUBJV.INDIRECT)

Two broad classes of analyses exist for the forms in (31): (i) head-movement qua X^0-movement (Branigan 2012; Oxford 2017), and (ii) phrasal movement qua XP-movement (Déchaine 1999; Barrie and Mathieu 2016). Although both account for the surface linearization of Innu Vforms, they differ in the predictions they make about input ordering. We illustrate this in (32) with (*ka*)*nipêtuananatakuati*, the 1pl>3pl form of 'We hear them', inflected with indirect *-atak* and subjective (*ka*)... *-wa*. Example (32a) gives the input form for an X^0-movement account, where *pêtu* 'hear.TA' associates with Voice (direct *a*), and in turn $Infl_{AGR}$ (person features, here 1pl *-nan*), the two Mode suffixes (indirect *-atak* and subjective *-ua*), and then C_{AGR} (number and obviation features, here 3obv *-ti*.) X^0-movement has mirror-image ordering of heads (Baker 1985), so the input is the opposite of the output. (32b) gives the input form for XP-movement where, except for the position of the *v*P constituent, input and output order are the same.

(32) input for *nipetuananatakuati* realis+subjective+indirect 'We hear them'

a. X^0 [$_{\text{C:3PL}}$ -***ti*** [$_{\text{SBJV}}$-***ua*** [$_{\text{INDIR}}$ -***atak*** [$_{\text{I:1PL}}$-***nan*** [$_{\text{VCE:DIR}}$-*a* [$_{v}$ *pêtu*]

b. XP [$_{\text{C}}$ ***ni***$_1$=__ [$_{\text{PERS:1PL}}$ =***nan*** [$_{\text{INDIR}}$__=***atak*** [$_{\text{SBJV}}$__=***ua*** [$_{\text{NUM:3PL}}$__=***ti*** [$_{v\text{P}}$ *pêtua*]

The input strings in (32) are associated with the derivations in (33) for X^0-movement and (34) for XP-movement. The X^0-movement derivation (based on Oxford 2017) treats direct as a Voice head (33a) that triggers *v*-to-Voice movement, and each successive head similarly triggers head-movement: Voice-to-Infl (33b), Infl-to-Mode (33c), Mode-to-Mode (35d), and Mode-to-C (33e).[12] In the XP-movement derivation (based on Déchaine 1999), the target of movement is *v*P, which moves Spec-to-Spec through Spec,NumP (34a), SpecModeP (34b-c), and SpecPersP (34d).[13]

(33) Step-by-step derivation via X^0-movement

a.	[$_{\text{VCE:DIR}}$ -*a* [$_{v}$ *pêtu*]]	[$_{\text{VCE:DIR}}$ *pêtu-a* [<*v*>]]
b.	[$_{\text{I:1PL}}$ -***nan*** [$_{\text{VCE}}$ *pêtua*]]	[$_{\text{I:1PL}}$ *pêtua-nan* [<~~VOICE:DIRECT~~]]
c.	[$_{\text{INDIR}}$ -***atak*** [$_{\text{INFL:1PL}}$ *pêtuanan*]]	[$_{\text{INDIR}}$ *pêtuanan-atak* [< ~~INFL:1PL~~>]]
d.	[$_{\text{SUBJV}}$ -***ua*** [$_{\text{INDIR.1/2}}$ *pêtuananatak*]]	[$_{\text{SUBJV}}$ *pêtuananatak-ua* [<~~MODE:INDIR~~>]]
e.	[$_{\text{C.3PL}}$ -***ti*** [$_{\text{SUBJV}}$ *pêtuananatakua*]]	[$_{\text{C.3PL}}$ *pêtuananatakua-ti* [<~~MODE:SBJV~~>]]
	(not discussed: attachment of ***ni***-)	

(34) Step-by-step derivation via XP-movement

[$_{\text{C}}$ ***ni***$_1$= [$_{\text{PERS:1PL}}$____=***nan*** [$_{\text{INDIR}}$____=***atak*** [$_{\text{SBJV}}$____=***ua*** [$_{\text{NUM:3PL}}$____=***ti*** [$_{v\text{P}}$ *pêtu-a*]

a. [$_{v\text{P}}$ *pêtua*]

b. [$_{v\text{P}}$ *pêtua*]

c. [$_{v\text{P}}$ *pêtua*]

d. [$_{v\text{P}}$ *pêtua*]

As shown in (35), X^0- and XP-movement analyses make opposite claims about morpheme ordering. Relative to Mode, an X^0-movement analysis has as input [subjective>indirect], while an XP-movement analysis has [indirect>subjective].

(35) morpheme ordering

a. X^0 $[_{\text{C.AGR.3PL}}$ $[\textbf{Mode}_{\text{SBJV}}$ $[\textbf{Mode}_{\text{INDIR:\{1,2\}}}$ $[_{\text{I.AGR.1PL}}$ $[_{\text{VCE:DIR}}$ $[_{\nu P}$

b. XP $[_{\text{C.PERS}}$ $[_{\text{PERS.1PL}}$ $[\textbf{Mode}_{\text{INDIR:\{1,2\}}}$ $[\textbf{Mode}_{\text{SBJV}}$ $[_{\text{NUM.3PL}}$ $[_{\nu P}\ \nu$ [DP]

Three types of evidence bear on the order of the two Mode heads, and they all point to [indirect>subjective] ordering.[14] First, indirect is restricted to root CPs, indicating it is selected by C_{ROOT}. Second, the form of indirect is conditioned by pronominal agreement, as it is realized as *-atak* with first/second person. In an XP-movement analysis, the sensitivity of the indirect to person is consistent with treating person as a C-head that selects indirect as sister. Third, and most compelling, the form of indirect is conditioned by clause-type. This is illustrated in (36): C_{PERS} conditions the *-atak* allomorph; C_{OP} selects the *u . . .* ê allomorph. This follows if C_{FORCE} selects for (in)direct, as claimed by the XP-movement analysis.[15] This establishes that X^0- and XP-movement analyses both account for the integration of mode suffixes in the verb complex; however, only an XP-movement analysis provides a principled account for [indirect>subjective] ordering.[16]

(36) a. **nipêtuananatakat**
ni-[pêtu-a]-nan-atak-at
1-hear-DIR-1pl-INDIR-SBJV-3PL(IND)
'We heard them' (INDIRECT)

b. **pêtuauatshitshênit**
[pêtu-a]-u -atshi-tsh-ê-nit
hear-DIR-SBJV-1PL -3-SBJV-3PL(CJ)
'. . . we heard them' (INDIRECT)

Integrating Prefixes and Proclitics via X^0- versus XP-Movement

X^0- and XP-movement analyses diverge when we compare their treatment of the left edge of the Vcomplex. Here we focus on person proclitics and irrealis *ka*. Some analyses assign the same set of features to independent and conjunct orders (Oxford 2017; Lochbihler 2012; Brittain 1999), but there are reasons to think they are distinct. The crucial evidence comes from the person proclitics *ni-* (first person) and *tshi-* (second person). See Table 9, which shows the independent (C_{PERS}) and conjunct (C_{OP}) orders for the TA mixed series (1/2>3).

The two paradigms differ in how they resolve 1sg and 2sg, as seen by the shaded cells in Table 9. With C_{PERS}, *ni-* and *tshi-* realize first and second person; in the absence of any additional marking—specifically in the absence of plural-specified nan_{1PL} and $\text{-}uau_{PL}$ in $Agr_{1/2}$—they are construed as "singular." Thus, the interpretation

TABLE 9. Innu VTA indicative, mixed series: 1/2 > 3 (adapted from D2014: 530f., 551f.)

C_{PERS} (INDEPENDENT ORDER)					C_{OP} (CONJUNCT ORDER)			
	PERS	(OBV)-DIR	$AGR_{1/2}$	$AGR_{3/PL/OBV}$		(OBV)	$AGR_{1/2}$	$AGR_{3/PL/OBV}$
1	ni-	... a	$(\varnothing_{1SG})$	u_3	1	...	(a)k_1	$\varnothing_3$
				u_3at_{3PL}				$\varnothing_3au_{PL}$
		... m-a		u_3a_{OBV}		... (i)m		$\varnothing_3i_{OBV}$
1PL		... a	nan_{1PL}	$\varnothing_3$	1PL	...	(a)tsh_1 <(a)k_1	it_3
				$\varnothing_3at_{3PL}$				$ih_{PL}t_3$
		... m-a		$\varnothing_3a_{3OBV}$		... (i)m		it_3i_{OBV}
2	tshi-	... a	$(\varnothing_{2SG})$	u_3	2	...	(a)t_2	$\varnothing_3$
				u_3at_{3PL}				$\varnothing_3au_{PL}$
		... m-a		u_3a_{3OBV}		... (i)m		$\varnothing_3i_{OBV}$
21		... a	nan_{1PL}	$\varnothing_3$	21	...	a_{21}-$k^u{}_{2PL}$	$\varnothing_3$
				$\varnothing_3at_{3PL}$			a_{21}-ku_{2PL}	$\varnothing_3$-t_{PL}
		... m-a		$\varnothing_3a_{3OBV}$		... (i)m		$\varnothing_3$-i_{OBV}
2PL		... a	uau_{PL}	$\varnothing_3$	2PL	...	e_2-$k^u{}_{2PL}$	$\varnothing_3$
				$\varnothing_3at_{3PL}$			e_2-ku_{2PL}	$\varnothing_3t_{PL}$
		... m-a		$\varnothing_3a_{3OBV}$		... (i)m		$\varnothing_3i_{OBV}$

of a form as "singular" in the absence of "plural" is a form of implicature (Grice 1981). This leads to the conclusion that agreement is compositional and additive (Hockett 1992; Déchaine 1999). Conjunct order agreement shows a different featural organization, as it has dedicated morphemes for 1sg and 2sg, namely, -(*a*)k_1 and -(*a*)t_{2SG}.[17] The main difference between C_{PERS} and C_{OP} lies in the existence of dedicated left-peripheral person-marking with C_{PERS}, and its absence with C_{OP}. In some analyses, the existence of a 1sg/2sg contrast with central agreement ($Agr_{1/2}$) in the conjunct order (C_{OP}) is taken as evidence for a parallel 1sg/2sg contrast in the independent order (C_{PERS}), leading to the postulation of zero-marked 1sg/2sg in the independent order. However, it is curious that zero-marked 1sg/2sg is invoked for Vforms that have first and second person proclitics at the left edge. We reject this approach, and instead adopt the view that in the independent order, singular construals for first and second person are recoverable from general principles of compositional interpretation. But there remains the question of how to integrate left-edge person proclitics into the verb complex. This issue arises for all left-edge (i.e., prefixal) morphology, so is relevant to irrealis *ka*. To see how this bears on the syntax of C-typing, look at (37), which illustrates the appearance of left-edge morphemes with C_{PERS} (37a) and C_{OP} (37b).

(37) a. **nika pêtuananat**
ni-ka pêtu-a-nan-at
1-IRR hear-DIR-1PL-3PL
'We will hear them'

b. **tshê pêtutshiht**
IC+ka pêtu-tsh-iht
C-IRR hear-1PL-3PL
'. . . when we will hear them'

Consider how X^0- and XP-movement analyses account for the integration of irrealis *ka* into the verb complex. In an X^0-movement analysis (e.g., Oxford 2017), the anchor for C-typing is right-edge peripheral agreement ($Agr_{3/PL/OBV}$), which realizes C_{AGR}. In an XP-movement analysis (e.g., Déchaine 1999), the anchor for C-typing is proclitic agreement (ni_1 and $tshi_2$), which realizes C_{PERS}. In our implementation, C_{PERS} is an allomorph of C_{FORCE}, which (as discussed earlier) correctly predicts that C_{FORCE} selects C_{FIN} (the locus of (ir)realis). As far as we can determine, the C_{AGR} analysis cannot account for the C_{FORCE} and C_{FIN} dependencies attested in Innu.[18]

Prospects

We have argued that the Innu C system is conditioned first and foremost by the (ir) realis partition. Tracking this partition yields two positive results: (i) Empirically, it provides a clear basis for the rich inventory of Innu realis clause-types that are conditioned by (realis) evidential contrasts, most notably the direct/indirect and the indicative/subjective; (ii) theoretically, it successfully applies the layered CP analysis (which distinguishes C_{FORCE} from C_{FIN}) to Innu, and in so doing contributes to a broader understanding of cross-linguistic C-typing. There remain open questions relative to how irrealis *ka* interacts with other irrealis contexts (e.g., subjunctive, negation, and dubitative) and with past-oriented temporal operators (e.g., past *tshi-*, preterit *-pan*). More broadly, there is the question of how the Innu (ir)realis partition compares to other varieties of Cree, and to other (Algonquian) languages.

NOTES

1. Innu data from Drapeau (2014) is presented with the original French translation and its counterpart English translation. Departing from the standard orthography (which does

not represent vowel length), vowel length is represented as a macron: e.g., long /i:/ = î. Innu ǹ = Proto-Algonquian *l, realized as /l/ or /n/ depending on the dialect. For many fruitful exchanges, thanks to J. Bohnemeyer, H. Burge, S. Cable, T. Cardinal, S. Chen, J. Crippen, A. Dahlstrom, L. Drapeau, J. Gambarage, H. Keupdjio, L. Matthewson, A. Osa-Gomez, W. Oxford, C. Reinholtz, R. Rhodes, and H. C. Wolfart.

2. Conventions: 1 = 1st person, 2 = 2nd person, 3 = 3rd person animate, 0 = 3rd person inanimate, Agr1/2 = 1st or 2nd (central) person agreement, Agr3/3PL/3OBV = 3rd person (peripheral) agreement, AI = animate intransitive verb stem, ANIM = animate, C = complementizer, CJ = conjunct order, d2014 = Drapeau 2014, DEM = demonstrative, DIR = direct voice, EMPH = emphatic, FIN = finiteness, IC = initial change, II = inanimate intransitive verb stem, IMVE = imperative, INANIM = inanimate, IND = independent order, INDIR = indirect mode, IRR = irrealis, LOC = local 1st or 2nd person agreement, MED.DST = medio-distal, NEG = negation, P = preposition, PERS = 1st or 2nd person proclitic agreement, PRN = pronoun, OBV = obviative, PL = plural, REAL = realis, SBJ = subjunctive, SBJV = subjective mode, TA = transitive animate verb stem, TI = transitive inanimate verb stem.
3. (Ir)realis diagnostics are from Déchaine et al. (in prep.), who investigate (ir)realis in Plains Cree, Swampy Cree, and Innu.
4. See Déchaine et al. (in prep.) for discussion of how (ir)realis diagnostics bear on micro- and macro-parametric variation.
5. Here we focus on the syntax of proclitic agreement; see later discussion for enclitic agreement.
6. Innu has a rich neg inventory: in addition to *apu* and êka, there are (i) *ma* with yes/no questions and interjections expressing surprise; (ii) *mauat* with independent order verbs to denote a state of affairs contrary to what is expected or presupposed; and (iii) *nama/namaieu* with nominal predication.

(i) ma takuana mitshuapa
neg exist.ii.3pl(ind) house.ni.pl
'Aren't there any houses?' ('N'y a-t-il pas de maisons?' D314)

(ii) êshkau mauat punitakanu
wait neg stop.ti.psv.3(ind)
'Up to now, to the contrary, they didn't stop that'
('Jusqu'ici, au contraire, on a pas arrêté ça' D315)

(iii) namaiêu tshiǹ
neg 2sg.prn
'It's not you'
('Ce n'est pas toi' D316)

7. We distinguish indicative from subjective; this departs from Drapeau (2014), who uses indicative for Vforms that we treat as realis.

8. Subjective *ka-* (i) precedes independent order person proclitics, is optional, and is conditioned by subjective *-ua*; the latter is located between Agr1/2 ('central agreement') and Agr3/3PL/3OBV ('peripheral agreement'). Irrealis *ka* (ii) is a preverb (Wolvengrey 2006) between person proclitics and the Vstem.

(i)	(kaSUBJECTIVE)	Pers-	[Vstem]-Agr1/2-uaMODE	-Agr3/3PL/3OBV
(ii)		Pers-kaIRR	[Vstem]-Agr1/2	-Agr3/3PL/3OBV

9. For related discussion, see Cook (2014) and Déchaine, Cook, Muehlbauer, and Waldie (2017).
10. A reviewer asks whether, in (20), êku nê 'and then' might trigger the conjunct order. Our answer is a qualified "yes." Yes, because anaphoric clauses are in the conjunct mode, and *êku nê* introduces anaphoric clauses; this accounts for the form of the conjunct. But the "yes" is qualified because the conjunct mode has semantic force: Conjunct order CPs present direct eyewitness (Drapeau 2014:193) and contrast with independent order CPs, which present direct experience (Drapeau 2014:175). This predicts that if (20) were to be used in the independent order, to remain felicitous, it would likely switch to first person plural form, as in (i). See Cook (2014) for similar observations about Plains Cree.

    (i) <context: speaker participated in the event of seeing>
    niuapamaunan anitê iǹnua
    ni-∅-∅-uapama-nan anitê iǹnu-a
    1-∅-real-see.ta-1pl(ind) there Innu-obv
    'We saw an Innu'

11. These definiteness effects—also observed in Plains Cree (Cook 2014) and Swampy Cree (Ellis 1971)—may be related to Salish 'assertion-of-existence" (Matthewson 1998) and Bantu 'belief-of-existence' (Gambarage 2019). If so, we expect polarity-sensitive effects; this remains to be determined.
12. X^0-movement analyses derive the placement of the person proclitic ni- via other mechanisms (see Brittain 1999; Lochbihler 2012; Oxford 2017).
13. vP-movement is a species of predicate fronting; see Massam and Smallwood (1996) for related discussion. For discussion of how the morphophonology reacts appropriately to the phasal boundaries, see Déchaine and Weber (2015).
14. An X^0-movement analysis accounts for the ordering of Mode via additional mechanisms; see Oxford (2017). The discussion in the main text aims to show that an XP-movement analysis need not invoke additional mechanisms.
15. Mode suffixes partition third person agreement into two positions: (number-neutral)

third person followed by pl/obv. As documented by Drapeau (2014), the [3- . . . -pl/obv] frame hosts subjective *-ua*, dubitative *-tshê*, preterit *-pan*, preterit subjective *-pan-ua*, preterit dubitative *-ku-pan*, preterit indirect *-sha-pan*.

16. The [indirect>subjective] order predicts indirect scopes over subjective; this remains to be confirmed.
17. In the conjunct order in Table 8, an allomorph of the 1sg is used for 1pl, as (*a*)*k1* surfaces as palatalized (*a*)*tsh1*. This suggests that the Innu conjunct order has number-neutral first person marking.
18. Not discussed are the details of allomorphy and suppletion; see Oxford (2014) for a Distributed Morphology account that invokes postsyntactic fission. We eschew this mechanism, and conjecture that suppletion and allomorphy are syntactically (rather than phonologically) conditioned. We leave this to future work.

REFERENCES

Aikhenvald, Alexandra Y. 2004. *Evidentiality*. Oxford: Oxford University Press.

Baker, Mark. 1985. The Mirror Principle and Morphosyntactic Explanation. *Linguistic Inquiry* 16:373–415.

Baraby, Anne-Marie. 2017. Imperatives and Evidentiality in Innu. *Imperatives and Directive Strategies*, ed. by Daniël Van Holmen and Simone Heinold pp. 53–77. Amsterdam: John Benjamins.

Barrie, Michael, and Éric Mathieu. 2016. Noun Incorporation and Phrasal Movement. *Natural Language & Linguistic Theory* 34(1):1–51.

Branigan, Phil. 2012. Macroparameter Learnability: An Algonquian Case Study. Unpublished manuscript, Memorial University of Newfoundland.

Brittain, Julie. 1999. A Reanalysis of Transitive Animate Theme Signs as Object Agreement: Evidence from Western Naskapi. *Papers of the 30th Algonquian Conference*, ed. by H. David Pentland, pp. 34–46, Winnipeg: University of Manitoba.

Bybee, Joan L. 1998. Irrealis as a Grammatical Category. *Anthropological Linguistics* 40(2):257–271.

Cook, Clare. 2008. The Syntax and Semantics of Clause-Yyping in Plains Cree. PhD thesis, UBC.

Cook, Clare. 2014. *The Clause-Typing System of Plains Cree: Indexicality, Anaphoricity, and Contrast*. Oxford: Oxford University Press.

Déchaine, Rose-Marie. 1999. What Algonquian Morphology is Really Like: Hockett Revisited. *MIT Occasional Papers in Linguistics* 17:25–72.

Déchaine, Rose-Marie, Clare Cook, Jeffrey Muehlbauer, and Ryan Waldie. 2017. (De-)

constructing Evidentiality. *Lingua* 186–187:21–54.

Déchaine, Rose-Marie, Monique Dufresne, and Charlotte Reinholtz. [In prep.]. The Reality of the (IR)REALIS Parameter.

Déchaine, Rose-Marie, and Natalie Weber. 2015. Head-Merge, Adjunct-Merge, and the Syntax of Root Categorization. *Proceedings of the Poster Session of the 33rd West Coast Conference on Formal Linguistics* (*WCCFL 33*), ed. by Pocholo Umbal and Kyeong-min Kim, pp. 38–47. Simon Fraser University Working Papers in Linguistics.

Demonte, Violeta, and Olga Fernández-Soriano. 2009. Force and Finiteness in the Spanish Complementizer System. *Probus* 21(1):23–49.

Drapeau, Lynn. 2005. Epistemic Modality in Innu-Montagnais. Paper read at the 37th Algonquian Conference, University of Ottawa.

Drapeau, Lynn. 2014. *Grammaire de la Langue Innue*. Québec City, QC: Les Presses de l'Université du Québec.

Ellis, C. Douglas. 1971. Cree Verb Paradigms. *International Journal of American Linguistics* 37:76–95.

Gambarage, Joash Johannes. 2019. Belief-of-Existence Determiners: Evidence from the Syntax and Semantics of Nata Augments. PhD thesis, University of British Columbia.

Givon, Thomas. 1994. Irrealis and the Subjunctive. *Studies in Language* 18(2):265–337.

Goddard, Ives. 1979a. Comparative Algonquian. *The Languages of Native America*, ed. by Lyle Campbell and Marianne Mithun, pp. 70–132. Austin: University of Texas Press.

Goddard, Ives. 1979b. *Delaware Verbal Morphology: A Descriptive and Comparative Study*. New York: Garland.

Grice, H. Paul. 1981. Presupposition and Conversational Implicature. *Radical Pragmatics*, ed. by P. Cole, pp. 183–98. New York: Academic Press. Reprinted in *Studies in the Ways of Words* [1989], ed. H. Paul Grice, pp. 269–282. Cambridge, MA: Harvard University Press.

Hockett, Charles F. 1992. Direction in the Algonquian Verb: A Correction. *Anthropological Linguistics* 34:311–315.

Ilkhanipour, Negin. 2018. On Subjunctive Clauses and Irrealis Mood in Persian. *CJL/RCL* 63(1):100–111.

Lochbihler, Bethany 2012. Aspects of Argument Licensing. PhD thesis, McGill University.

Massam, Diane, and Caroline Smallwood. 1996. Essential Features of Predication in Niuean and English. *Proceedings of NELS 27*, GLSA, ed. by Kiyomi Kusumoto, pp. 236–272. Amherst: University of Massachusetts.

Matthewson, Lisa. 1998. *Determiner Systems and Quantificational Strategies: Evidence from Salish*. The Hague: Holland Academic Graphics.

Michael, Lev. 2014. The Nanti Reality Status System: Implications for the Typological Validity of the Realis/Irrealis Contrasts. *Linguistic Typology* 2:251–288.

Oxford, Will. 2014. Microparameters of Agreement: A Diachronic Perspective on Algonquian Verb Inflection. PhD thesis, University of Toronto.

Oxford, Will. 2017. Inverse Marking as Impoverishment. *Proceedings of the 34th West Coast Conference on Formal Linguistics*, ed. by Aaron Kaplan et al., pp. 413–422. Somerville, MA: Cascadilla Proceedings Project.

Peterson, Tyler. 2015. Grammatical Evidentiality and the Unprepared Mind. *Review of Cognitive Linguistics* 13(2):314–352 (published under the auspices of the Spanish Linguistic Association).

Rizzi, Luigi. 1997. The Fine Structure of the Left Periphery. *Elements of Grammar*, ed. by Liliane. Haegeman, pp. 281–337. Amsterdam: Kluwer.

Waldie, Ryan James. 2012. Evidentiality in Nuu-chah-nulth. PhD thesis, UBC.

Wolvengrey Arok. 2006. Prospective Aspect in the Western Dialects of Cree. *International Journal of American Linguistics* 72(3):397–407.

A Ditransitive Analysis of Possessor Raising in Mi'kmaw

Distinct Licensing for Possessor and Possessum

Yvonne Denny, Arlene Stevens, Elizabeth Paul,
Barbara Sylliboy, and Dianne Friesen

One widely discussed feature of Algonquian languages is discontinuous noun phrases: that is, two nominal elements—such as a noun and determiner—that seemingly function as a constituent but are separated by other clausal elements (Dahlstrom 1987; Reinholtz 1999; Bruening 2001, 2006; LeSourd 2006, 2013; Lochbihler 2009; Bliss 2012; Johnson and Rosen 2015; Kitaoka 2016).[1] Discontinuous possessor phrases are analyzed as involving "possessor raising," construed as a possessor being raised out of its containing noun phrase to become a verbal object in its own right (Bruening 2001; LeSourd 2010). Our study of what appeared to be discontinuous possessor phrases in Mi'kmaw shows that possessors and their objects can be grammatically indexed by distinct morphemes within the verb stem. As such, they are independent arguments in the clause and the clause is ditransitive. These findings are contra a recent analysis of Mi'gmaq by Hamilton (2017) that possessor raising constructions are not ditransitive.[2] We first present some background about verb morphology and licensing in Mi'kmaw.

Methodology

Mi'kmaw is the first language of the first four co-authors of this paper; this research is done in the context of Friesen's language learning following Wilson's (2007) Indigenist paradigm. Because they are foundational to the results of this paper, we reproduce his guiding principles for research here (Wilson 2007:195):

- Respect for all forms of life as being related and interconnected.
- Conduct all actions and interactions in a spirit of kindness and honesty; compassion.
- The reason for doing the research must be one that brings benefits to the Indigenous community.
- The foundation of the research question must lie within the reality of the Indigenous experience.
- Any theories developed or proposed must be grounded in an Indigenous epistemology and supported by the Elders and the community that live out this particular epistemology.
- The methods used will be process-oriented, and the researcher will be recognized and cognizant of his or her role as one part of the group in process.
- It will be recognized that transformation within every living entity participating in the research will be one of the outcomes of every project.
- It will be recognized that the researcher must assume a certain responsibility for the transformations and outcomes of the research project(s) which he or she brings into a community.
- It is advisable that a researcher work as part of a team of Indigenous scholars/thinkers and with the guidance of Elder(s) or knowledge-keepers.
- It is recognized that the integrity of any Indigenous people or community could never be undermined by Indigenous research because such research is grounded in that integrity.
- It is recognized that the languages and cultures of Indigenous peoples are living processes and that research and the discovery of knowledge is an ongoing function for the thinkers and scholars of every Indigenous group.

As teachers, learners, and speakers of Mi'kmaw, we observed that there are two ways to translate sentences like 'we saw Peter's house' into Mi'kmaw. One of our goals with this paper is to understand the grammar of the two patterns, in order to incorporate these insights into our understanding of the expressive power of Mi'kmaw and into the creation of learning materials for students of Mi'kmaw language. Looking at transitivity is a key to looking at this grammatical patterning. Sylliboy et al. (2019) showed that two sets of morphemes are involved in determining the transitivity of a clause; in order to study the licensing of arguments in possessor phrases and how these morpheme sets are involved, we expanded the scope of the research. We studied about 150 stems, considering as many combinations of the two sets of morphemes as we could. In the end we entered 1,200+ sentences in Excel for analysis and comparison. We investigate here the functions of the morphemes in the two sets and how they license the participants in the clause. We focus our attention on sentences with possessed noun objects and the corresponding verb morphology.

Possessed Noun Objects and Verb Morphology

The Mi'kmaw language is often described as having free word order, since practically any three- or four-word sentence can be uttered with any word order while preserving meaning. This study focuses on 'discontinuous possessor phrases'; an inanimate possessum (*wtwi'katiknm* 'his/her letter') is illustrated in (1) and an animate possessum (*wkwijl* 'his/her mother') in (2). Morphemes are not parsed in these two examples. The two 'parts' of each 'discontinuous possessor phrase' are underlined.[3]

(1) <u>Pie'l</u> eskmatmaq <u>wtwi'katiknm</u>
Peter wait.for his/her.letter
'I am waiting for Peter's letter.'

(2) <u>wkwijl</u> eskmatmaql <u>Pie'l</u>
his/her.mother wait.for Peter
'I am waiting for Peter's mother.'

Sylliboy et al. (2019) show that, in addition to the inflection, there are at least two morpheme sets within the verb word that license and place restrictions on subjects and objects. In this work, we follow Brittain (1999, 2003), Hirose (2003),

Branigan et al. (2005), and Slavin (2012) and refer to the first as little *v*; the second is termed Voice. These morphemes are glossed in (3).

(3) Malklit eskm-al-Ø-a-t-l Pie'l-al
Margaret wait-*V*-VOICE-3S.O-3S.S-OB Peter-OB
'Margaret is waiting for Peter.'

In transitive clauses, the animacy value of the little *v* morphemes agrees with that of the syntactic object (cf. Sylliboy et al. 2019). In (4)–(7), four different verb roots are shown, with inanimate objects in part (a) and animate objects in part (b). Inanimate-indicating morphemes and inanimate nouns are bolded; animate are underlined.

(4) a. jip-at-m-Ø **winikiskɨk**
fear-IN-VOICE-1s bad.weather(IN)
'I am afraid of bad weather.'

b. jip-al-Ø-k l'mu'j
fear-AN-VOICE-1s>3s dog(AN)
'I am afraid of the dog.'

(5) a. elm-a't-u-Ø **wasuek**
go.home-IN-VOICE-1s flower(IN)
'I am taking the flower home.'

b. elm-a'l-Ø-ɨk l'mu'j
go.home-AN-VOICE-1s>3s dog(AN)
'I am taking the dog home.'

(6) a. wel-o't-m-Ø **wasuek**
good-IN-VOICE-1s flower(IN)
'I keep the flower good.'

b. wel-ey-Ø-a-q l'mu'j
good-AN-VOICE-APPL-1s>3s dog(AN)
'I keep the dog good.'

(7) a. pew-it-u-Ø **wasuek**
dream-IN-VOICE-1s flower(IN)
'I am dreaming about a flower.'

b. pew-i'-Ø-k l'mu'j
dream-AN-VOICE-1s>3s dog(AN)
'I am dreaming about a dog.'

Inglis (1986; see also McCulloch 2013) noted that many of what she called 'finals' in Mi'kmaw (little *v*) occur in pairs, with one member of the pair indicating an inanimate object (here glossed -IN) and the other an animate object (glossed -AN).[4] In part (a) of each example, the little *v* morpheme indexes the inanimate *winikiskik* 'bad weather' or *wasuek* 'flower', and in part (b), the little *v* morpheme indexes the animate *l'mu'j* 'dog'. Note that an inanimate object (part a) is unmarked in Mi'kmaw inflections; inflections on verbs in transitive clauses with inanimate objects index subject only (cf. Wolfart 1973:39, who noted that "the transitive inanimate (TI) paradigm, while clearly transitive in derivation, syntax, and meaning, in Cree shows no suffixes for the goal at all"). In part (b), the inflections (*ɨ*)*k* and *a-q* (both indicating a 1s subject with a 3s animate object; Francis and Hewson 2016:135, 149) also correspond with the animate object. We analyze the *-a* suffix as an applicative morpheme.[5] Thus, the animacy features of *v* accord with the animacy features of the object, regardless of whether the inflection indexes the object.

Clauses that include possessed nouns have an extra layer of precision in that a speaker can choose to index both possessor and possessum in the verb using these same morphemes. Two forms of the verb *nem-* 'see' are shown in (8) and (9).

(8) Nem-it-u-Ø Pie'l w-i'k
see-IN-VOICE-1s Peter(AN) 3S.POSS-house(IN)
'I see Peter's house.'

(9) Nem-it-Ø-a-q Pie'l w-i'k
see-IN-VOICE-APPL-1s>3s Peter(AN) 3S.POSS-house(IN)
'I see Peter's house.'

The possessor phrase is identical in both examples but the verb morphology is different. Both are glossed 'I see Peter's house'. Speakers say that they would use

TABLE 1. Discontinuity correlates with verbal morphology

VERB MORPHOLOGY LICENSES INANIMATE OBJECT ONLY; POSSESSOR AND POSSESSUM MUST BE CONTIGUOUS	VERB MORPHOLOGY LICENSES INANIMATE AND ANIMATE OBJECTS; FREE WORD ORDER IS POSSIBLE
'I see Peter's house.'	'I see Peter's house.'
***Nemitu** Pie'l wi'k.*	***Nemitaq** Pie'l wi'k.*
***Nemitu** wi'k Pie'l.*	***Nemitaq** wi'k Pie'l.*
*Pie'l wi'k **nemitu**.*	*Pie'l wi'k **nemitaq**.*
*Wi'k Pie'l **nemitu**.*	*Wi'k Pie'l **nemitaq**.*
Pie'l **nemitu wi'k.*	*Pie'l **nemitaq** wi'k.*
Wi'k **nemitu Pie'l.*	*Wi'k **nemitaq** Pie'l.*

(9) when they wanted to stress that the home is owned by Peter, for example, in situations where they might be looking for Peter and they see his house (even if he himself is not visible). In (8), only the inanimate possessum is indexed: the bolded morpheme *-it* indexes the inanimate possessed object *w-i'k* 'his home'. In (9), both possessor and possessum are indexed: the bolded morpheme *-it* indexes the inanimate 'home' and the underlined morphemes (applicative suffix *-a,* and inflection *-q*) indicate an animate object, thus indexing the animate possessor *Pie'l* 'Peter'.

The grammaticality of free word order for verb, possessor, and possessum correlates with the verbal morphology (as shown in Table 1). When the verb morphology indexes only the inanimate object (left column, corresponding to (8)), the possessor must be adjacent to the possessum (final two entries are ungrammatical). However, when the verb morphology indexes both an animate and inanimate object (right column, corresponding to (9)), any word order is permitted, including those where the possessor and possessum are separated by the verb—the 'possessor phrase' is apparently discontinuous. (Verbs are bolded but words are not parsed in Tables 1 and 2.)

Similarly, discontinuity of possessor and possessum is also grammatical when both are animate and both noun phrases correlate with distinct verb marking. Compare (10) and (11), which both have the same gloss, 'I am looking after Peter's child'.

(10)	#Ank-wey-Ø-a-q	Pie'l	wu-nijan-n
	care-AN-VOICE-APPL-1S>3S	Peter	3S.POSS-child(AN)-OB
	'I am looking after Peter's child.'		

TABLE 2. Animate possessor and possessum

VERB MORPHOLOGY LICENSES ONLY ONE ANIMATE OBJECT; POSSESSOR AND POSSESSUM MUST BE CONTIGUOUS	VERB MORPHOLOGY LICENSES INANIMATE AND ANIMATE OBJECTS; FREE WORD ORDER IS POSSIBLE
'I am looking after Peter's child.'	'I am looking after Peter's child.'
*#**Ankweyaq** Pie'l wnijann*	***Anko'tmaql** Pie'l wunijann.*
*#**Ankweyaq** wnijann Pie'l*	***Anko'tmaql** wunijann Pie'l.*
*#Pie'l wnijann **ankweyaq***	*Pie'l wunijann **anko'tmaql**.*
*#Wnijann Pie'l **ankweyaq***	*Wunijann Pie'l **anko'tmaql**.*
Pie'l **ankweyaq wnijann*	*Pie'l **anko'tmaql** wunijann.*
Wnijann **ankweyaq Pie'l*	*Wunijann **anko'tmaql** Pie'l.*

(11) Ank-**o't**-m-a-q-l   Pie'l   wu-nijan-n
care-IN-VOICE-APPL-1S>3S-OB   Peter   3S.POSS-child(AN)-OB
'I am looking after Peter's child.'

Note however, that (10) is considered awkward by some speakers (which we show with the # symbol), since it has two possible object referents, *Piel* 'Peter' and *wunijann* 'his child'. In (10), *-wey* indexes one animate object. In (11), the animate possessor *Pie'l* 'Peter' is indexed by the applicative inflection (underlined). The possessum receives inanimate object verb marking, even though the referent, *nijan* 'child', is animate: *-o't* (bolded) is used ordinarily to index an inanimate object (see (4)–(7)). The obviative marking on both the verb and the possessum makes it clear that the object referent is animate, however, since the obviative disambiguates two third-person *animate* referents (Manyakina 2012).

Table 2 shows that when only one object is indexed (10), all sentences are considered awkward by some speakers but discontinuity is not permitted (final two entries of left column). However, any word order of the elements in (11) is acceptable since all arguments are indexed by the verb (right column).

Discussion

The distinct morphological licensing of the possessor and possessum strongly suggests that this is not a case of Mi'kmaw grammar allowing discontinuous possessor phrases. Instead, there are two distinct noun phrases each licensed by different suffixes on the verb; that is, the clauses in (9) and (11) are ditransitive. Compare the verb and clause structure in these examples to a known ditransitive event: *iknm-* 'give' illustrated in (12) and (13).

(12) Iknm-Ø-Ø-a-q Pie'l **kutputi**
give-IN/AN-VOICE-APPL-1S>3S Peter chair(IN)
'I am giving Peter a chair.'

(13) Iknm-Ø-Ø-a-q-l Pie'l **l'mu'j-l**
give-IN/AN-VOICE-APPL-1S>3S-OB Peter dog(AN)-OB
'I am giving Peter a dog.'

All examples have matching structures for inanimate object (9) and (12) and animate object (11) and (13). For the verb *iknm-* 'give', the recipient is the applied object, agreeing with the applicative inflection (underlined). The objects 'chair' and 'dog' both agree in animacy with zero little *v*, which allows an object of either animacy and is glossed -IN/AN (little *v* and object are bolded).

Our findings follow Bliss (2012:9, 11) who noted that "discontinuity in Blackfoot requires a morphological index on the verb," which can be in the form of a prefix or agreement morphology. Similar to Blackfoot, part of the indexing in Mi'kmaw verbs happens through agreement in the inflections. However, the morphology that Bliss identifies for Blackfoot is other than what we call little *v* and Voice suffixes. What is clear is that each language has a means of indexing two objects in the verb. Bruening (2001:29) also concludes that possessor raising is ditransitive in Passamaquoddy. Payne and Barshi (1999:18) note that "the very basis of the raising analysis is that the possessor and possessed items no *longer* form a constituent but behave as syntactically independent NPs."

Verb Licensing of Possessor Phrases—A Ditransitive Clause?

With the preceding background we can now turn to Hamilton (2017) and our objections to his analysis. In his study of possessor raising in Mi'gmaq,[6] Hamilton rejects the possibility that this construction is ditransitive in Mi'gmaq, giving three arguments. The first relates to "the optional and discourse related characterization of P[ossessor] R[aising]" (Hamilton 2017:10). The "topicality of the possessor DP seems to condition the presence of PR and an APPLP. This is different from ditransitives, which always have an ApplP." (Hamilton 2017:11). We agree that possessor raising is optional for the most part; a speaker can choose to license the entire possessor phrase as an object in a monotransitive construction or they can use the possessor raising construction, which is structurally identical to the ditransitive construction. This fact, however, is not an argument against the two constructions having the same syntactic structure, only that a Mi'kmaq speaker can be very precise about whether a clause is transitive (with the possessum as the object) or ditransitive (when the possessor and possessum must both be marked as participants).

Second, Hamilton argued that not all possessors in Mi'gmaq possessor raising constructions have an affectee role. We agree with Hamilton in this, but we note that an affectee role is not a necessary condition for a possessor in possessor raising. Payne and Barshi (1999:20) report that external possession constructions "manipulate which participants or semantic roles receive prominent syntactic coding as core grammatical relations of the clause." That coding is often but not necessarily the affectee role. In the same volume, Aissen (1999) argues that topicality of the possessor is relevant to External Possessor Constructions in Tz'utujil, a finding that Hamilton has attributed to possessor raising in Mi'gmaq.

In his third and major objection, Hamilton (2017) argues that "while goal DPs can be the primary internal argument in passives and reflexives, the possessor DP in P[ossessor] R[aising] cannot." He provides examples, which are reproduced here as (14a–c).

(14) PASSIVE

a. DITRANSITIVE
elugw-atm-(u)-ugsi-eg-p a'pi-l
fix-DFLT-APPL-3>S.APPL/PASS-1.PL-PST net-OB
'We were fixed a/the net (AN).' Hamilton (2017:13)

b. PR
*ges-atm-(u)-ugsi-eg-p 'nt-gij-inen
love-DFLT-APPL-3>S.APPL/PASS-1.PL-PST 1.POSS-mother-1.PL
intended: 'Our mother was loved.' Hamilton (2017:13)

c. NON-PR: VTA
ges-al-u't-'p 'nt-gij-inen
love-AN-3.PASS-PST 1.POSS-mother-1.PL
'Our mother was loved.' Hamilton (2017:13)

In response, although we agree that the clause in (14b) is ungrammatical (or at least not felicitous), we find that a passive with possessor raising is in fact a productive construction in the language. Examples (15)–(21) show this construction with seven verb roots.

(15) nis-a't-u-t-l Pie'l w-nijan-n l'kusuaqn-iktuk
down-IN-VOICE-3S-OB Peter 3.POSS-child-OB ladder-LOC
'Peter's child is being taken down from the ladder.'/'They are taking Peter's child down from the ladder.'

(16) tukw-a't-u-t-l Sa'n w-nijan-n
wake.up-IN-VOICE-3S-OB John 3.POSS-child-OB
'John's child is being woken up.'

(17) kejkap-a't-u-t-l Sa'n w-nijan-n
scratch-IN-VOICE-3S John 3.POSS-child-OB
'John's child is being scratched.'

(18) tew-a't-u-t-l Sa'n w-nijan-n
out-IN-VOICE-3S-OB John 3.POSS-child-OB
'John's child is being taken out.'

(19) pem-a't-u-t-l Sa'n w-nijan-n
along-IN-VOICE-3S-OB John 3.POSS-child-OB
'Somebody is going by with John's child.'

(20) enq-a't-u-t-l Sa'n w-nijan-n
stop-IN-VOICE-3S-OB John 3.POSS-child-OB
'John's child is being stopped.'

(21) aj-a't-u-t-l Sa'n w-nijan-n
move-IN-VOICE-3S-OB John 3.POSS-child-OB
'John's child is being moved.'

Our examples have third person proximate subjects to avoid the use of *-uksi,* a morpheme we find with non-third person proximate subject inflections but for which the parsing is still a matter to be solved. We also show examples using different roots than in Hamilton 2017 because we find the sequence *m-u* (e.g., *elugwatm-*(*u*)*-ugsi-eg-p*) also difficult to interpret.

In the intransitive passive construction as in (14c), the subject is the possessor phrase, whereas in the transitive (possessor raised) passive construction as in (15)–(21), the subject is the possessor and the possessum is marked by the inanimate little *v* and the obviative (there is no evidence for an applicative).

Object Animacy and Verb Morphology

Bruening (2001:261) noted that the possessor raising construction used a stem with morphemes indicating an inanimate object even though the actual object was animate. He concluded that "the actual animacy values of the internal arguments do not play a role: both arguments can be animate, and the base will still be a T[ransitive] I[nanimate]. This suggests that the TI form is a default, and does not agree with anything; if it were not, a clash in features would arise." Our results lead us to a different interpretation—that there is a clash in features and the actual animacy values do play a role in discourse.

In the possessor raising construction, an animate possessum is indexed by *v* morphemes that usually mark an *inanimate* object. This clash in animacy is not the only place in the grammar where Mi'kmaw morphology indicates that an object is inanimate even when the referent is animate. Sylliboy et al. (2019) reported for the Voice morpheme *-eke* that "one way that *-eke* functions is to give inanimate status to a semantically animate object referent, perhaps taking it out of focus for discourse reasons. This discourse function of *-eke* has also been noted with respect to a similar morpheme in Nishnaabemwin." Valentine considers the morpheme *-ge* an "actor focus detransitive" that "focuses on the actor by making it the only role" (Valentine 2001:403). Mi'kmaw speakers explain that *-eke* is used in contexts where the focus is on the event, not the participants. While *-eke* is not detransitivizing (see Sylliboy et al. 2019), morphologically rendering the object referent inanimate might contribute to a focus on the event expressed by the verb.

To illustrate, we provide three examples with the same root *ank-* 'care' (22a–c) and three with *pun-* 'stop' (23a–c). The little *v* morphemes are bolded.

(22) a. Ank-**o't**-m-Ø wasuek
care-IN-VOICE-1s flower
'I am taking care of a flower.'

b. Ank-**wey**-Ø-a-q mijua'ji'j
care-AN-VOICE-APPL-1s>3s child
'I am taking care of the child.'

c. Ank-**o't**-eke-y
care-IN-VOICE-1s
'I am babysitting.'

(23) a. Pun-a't-u-Ø pɨtewey
stop-IN-VOICE-1s tea
'I am quitting [drinking] tea.'

b. Pun-a'l-Ø-ɨk Sa'n
stop-AN-VOICE-1s>3s John
'I am breaking up with John.'

c. Pun-a't-eke-y
stop-IN-VOICE-1s
'I am breaking up with somebody.'

Part (a) in each example has an inanimate object and the Voice morphemes *-m* or *-u;* the little *v* morphemes are *-o't* and *-at.* Part (b) has an animate object and the zero Voice morpheme; the little *v* morphemes are the animate counterparts of those in part (a): *-wey* and *-al.* The clause in part (c) has no object (this construction with *-eke* is ungrammatical with an object); however, there is an animate implied referent (people) in both (22c) and (23c). The little *v* morpheme that *-eke* selects is the one that indicates an inanimate object (*-o't* and *-at*). Note we have glossed *-eke* as a morpheme that indicates either an inanimate or an animate referent, since in other constructions *-eke* allows objects of any animacy (see Sylliboy et al. 2019).

Hamilton (2017:10–11) says that the marked possessor construction in Mi'gmaq is "discourse-driven and speakers report that the possessor DP is interpreted as being topical when used . . . the topicality of the possessor DP seems to condition the presence of P[ossessor] R[aising]." Anderson (1997:234) also reports for Meskwaki that the possessor, when indexed on the verb, is likely "to exhibit a high degree of discourse salience." The fact that an animate possessum is given inanimate status by the verb construction indicates that its referent might be somehow out of sight or not an active participant in the event represented by the verb as compared with the marked possessor.

Conclusion and Further Studies

This article presents arguments against a recent analysis of Mi'kmaw by Hamilton (2017) where he argues that possessor raising constructions are not ditransitive. We provide evidence instead that these constructions are ditransitive and that possessor raising constructions in which the possessor is not adjacent to the possessum are not instances of discontinuous constituents, but rather familiar cases of the first object and second object of a ditransitive occurring in different locations in the clause. Mi'kmaw has a means of distinctly indexing the two objects by means of verb suffixes. Possessors and their objects can be grammatically indexed by distinct morphemes within the verb stem, and any word order is grammatical. Word order is thus freed up to express other facets of discourse. Also, suffixes that indicate an INANIMATE object are employed in verb stems to index possessed nouns, regardless of the animacy of the referent. Current research investigates narratives to determine whether this 'assigned' animacy value is linked to discourse features in the texts.

Payne and Barshi (1999:15) say that possessor raising constructions "bring together central questions in language processing and in syntax, including the intersection of verbal valence and . . . event construal and voice. Their particular interest is that they are a limiting case in terms of argument structure, and thus hold some fundamental keys for understanding the connection between verbal argument structure and syntactic clause structure." Regarding *v* and Voice in Mi'kmaw, current research indicates that these suffixes also carry other information about the nature of the event and the argument structure.

NOTES

1. For their expert guidance and insights, we are indebted to Friesen's doctoral committee: Drs. Leslie Saxon, Heather Bliss, Charlotte Loppie, and Barbara Sylliboy. The mentor–apprentice program is funded by Canadian Heritage and Mi'kmaw Kina'matnewey; the project was carried out in collaboration with Drs. Onowa McIvor and Peter Jacobs in the 'One Mind One People' language revitalization project supported by SSHRC. This work is

partially supported by a SSHRC doctoral fellowship.

2. 'Mi'kmaw' and 'Mi'gmaq' represent different dialects and orthographies of the same language found in different regions. Mi'kmaw uses the Francis-Smith orthography (as described in Francis and Hewson 2016) where stops are represented by the voiceless <p, t, k>. The letters <q>, <y>, and <j> correspond to phonetic [χ], [j], and [ʧ], respectively. Apostrophe indicates vowel length. Schwa is written as <ɨ>.
3. Abbreviations include 1s = first person singular, 3s = third person singular (animate), 3P = third person plural (animate), 1s>3s = first person singular acts on animate third person singular object, AN = animate, APPL= applicative morpheme, IN = inanimate, LOC = locative, O = object, OB = obviative marking, POSS = possessive marking, S = subject, VOICE = Voice morpheme, -Ø = zero morpheme.
4. Friesen and Denny (2019) noted that little *v* morphemes that end in [t] correspond with inanimate objects and those that end in [m], [y], or [l] (or long [i'], which could be an [iy] sequence) correspond with animate objects.
5. Hamilton (2015) first reported the applicative morpheme *-w/-u* in Mi'gmaq. In our study of the complete Mi'kmaw verb paradigms, we noticed that when the verb stem ends in a vowel, the applicative is invariably [w]. With stems ending in a consonant, [a] occurs when the inflection begins with a consonant and [w] when it begins with a vowel. We conclude that /w/ can undergo a phonological change to [a] between consonants. Note also the phonological change in the inflection: *-k* becomes *-q* [χ] when it follows a back vowel like /a/. See Friesen (in prep.) for a more complete discussion of these processes.
6. Hamilton (2017) studied the dialect of Mi'kmaq spoken in the Restigouche area. This orthography, where different from the Francis-Smith, writes the stops [p, t, k] as <b, d, g>. Apostrophe indicates both schwa and long vowels. Hamilton's abbreviations where different from ours include DFLT = default, SAP = speech act participant, PASS = passive, PST = past, and PL = plural.

REFERENCES

Aissen, J. 1999. External Possessor and Logical Subject in Tz'utujil. *Typological Studies in Language* 39:167–194.

Anderson, Gregory. D. 1997. On "Animacy Maximization" in Fox (Mesquakie). *International Journal of American Linguistics,* 63(2):227–247.

Bliss, Heather. 2012. A split DP Analysis of Blackfoot Nominal Expressions. *Proceedings of the 2012 Canadian Linguistic Association,* ed. by P. Cajax, pp. 1–15. Waterloo, ON: Wilfred Laurier.

Branigan, Phil, Julie Brittain, and Carrie Dyck. 2005. Balancing Syntax and Prosody in the Algonquian Verb Complex. *Papers of the 36th Algonquian Conference,* ed. by H. Christoph Wolfart, pp. 75–93. Winnipeg: University of Manitoba.

Brittain, Julie. 1999. A reanalysis of transitive animate theme signs as object agreement: Evidence from Western Naskapi. *Algonquian Papers-Archive* 30:34–46.

Brittain, Julie. 2003. A Distributed Morphology Account of the Syntax of the Algonquian Verb. *Proceedings of the 2003 Annual Conference of the Canadian Linguistic Association,* ed. by Stanca Somesfalean and Sophie Burel, pp. 26–41. Montreal: Université du Québec à Montréal.

Bruening, Benjamin. 2001. Syntax at the Edge: Cross-Clausal Phenomena and the Syntax of Passamaquoddy. PhD thesis, Massachusetts Institute of Technology, Cambridge.

Bruening, Benjamin. 2006. Discrepancies between Projection and Selection: Split Coordination and Raising to Object in Passamaquoddy. Unpublished manuscript, University of Delaware, Newark.

Dahlstrom, Amy. 1987. Discontinuous Constituents in Fox. *Native American Languages and Grammatical Typology: Papers from a Conference at the University of Chicago,* ed. by Paul D. Kroeber and Robert E. Moore, pp. 53–73. Bloomington: Indiana University Linguistics Club.

Francis, Bernie, and John Hewson. 2016. *The Mi'kmaw Grammar of Father Pacifique.* Sydney, NS: Cape Breton University Press.

Friesen, Dianne. In prep. A Grammar of Relationship. How Mi'kmaw Verbs Indicate the Relationship between Participants in a Sentence. PhD thesis, University of Victoria.

Friesen, Dianne, and Yvonne Denny. 2019. Zero Morphemes in Two Categories in Mi'kmaw. *Proceedings of the 23rd Workshop on Structure and Constituency in Languages of the Americas.* Ottawa: University of Ottawa.

Hamilton, Michael D. 2015. The Syntax of Mi'gmaq: A Configurational Account. PhD thesis, McGill University, Montréal.

Hamilton, Michael D. 2017. Ditransitives and Possessor Raising in Mi'gmaq. *Papers of the 46th Algonquian Conference,* ed. by Monica Macaulay and Margaret Noodin, pp. 81–100. East Lansing: Michigan State University Press.

Hirose, Tomio. 2003. Origins of Predicates: Evidence from Plains Cree. Outstanding Dissertations in Linguistics. PhD thesis, University of British Columbia.

Inglis, Stephanie. 1986. The Fundamentals of Micmac Word Formation. MA thesis, Memorial University of Newfoundland, St. Johns.

Johnson, Meredith, and Bryan Rosen. 2015. The Syntax of Discontinuous Noun Phrases in Algonquian Languages: Left Branch Extractions and Focus Movements. *Papers of the 43rd*

Algonquian Conference, ed. by Monica Macaulay and J. Randolph Valentine, pp. 135–150. Albany: State University of New York.

Kitaoka, Daiho. 2016. Discontinuous Quantifiers in English, Japanese, and Algonquian Languages. Paper read at the Canadian Linguistic Association, University of Calgary, Calgary.

LeSourd, Philip S. 2006. Problems for the Pronominal Argument Hypothesis in Maliseet-Passamaquoddy. *Language* 82(3):486–514.

LeSourd, Philip S. 2010. On Raising to Object in Maliseet-Passamaquoddy. *Proceedings of the 14th Workshop on Structure and Constituency in Native American Languages*, pp. 171–182. Vancouver: University of British Columbia Working Papers in Linguistics.

LeSourd, Philip S. 2013. On Split Coordination in Passamaquoddy. *Papers of the 41st Algonquian Conference*, ed. by Karl S. Hele and J. Randolph Valentine, pp. 120–142. Albany: SUNY Press.

Lochbihler, Bethany. 2009. Discontinuous DP Constructions. *Proceedings of the 2009 Annual Conference of the Canadian Linguistic Association*, ed. by Frederic Mailhot, pp. 1–13. Toronto: University of Toronto Press.

Manyakina, Yulia. 2012. An Analysis of Obviation in Mi'gmaq. BA Honors thesis, Concordia University, Montreal.

McCulloch, Gretchen. 2013. Verb Stem Composition in Mi'gmaq. MA thesis, McGill University, Montreal.

Payne, Doris L., and Immanuel Barshi (eds.). 1999. *External Possession* (Vol. 39). Amsterdam: John Benjamins Publishing.

Reinholtz, Charlotte. 1999. On the Characterization of Discontinuous Constituents: Evidence from Swampy Cree. *International Journal of American Linguistics* 65(2):201–227.

Slavin, Tanya. 2012. The Syntax and Semantics of Stem Composition in Ojicree. PhD thesis, University of Toronto.

Sylliboy, Barbara, Elizabeth Paul, Serge Paul, Arlene Stevens, and Dianne L. Friesen. 2019. The Light Verb *-eke* in Mi'kmaq. *Papers of the 48th Annual Algonquian Conference*, ed. by Monica Macaulay and Margaret Noodin, pp. 255–274. East Lansing: Michigan State University Press.

Valentine, J. Randolph. 2001. *Nishnaabemwin Reference Grammar*. Toronto: University of Toronto Press.

Wilson, Shawn. 2007. Guest Editorial: What Is an Indigenist Research Paradigm? *Canadian Journal of Native Education* 30(2):193–195.

Wolfart, H. Christoph. 1973. Plains Cree: A Grammatical Study. *Transactions of the American Philosophical Society* 63(5):1–90.

Nominalization Strategies in Plains Cree

An Analysis of the *-win* Suffix

Lex Giesbrecht and Jordan Lachler

The main focus of this work is to investigate the semantic properties and usage patterns of the *-win* nominalizer in Plains Cree. Nominalization is the process of deriving nouns from other parts of speech, such as verbs or adjectives. Deverbal nominalization, specifically, is the derivation of nouns from verbs, often through the use of affixes on the verb stem.

Plains Cree utilizes several different suffixes for the purposes of derivation. One such suffix, the nominalizer *-win*, is broadly used for deverbal nominalization in Plains Cree. According to Ahenakew (1987:165), "Almost any VAI stem can be used as the base of an inanimate noun; all that needs to be done is to add the suffix *-win*[. . .]. The meaning of these nouns is often the same as the meaning of the verbs from which they are derived, or at least closely related."

However, there are attested *-win* nominals in Wolvengrey (2001) with VTI, VTA, and VII verb stems. Additionally, it is not clear from this description exactly what the semantic relationship is between a *-win* nominal and its stem.

Herein, we seek to answer the following questions: What are the tendencies of usage for the *-win* suffix? In what way is the meaning of a nominalized form related to the meaning of its stem? And, finally, are the meanings of these forms predictable?

The Structure of Plains Cree Verb Stems

Cree verb stems are composed of three different types of morphemes, as described by Dahlstrom (2014:134):

- Initials: Verb initials always take the first position, and usually act as the lexical root.
- Medials: Optional. Medials may be inserted to denote such things as a relationship or a nominal entity.
- Finals: Finals are suffixed after the initial (and, optionally, the medial), and may denote an additional lexical root, a change in aspectual construal, or verb class membership, among other functions.

As mentioned above, verb finals are generally the determining factor for which stem class a verb belongs to. This is because they provide information on valency and gender agreement. That is, VII stems take an inanimate subject, VAI take an animate subject, VTI are transitive and take an inanimate object, and VTA are transitive and take an animate object. It is important to note that VII stems have no animate participants, VTA stems have two animate participants, and both VAI and VTI stems have one animate participant. This will be important later in this paper.

Verb finals can also be used recursively, as demonstrated in (1), from Dahlstrom 2014.[1]

(1) sakihisosihkasoskiw
saki-h-iso-isi-hkaso-iski-w
love-VTA-DETR.REFL.VAI-DIM-pretend.to-HAB-3S.IND
'He's in the habit of pretending to love himself a little bit.' (Dahlstrom 2014:135)

Here, we see an example of a verb final, *-h*, that establishes *sakih-* as a VTA verb stem. However, we also see another verb final, the reflexive marker *-iso*, which changes the meaning of the verb to refer to the agent as doing the predicated action to themselves. A Cree verb bearing the reflexive marker only needs to be inflected for one participant, who is both the subject and the object of the action. The *-iso* verb final is a detransitivizer, meaning that it reduces the grammatical transitivity of the verb it affixes to, thus changing the VTA stem to a VAI stem. Detransitivizing verb finals are an important part of the analysis to follow. We have included those relevant to our data set in (2).

(2) Detransitivizing verb finals

a. -ikê 'unspecified goal'
nôtinikêw (VAI)
nôtin-ikê-w
fight.VTA-DETR.UNSPEC-3SG
'S/he fights people'

b. -iwê 'unspecified goal'
sâkihiwêw (VAI)
sâkih-iwê-w
love.VTA-DETR.UNSPEC-3SG
'S/he loves others'

c. -ito 'reciprocal'
wîcihitowak (VAI)
wîcih-ito-wak
help.VTA-DETR.RECP-3PL
'They help each other'

d. -iso 'reflexive'
nipahisow (VAI)
nipah-iso-w
kill.VTA-DETR.REFL-3SG
'S/he kills him/herself'

e. -o 'middle reflexive'
mamihcimow (VAI)
mamihcim-o-w
brag.VTA-DETR.MREFL-3SG
'S/he brags about him/herself'

Plains Cree Nominalizers

In addition to the *-win* suffix, Cree employs a multitude of suffixes to derive nouns from verbs, particles, and even other nouns. Okimâsis (2004:10) provides an expansive list of such suffixes, including those found in (3).

(3) Derivational suffixes in Plains Cree

a. -kan 'tool/instrument'
kitohcikê 'make music'
kitohcikêkan 'a musical instrument'

b. -hkan 'artificial object'
mohcowi 'be foolish'
mohcohkan 'a clown'

c. -wikamik 'building'
atâwê 'buy it'
atâwêwikamik 'a store'

d. -âpoy 'liquid'
sîwâw 'it is sweet'
sîwâpoy 'pop/any sweet drink'

e. -imin 'berry'
takwaha 'crush it'
takwahimin 'a chokecherry'

One thing that separates the *-win* suffix from those seen above is that it is relatively semantically neutral. That is, other nominalizers in Plains Cree provide additional lexical meaning to the noun they derive, while *-win* acts as more of a 'general use' nominalizer.

Building the Data Set

The data for this project was selected from the *nêhiyawêwin: itwêwina* Plains Cree dictionary, compiled by Arok Wolvengrey. The database was built from a query of entries for words that contained the *-win* nominalizer.

The original set of nominalizations comprised more than 700 entries, which were then pared down to exclude (a) forms that created duplicate verb stem entries through the presence of pre-particles, (b) *-win* forms that had undergone further derivation, and (c) forms that did not have direct correspondence with an attested verb form.

This paring down of terms resulted in a set of 552 noun–verb pairs. Subsequently, a reanalysis was conducted in order to take detransitivizing verb finals into account, and as a result, several nominals that had been removed from the data set were reintroduced. In such cases, the absence of a corresponding verb stem was due to the absence of the detransitivized form of the verb in Wolvengrey 2001, and a corresponding verb stem (without the detransitivizer) was attested. This reintroduction of entries into the database brought the number of noun–verb pairs up to 584 entries in the revised analysis.

This was done in the interest of observing how closely the proportions of verb classes in the data set fit the proportions of verb classes in the dictionary overall, as well as to observe the relative frequency of different detransitivizers as they occur in the data.

A second query was done to obtain the counts of verb stems in the dictionary overall by verb class. These counts can be found in Table 1 and are used for comparison with our database in Figure 4.

Verb Class Distribution

We begin by looking at the overall distribution of verb class as it is recorded in Wolvengrey 2001. These are given in figure 1. In Table 1, we have included the raw frequencies and percentages that are displayed.

We see that VAI verbs account for the largest portion of verbs in Wolvengrey 2001, representing nearly 45% of the dictionary's verb entries, while VTA verbs make up approximately 23%, VTI verbs make up approximately 18%, and VII verbs comprise only about 14% of the verbs in the dictionary.

FIGURE 1. Verb class distribution in Wolvengrey 2001.

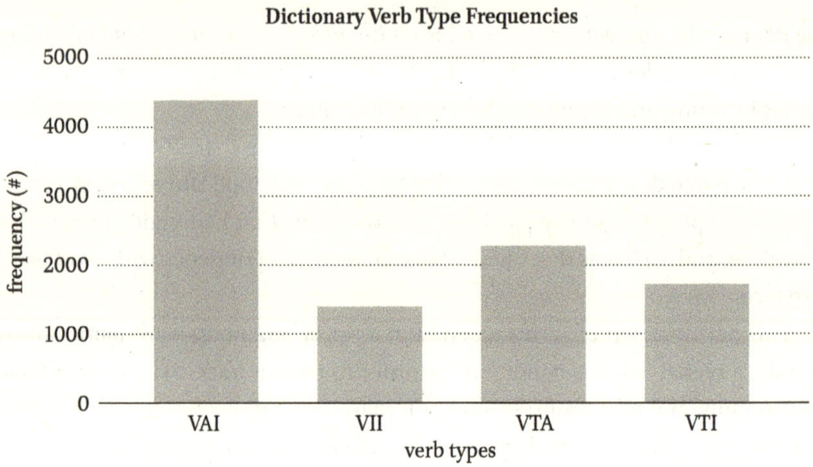

TABLE 1. Verb class distribution in Wolvengrey 2001

	FREQUENCY (#)	PERCENT (%)
VAI	4373	44.91
VII	1374	14.11
VTA	2262	23.23
VTI	1729	17.76

Next, we look at the verb class distribution for the initial data set of 552 terms in figure 2 and Table 2.

What we see here seems to confirm the statement made by Ahenakew (1987:165). With nearly 90% of the *-win* nominals in our data set coming from a VAI verb stem, it seems that all others are relatively rare exceptions. However, there are more than a few exceptions regarding VTI stems, and this seems to indicate that there is more to the story.

Detransitivization: A Complication

Although the difference in number of entries between the initial and revised analyses is the reintroduction of only 32 entries in the latter, the revised analysis reveals the presence of 194 detransitivizers among the *-win* nominals in Wolvengrey 2001. This means the other 162 detransitivized verb stems have been given their

FIGURE 2. Verb class distribution in the data set (first analysis).

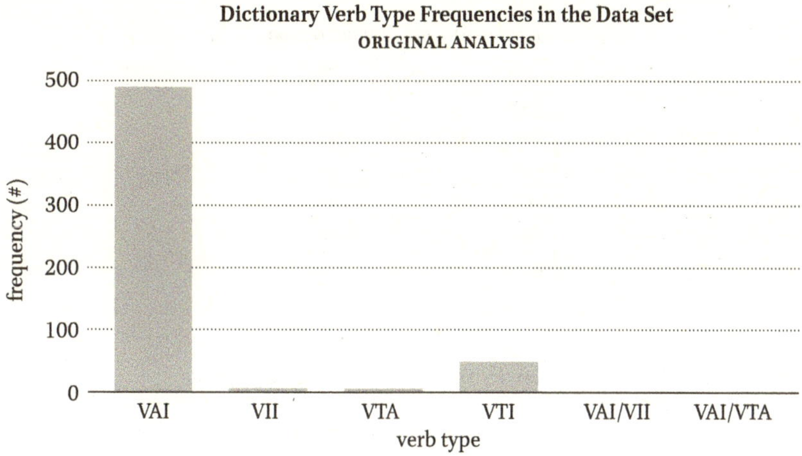

TABLE 2. Verb class distribution in the data set (first analysis)

	FREQUENCY (#)	PERCENT (%)
VAI	491	88.95
VII	6	1.09
VTA	3	0.54
VTI	50	9.06
VAI/VII	1	0.18
VAI/VTA	1	0.18

own entry in the dictionary, possibly having been lexicalized in the language itself. The frequency counts of each detransitivizer, as well as the few instances of the inverse theme marker *-iko*, are detailed in Table 3.

In figure 3 and Table 4, we see the distribution of verb classes in the data set after revising it to account for these detransitivizers.

Here, we can confirm that there is more to the story. The revised set has a distribution resembling that which we find in Wolvengrey 2001, apart from it still lacking VII verb stems. This comparison is demonstrated in figure 4.

Figure 4 shows us that, with the exception of VII stems, the proportions of each verb type in the data set somewhat resembles the verb type proportions found in the dictionary, once the presence of detransitivizers is accounted for.

This result further bolsters Ahenakew's claim that VAI stems are the affixal

TABLE 3. Detransitivizing verb finals in the data set

DETRANSITIVIZER	FREQUENCY (#)
-ikê	69
-iwê	14
-ito	46
-iso	15
-o	46
-iko	4
Total	*194*

FIGURE 3. Verb class distribution in the data set (revised analysis).

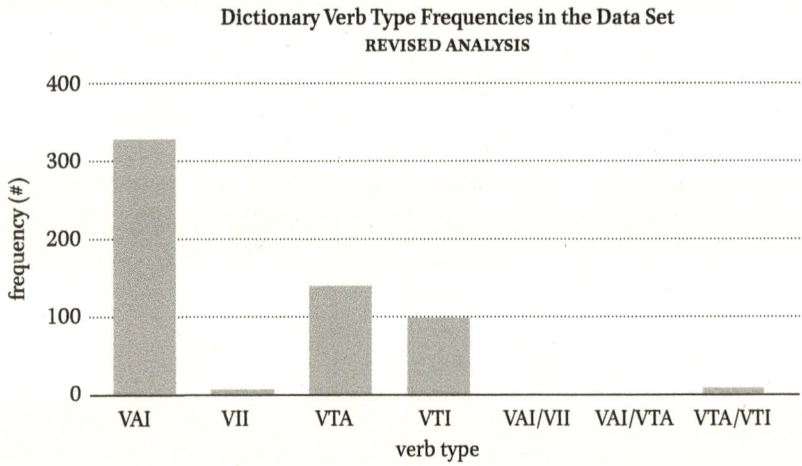

TABLE 4. Verb class distribution in the data set (revised analysis)

	FREQUENCY (#)	PERCENT (%)
VAI	329	56.34
VII	6	1.06
VTA	140	23.97
VTI	99	16.95
VAI/VII	1	0.17
VAI/VTA	1	0.17
VTA/VTI	8	1.37

FIGURE 4. Comparison of dictionary and data set (initial and revised) distributions.

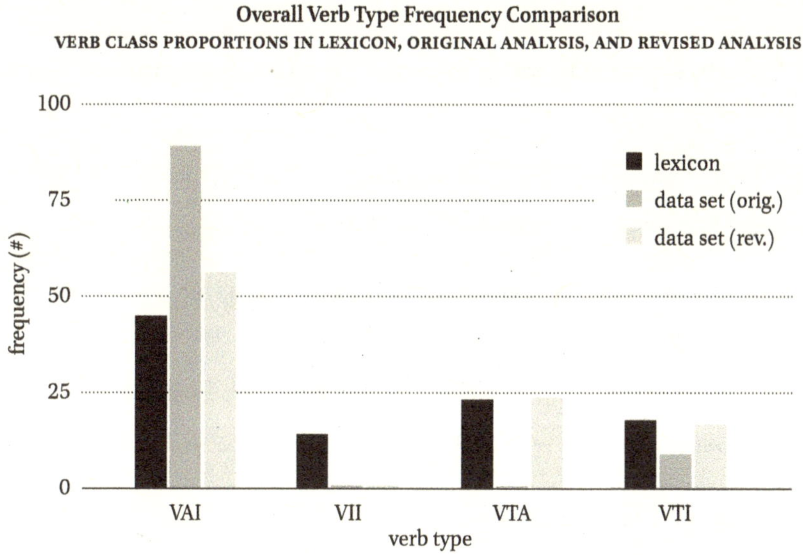

environment of the *-win* suffix, as transitive verb stems will largely undergo detransitivization to a VAI stem for the purposes of *-win* nominalization.

However, we cannot ignore the 50 VTI stems in the initial analysis of the data set. Recall that VTA stems have two animate participants, while VTI stems, like VAI stems, have only one. With the exception of three entries, nearly all VTA stems in the data were detransitivized to VAI stems, whereas VTI stems are demonstrably more acceptable as the affixal environment for the *-win* suffix without the addition of a detransitivizer. It is also notably rare to see VII stems, which have zero animate participants, as the affixal environment for the *-win* suffix. This leads us to suspect that the number of animate participants involved is a factor in whether a verb stem can take the *-win* suffix. Specifically, the *-win* suffix seems to prefer verb stems that take exactly one animate participant.

Semantic Analysis

The following list details the operational definitions used to sort the nominalizations in the revised data set. The focus is on the relationship a nominalization has to its verb stem, that is, what part of the verb's meaning is being referenced by its derivation.

- Predicate: The nominalization references the action, event, attribute, or state predicated by the verb, e.g.:

(4) kwâskwêpicikêw (VAI) 's/he angles, s/he fishes (with rod and reel)'
kwâskwêpicikêwin (NI) 'angling; fishing with a rod and reel'

- Patient: The nominalization references the entity being acted on by the verb's actor, with or without any change to that entity, e.g.:

(5) mîciw (VTI) 's/he eats s.t.'
mîciwin (NI) 'food, groceries; meal'

- Instrument: The nominalization references an instrument or tool used to carry out the predicated action, e.g.:

(6) micimahpisow (VAI) 's/he is tied, s/he is bound'
micimahpisowina (NI) 'manacles, handcuffs'

- Product: The nominalization references something created through the process of the verb, e.g.:

(7) pwâkamow (VAI) 's/he vomits; s/he is sick'
pwâkamowin (NI) 'vomit'

- Result: The nominalization references the outcome of the verb, unless this outcome pertains to something 'created' through the process (cf. 'product'), e.g.:

(8) matwêkahikêw (VAI) 's/he chops noisily'
matwêkahikêwin (NI) 'sounds of chopping heard at a distance'

- Location: The nominalization references the place where the predicated action of the verb would typically take place, e.g.:

(9) kapâw (VAI) 's/he goes ashore, s/he lands; s/he gets out of a canoe or boat'
kapâwin (NI) 'dock; area for docking boats, landing area for boats'

- Manner: The nominalization references the way in which the predicated action of the verb is done, rather than referencing the predicate itself, e.g.:

(10) tôtam (VTI) 's/he does s.t., s/he does s.t. so'
tôtamowin (NI) 'way of doing (so)'

- Time: The nominalization references the time the predicated action would take place, e.g.:

(11) waniskâw (VAI) 's/he gets up, s/he arises from lying, s/he gets out of bed'
waniskâwin (NI) 'time to get up'

- Other: Used when the nominal was too difficult to categorize due to multiple or ambiguous glosses, or otherwise when the relationship between the nominalization and the verb is unclear.

A major limitation of this study is that it was undertaken with little prior knowledge of which semantic categories would be considered significant within the paradigm of the Algonquian languages. Also, it should be taken into consideration that the categorization of *-win* nominals is based on English glosses provided in the dictionary. As such, this analysis is only meant to be a starting point for further research, and consultation with fluent speakers will be necessary to properly tease out some patterns that only begin to emerge here.

Table 5 illustrates the prevalence of the above categories represented in the data set with frequency counts and percentages.

It is clear that the vast majority of *-win* nominalizations in the data set reference the action or quality being predicated by their verb stems. On the other hand, there is also a great deal of variation, from which we can conclude that the meaning of a *-win* nominal is not entirely predictable from its verb stem. Further investigation, primarily involving consultation with speakers of Plains Cree, will be necessary to fully understand speakers' intuitions about the variable semantic outcomes of this suffix.

TABLE 5. Semantic categories in the data set

CATEGORY	FREQUENCY (#)	PERCENT (%)
Predicate	413	70.72%
Patient	60	10.27%
Instrument	19	3.25%
Location	13	2.23%
Product	8	1.37%
Result	11	1.88%
Manner	5	0.86%
Time	2	0.34%
Other	53	9.07%

A Note on Nominalization and Animacy

Recalling the statement by Ahenakew (1987:165), nominalization with the *-win* suffix has been determined to result in inanimate (NI) nouns. This is borne out in our investigation, with the exception of two animate (NA) entries, given here in (12).

(12) NA -win derivations

a. ayisiyinîwiw (VAI) 's/he is a person, s/he is a human being'
ayisiyinîwiwin (NA) 'human life'

b. têhtapiw (VAI) 's/he mounts, s/he is mounted, s/he rides; s/he sits on horseback'
têhtapiwin (NA) 'mount, horse'

It is also important to note that, in the case of *têhtapiw*, two separate entries exist in the data set for nominalized forms. These are given in (13).

(13) NA and NI forms of têhtapiwin

a. têhtapiwin (NA) 'mount, horse'
b. têhtapiwin (NI) 'chair, seat; saddle'

The presence of both an NA and NI nominalization for *têhtapiw* indicates that there is nothing about the verb stem that determines the animacy of its nominal.

It seems clear from these two examples that *-win* nominals that are prototypically living, such as 'horse' and 'human life', will become grammatically animate on this parameter alone.

Summary

This study builds on our understanding of the Cree nominalizing suffix *-win* in a number of ways. While we have observed the *-win* suffix being used for VII, VTI, and VTA verb stems without the use of class-changing verb finals, this is far less common than the nominalization of VAI verb stems. In the data, it is more frequent that class-changing suffixes are used to condition transitive (VTA or VTI) verb stems for nominalization.

In addition to showing a clear preference for affixal environment, the *-win* nominalizer also shows a pronounced tendency to produce nominals that reference the predicate of their verb stem. Again, we have also witnessed a variety of other referent categories in the data, but these occur at a much lower frequency.

Considering the findings of this study, there are a number of possible directions for future research. For instance, despite the prevalence of predicate nominals resulting from *-win* nominalization, other patterns began to make themselves known during lexicography sessions in Maskwacîs, Alberta. In particular, a session exploring terms for different sorts of crafting yielded the observation that the nominalized forms of manufacturing verbs tend to refer to both the act of manufacturing and the product of that act.

This is also found in a significant number of entries in our data set, placed in the "other" category for having multiple glosses that fall under different semantic categories. In fact, the presence of multiple glosses denoting referents of different semantic categories in our method of analysis seems to indicate a need to revise that method.

There is also the matter of examining the semantic effect of certain detransitivizing verb finals on the nominalizations. Specifically, a pattern has emerged for the reciprocal and reflexive finals that suggests they have more of a role in nominal derivation than simply conditioning the necessary affixal environment.

During future research into this topic, it would be vital to conduct fieldwork in tandem with other analyses, to ensure that we are gaining the most insight possible into the patterns being investigated.

NOTES

1. Abbreviations used in this paper: DETR = detransitive, DIM = diminutive, HAB = habitual, IND = independent mode, MREFL = middle reflexive, NA = animate noun, NI = inanimate noun, RECP = reciprocal, REFL = reflexive, UNSPEC = unspecified goal, VAI = animate intransitive verb, VII = inanimate intransitive verb, VTA = transitive animate verb, VTI = transitive inanimate verb.

REFERENCES

Ahenakew, Freda. 1987. *Cree Language Structures, a Cree Approach*. Winnipeg, Manitoba: Pemmican Publications.

Dahlstrom, Amy. 2014. *Plains Cree Morphosyntax*. Hoboken, NJ: Routledge.

Okimâsis, Jean. 2004. *nehiyawewin: paskwawi-pikiskwewin/Cree: Language of the Plains*. Regina, SK: Canadian Plains Research Center.

Wolvengrey, Arok. 2001. *nehiyawewin: itwewina/Cree: Words*. Regina, SK: Canadian Plains Research Center.

The Acquisition of Obviation in Northern East Cree

Evidence from Possessive Constructions

Ryan E. Henke

This study presents an initial investigation of the first language (L1) acquisition of obviation in an Algonquian language by focusing on possessive constructions in Northern East Cree (NEC).[1] In contrast to the findings of research across a range of typologically diverse languages, the acquisition of obviative inflection in possessives does not clearly hinge upon consistency of inflectional marking across nominal types and categories of nouns, but children largely follow expected patterns regarding bare possessees, age of acquisition, and errors in production.

Northern East Cree

East Cree (ISO 639–3 crl) is spoken in nine Québec communities, and the northern dialect is found in four: Chisasibi, Wemindji, Whapmagoostui, and Eastmain (Junker et al. 2012). Data for this study come from Chisasibi and were collected during 2004–2007, when many children were still acquiring NEC as an L1 (Brittain et al. 2007).

The Acquisition of Polysynthesis and Possession

Polysynthetic languages are underrepresented in L1 acquisition research (see, e.g., Kelly et al. 2014). Outside of decades-long work on Inuit languages (Allen 2017), for instance, the L1 acquisition of most of Canada's Indigenous languages is unexplored territory.

However, the Chisasibi Child Language Acquisition Study (CCLAS) (mun.ca/cclas) has examined the L1 acquisition of NEC since 2004. Brittain et al. (2007) provide a description of CCLAS history and methodology. CCLAS has primarily approached the acquisition of phonological elements (e.g., Rose et al. 2010; Swain 2008) and verb types/inflection (Johansson 2012; Terry 2010), rather than nominal inflection. This focus resembles the general tendency in linguistic approaches to polysynthesis, which often center on verb structure and/or phonological considerations such as fusion or prosodic wordhood (see, e.g., various chapters in Fortescue et al. 2017).

Yet nominal elements in polysynthetic languages can also have multifaceted morphological structure, particularly in marking the possessee in possessive constructions (Mithun 1999). The acquisition of possessive marking in polysynthesis has largely been ignored, especially compared to the body of cross-linguistic research on the acquisition of encoding possession.

For example, it is well established that children from a young age understand aspects of the concept of possession, and they express possession before they have acquired their target language's system of encoding possession (e.g., Golinkoff and Markessini 1980; Tomasello 1998). The acquisition of this encoding has received treatment across a variety of non-polysynthetic languages, including English, French, German, Greek, Hebrew, and Japanese (e.g., Brown 1973; Clancy 1985; Eisenbeiß et al. 2009; Leroy-Collombel and Morgenstern 2012). One important pattern that has emerged from this work (Marinis 2016) is that children initially omit grammatical marking for possession (e.g., adpositions or case marking), and mastery of encoding possession can take a few years.

No dedicated study has expressly approached the acquisition of possessive encoding in polysynthetic languages, but some similar patterns can be found in existing literature. For example, Feurer (1980) describes a Mohawk-speaking child at age 2;10 producing possessors with uninflected nouns as possessees (p. 31).[2] Feurer also reports that this child acquires possessive inflection "late," although no age is given (p. 35). Children acquiring Mayan languages have also expressed possession early but without obligatory grammatical marking (e.g., Pye 1992). For example, Brown (1998:738) reports two Tzeltal-speaking children before age 2;05 producing

TABLE 1. Obviative suffixes

ANIMACY	SINGULAR	PLURAL
Animate	iiyikh 'frog/frogs'	
Inanimate	ashtutiniyiu 'hat'	ashtutinh 'hats'

combinations of possessor and possessee lacking inflection, and Pye (1979:460) describes similar constructions from a K'iche-acquiring child around age 2;09.

No research has explored how children acquiring Algonquian languages master the mechanics of obviative inflection in possession, so general findings from the cross-linguistic acquisition of inflection can provide some clues into how the process may unfold in NEC. Deen's (2012) review offers some useful rules of thumb: (1) Regular inflectional systems are easier to acquire, and children acquire them more rapidly than irregular systems (e.g., systems with syncretism in marking or exceptions to marking); (2) children should have mastery of inflection by about age 5; and (3) errors of omission (of inflectional material) are much more common than errors of commission.

Obviation in Possession: A Quick Overview

A famously Algonquian phenomenon, obviation, distinguishes between third-person referents in a particular syntactic or discourse span (see, e.g., Bloomfield 1946). The workings of obviation are multidimensional and dependent upon syntactic and discourse factors (e.g., Dahlstrom 1996; Goddard 1990; Hasler 2002; Russell 1996), but possession creates an obligatory morphosyntactic context for obviation (e.g., Rhodes 1990): In constructions with a third-person possessor, the possessee must be designated obviative.

NEC nouns take a suffix that encodes their obviative status. Adapted from Junker et al. (2013), Table 1 lays out the inflectional paradigm for obviation. Animate nouns take only *-h,* with no marking distinguishing between singular and plural referents. Inanimate singular nouns can take the suffix *-(i)yiu,* while inanimate plurals take an *-h* that is homophonous with the animate obviative suffix.

The final *-h* involved in obviation is indeed a phonemic /h/, which surfaces in particular ways across different phonetic environments. Readers are encouraged to review work by Dyck et al. (2006), O'Neill (2013), Rose et al. (2010), and Swain

(2008) for more on the phonetics involved. As this body of work has shown, stress/accent is the consistent phonetic correlate for final *-h:* NEC nouns by default have either antepenultimate or penultimate stress, but words that take final *-h* all have stress on the final syllable.

From an acquisitionist perspective, obviative marking on nouns presents a particular set of challenges for children: Some nouns as possessees of third persons always receive overt obviative marking, but others do not. This distinction hinges upon two factors:

1. **Animacy** (i.e., noun class) of the possessee
2. Whether the **possessor is obviative**

ANIMATE possessees of third persons bear an obviative suffix. A demonstrative agreeing with the possessee takes an obviative marker, too, as in (1).[3]

(1) Aniyaah maa (name) utaamh naatih

ani-yaah	maa	(name)	u-taam-h	naa-tih
DEM.DIST-OBV	EMPH	N	3-dog-OBV	DEM.REM-LOC

'(Name)'s dog there' (Adult, B1.14, 100)[4]

Adapted from Junker (2003), (2)–(4) illustrate that overt obviative marking works much differently for INANIMATE possessees: An inanimate noun does not bear an obviative suffix when it is possessed, unless the possessor is also obviative (Junker and Blacksmith 2001; Junker 2003). In (2) the third-person possessor is proximate, so the possessed noun *utashtutin* 'her/his hat' carries only the person prefix without an obviative suffix. In fact, the presence of the inanimate singular obviative suffix in (3) precludes the reading in (2).

(2) Waapihtim utashtutin

waapihtim ut-ashtutin

see.TI 3-hat see.TI

'S/he sees her/his (own) hat.'

(3) Waapihtim utashtutiniyiu

waapihtim ut-ashtutin-iyiu

3-hat-OBV

*'S/he sees her/his (own) hat.'

In (4), however, the possessor of the hat is necessarily obviative because the subject of the verb is proximate. Here the possessee does indeed bear an obviative suffix, but this morpheme does not encode the obviative status of the possessee. Although this obviative suffix has been referred to as 'further obviative' marking (e.g., Hockett 1966), others convincingly argue that the suffix actually indexes the obviative status of the possessor (Bloomfield 1946; Wolfart 1978).

(4) Waapihtimwaau utashtutiniyiu
waapihtim-w-aa-u ut-ashtutin-iyiu
see.TI-REL-DIR-3 3-hat-OBV
'S/he sees her/his (someone else's) hat.'

The presence of this obviative possessor in (4) is also signaled by relational morphology on the verb. A relational morpheme encodes an additional third-person entity (most often in the role of possessor) and follows the TI stem, which is then followed by a TA theme sign and person inflection. Because it occurs only three times in the speech sampled for the present study (Section 5), relational morphology is not discussed further here, but is addressed more fully by Junker (Junker 2002, 2003).

Constructions with obviative possessors are not frequent in the CCLAS corpus, but examples (5) and (6) from the corpus illustrate the marking involved. Prior to (5), Daisy has pulled a small toy garbage can out of a toy house, and the adult remarks that this garbage can is for throwing things away. The can is established as proximate, and in (5) the adult asks Daisy what is being thrown away, which establishes the object *chaakwaan* 'what' as obviative.

(5) Chaakwaayiu wiyaapinichaat
chaakwaa-yiu wiyaapinichaat
what-OBV s/he.throws.it.away
'What is s/he throwing away?' (Adult, B1.01, 576)

The child answers with the adult-like obviative form *maatiwaakinishh* '(little) toys', and the adult replies in (6). Because the garbage can is proximate, the possessor of the toys must be obviative. Therefore, the inanimate possessee in (6) receives the obviative possessor suffix.

(6) Awaayiuh umaatiwaanishiyiuh

awaa-yiuh u-maatiwaan-ish-iyiu-h

who-OBV 3-toy-DIM-OBV-PL

'Whose little toys?' (Adult, B1.01, 580)

Thus, the distinction between animate and inanimate nouns presents a specific challenge that children must navigate: The obviative for possessed animates indicates a property of the possessee, but the obviative suffix for possessed inanimates encodes a property of the possessor.

However, a demonstrative provides the crucial morphosyntactic clue within the noun phrase to indicate the covert obviative status of a possessed inanimate. For example, in (7) the demonstrative *aniyaa* bears an obviative suffix in agreeing with *uskaat* 'his leg'.

(7) Chichiih waapihtimwaan aa aniyaa uskaat

chi-chiih-waapihtim-w-aa-n aa ani-yaa u-skaat

2-PST-see.TI-REL-DIR-SAP Q DEM.DIST-OBV 3-leg

'Did you see his leg?' (Adult, B1.01, 379)

Demonstratives can also stand alone as overtly obviative possessees in nominal predicate constructions (Déchaine 1997), without the presence of a noun referring to the possessee. Examples (8) and (9) show demonstratives in equational null-copula constructions. The proximate form in (8) means that the demonstrative and the name "Daddy" have coreference. However, in (9) the demonstrative takes an obviative form and signifies the possessee of a third-person possessor.

(8) Daddy an

Daddy an

N DEM.DIST

'That is Daddy.' (Adult, A1.03, 631)

(9) Dora aniyaa

Dora ani-yaa

N DEM.DIST-OBV

'That is Dora's.' (Adult, A1.12, 319)

TABLE 2. Obviative marking on possessees

TYPE OF POSSESSEE	TAKES OVERT OBVIATIVE SUFFIX?
Demonstrative (as pronoun or modifier)	Yes
Animate noun	Yes
Inanimate noun	No
Inanimate noun (with obviative possessor)	Yes

Finally, English nouns inflected with Cree morphology occur in both child and child-directed speech in the CCLAS corpus (e.g., Pile 2018). There is no existing comprehensive account of how English nouns pattern in NEC, but the adult speech in CCLAS indicates that English nouns are categorized according to the animacy of their Cree counterparts. For example, English 'camera' occurs with inanimate intransitive verbs, as would inanimate NEC noun *misinaapiskihiikin* 'camera', and English 'earring' is treated the same as animate noun *taapishaahun* 'earring'. Accordingly, this analysis posits that English nouns in the target grammar of NEC should behave the same as Cree nouns with obviative inflection in possessive constructions.

Table 2 summarizes the target system of obviative marking with possessees, and the present study poses the question: How do children acquire this system?

Method

All data for this study come from CCLAS video recordings and transcripts involving three child participants acquiring NEC as their first language. Each recording features one child and an adult in a naturalistic home setting, with an individual recording session lasting for approximately 30 to 50 minutes. A regular expression was used to search through the CCLAS corpus and find all child utterances with a third-person possessor.

The youngest child, codenamed Ani, produced 23 such constructions from age 2;03 to 4;00. The middle child, codenamed Daisy, produced 167 from age 3;08 to 5;10. The oldest child, codenamed Billy, produced 50 from 4;05 to 5;10. All of Ani's and Billy's constructions are analyzed here. To achieve more parity between the children, Daisy's recording sessions were randomly sampled, which resulted in a final count of 56 possessives across eight sessions. The age ranges of each child are represented in Table 7 of the appendix, and the number of possessive constructions per age for each child is tallied there in Table 8.

Each possessive construction was coded along several dimensions, which are listed in Table 9 of the appendix. All coding was done in Phon (phon.ca), a freely available open-source software program developed for language acquisition data management and phonological analysis (Rose et al. 2006; Rose and MacWhinney 2014). After coding, utterances were exported for analysis in R (r-project.org), an open-source software package for statistical computation and graphical representation of data.

The analysis presented here is purely descriptive, so no measures of statistical association were calculated. A morphological pattern is considered here to be acquired if it is present in 80 percent of obligatory contexts at a given age. This 80-percent threshold represents a compromise between Brown's (1973) well-known 90-percent threshold for English morphology and Pedro's (2015) 75-percent threshold for Q'anjob'al Maya.

Research Questions and Results

This section poses the following research questions (RQ) and offers results and discussion for each. Each RQ pertains only to possessive constructions with third-person possessors.

RQ1: Which Types of Possessees Do the Children Produce?

As Table 2 shows, the type of possessee largely dictates how overt marking for obviation applies. Figure 1 counts the types of possessees produced by each child.

Each child produces a different range of possessee types. The majority of Ani's tokens (15/23, 65.2 percent) consist of a demonstrative only, as in (10).[5] Such constructions behave very consistently with marking obviation, regardless of the grammatical animacy of the referent. However, Ani does produce nouns in about one-third of her possessees (8/23, 34.8 percent), as in (11).

(10) Maaniyaa Dora
maani-yaa Dora
DEM.DIST-OBV N
'That is Dora's.' (Ani, 2;03, A1.06, 793)

FIGURE 1. Types of possessees produced by each child.

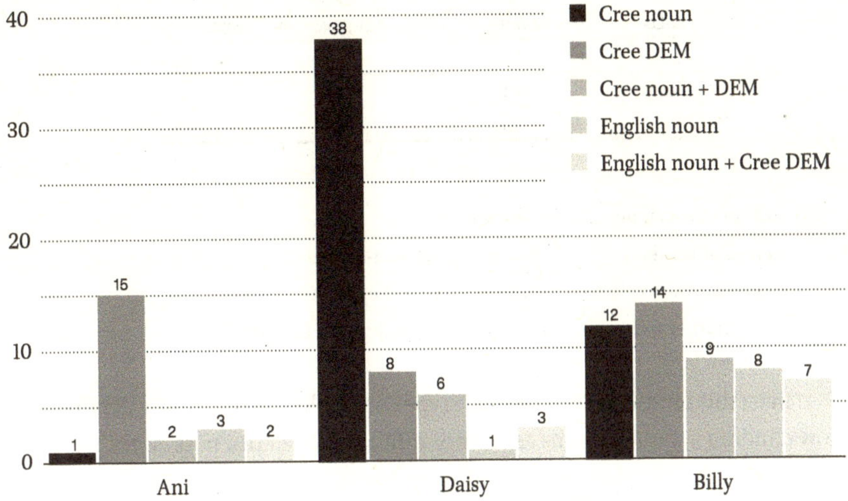

(11) Dora piyichiis

Dora *∅-piyichiis-*∅-*∅

N 3-pants-POSS-OBV

'Dora's pants' (Ani, 2;07, A1.12, 2)

On the other hand, the vast majority of Daisy's possessees contain nouns (48/56, 85.7 percent) as in (12), which means she contends to a much larger extent with the difference in marking between animate and inanimate nouns. She also produces demonstratives in her possessees (17/56, 30.4 percent), which need to inflect in a more consistent fashion.

(12) Umischisinishh

u-mischisin-ish-h

3-shoe-DIM-PL

'Her little shoes' (Daisy, 3;08, B1.01, 659)

Billy also produces a vast majority of noun possessees (36/50, 72 percent), as in (13). Most of his possessives also employ demonstratives (30/50, 60 percent), which inflect for obviation regardless of animacy.

TABLE 3. Demonstrative tokens with required obviative suffix

CHILD	ON-TARGET	OFF-TARGET/UNSURE	ACCURACY
Ani	17	2	89.5%
Daisy	14	3	82.4%
Billy	30	1	96.8%

(13) Chiih uhtinaakuu daycare ukaawih

chiih-uhtin-iku-u	daycare	u-kaawi-h
PST-take.TA-INV-4>3SG	ENG	3-mother-OBV

'His mother went to get him at daycare.' (Billy, 4;07, B3.06, 573)

Given this landscape of possessee types per child, the remaining RQs focus on how children acquire various aspects of inflecting obviative possessees.

RQ2: How Do Children Mark Their Demonstratives in Possessives?

This question centers on the most straightforward aspect of obviative marking in possession: Any demonstrative associated with a possessee should receive overt obviative marking. Table 3 tallies the tokens of such demonstratives produced by the children. Each demonstrative was counted as either (1) ON-TARGET, which means it received an obligatory obviative suffix, or (2) OFF-TARGET/UNSURE, which means either the demonstrative was lacking the required suffix, or it was impossible to discern from the recording whether the suffix was present. For each child, the number of on-target tokens was divided by the total number of tokens to calculate an accuracy rating.

Each child makes at least one clear error, and the errors all involve the omission of obligatory inflection: In (14)–(16), each child produces a demonstrative missing the required suffix.

(14) Waapim maa maau ubedim nimaa

waapim	maa	maau-*∅	u-bed-im	nimaa
see.TI	EMPH	DEM.PXL-OBV	3-ENG-POSS	right

'Look, this is her bed, right?' (Ani, 4;00, A1.35, 79)

(15) aai uwiichaawaakinh uu

aai u-wiichaawaakin-h uu-*∅

HES 3-friend-OBV DEM.PXL-OBV

'Ah . . . this is her friend.' (Daisy, 4;06, B1.15, 807)

(16) usledim uu Dora

u-sled-im uu-*∅ Dora

3-ENG-POSS DEM.PXL-OBV N

'This is her sled, Dora's.' (Billy, 5;06, B3.17, 365)

Each child mostly produces on-target demonstratives, but for Ani it is difficult to pinpoint an age of acquisition for this aspect of obviative inflection. She produces 15/15 correct demonstrative tokens at age 2;07, and her next demonstrative at age 2;08 is also on-target. But after this age, Ani produces no demonstratives involved with third-person possessors until age 4;00, and both of these tokens are not on-target.

Daisy's only demonstrative token at age 3;08 is correct, and three of four are correct at 3;09, but only one of her two tokens at 4;06 is on-target. During the next sampled recording session at age 4;10, though, all five of her demonstratives are on-target. This accuracy rating exceeds the 80-percent threshold for identifying acquisition.

Billy produces all on-target demonstratives until his final and only production at age 5;06, in (16). Given his high accuracy rate, it is possible that Billy has acquired obviative marking with demonstratives even before his first recording session at age 4;05.04.

In summary, it is unclear whether Ani has acquired the pattern of obviative inflection with demonstratives, but the two older children demonstrate a command of this obviative inflection by 5;00, which accords with cross-linguistic expectations.

RQ3: What Is the Animacy of the Children's Possessees?

This question focuses on the animacy balance of nouns in each child's speech. Table 4 presents a frequency count of the number of noun tokens produced by each child. English nouns are considered separately but categorized according to their putative Cree animacy.

Each child produces a different number and proportion of tokens across the

TABLE 4. Animacy of children's noun tokens as possessees

	ANIMATE NOUNS		INANIMATE NOUNS		
CHILD	CREE	ENGLISH	CREE	ENGLISH	TOTAL
Ani	1	0	3	5	9
Daisy	22	3	22	1	48
Billy	9	8	16	3	36

TABLE 5. Animate noun tokens with required obviative suffix

CHILD	ON-TARGET	OFF-TARGET/UNSURE	ACCURACY
Ani	0	1	0.0%
Daisy	21	1	96.0%
Billy	9	0	100.0%

animacy categories, and each child contends with the discrepancies in obviative marking across the two categories to a different extent.

Compared to the other children, Ani produces relatively few common nouns as possessees (just nine). The majority of these are inanimate (8/9 tokens, or 88.9 percent). This includes all five of her English noun tokens: 'bed', 'chair' (three tokens), and 'purse'. Her only animate noun is the Cree word *piyichiis* 'pants' in (11).

The two older children produce a nearly balanced picture of animacy. Daisy has 25 animate (52.1 percent) and 23 inanimate tokens (47.9 percent). Just one English token 'pencil' is inanimate, and her remaining three English tokens are all productions of animate 'friend'. Billy produces 17 animate (47.2 percent) and 19 inanimate tokens (52.8 percent). Three of these inanimates are English: 'toothbrush', 'goaliestick', and 'sled'.

RQ4: How Do the Children Mark Their Animate Possessees?

Animate nouns possessed by third persons should always take an overt obviative suffix. Table 5 tallies and codes the animate noun tokens produced by each child.

Ani produces only one animate possessee, and here she omits the obligatory obviative marking in (11). This bare possessee represents not just a lack of obviative marking but a complete omission of possessive inflection. In fact, until age 3;06

Ani's common nouns as possessees are missing all such inflection, including the person prefix, possessive suffix, and obviative marking. These productions resemble cross-linguistic findings, where children's initial possessive constructions lack obligatory grammatical encoding. From her sparse production, one cannot say that Ani has productively acquired obviative marking for animate nouns.

However, the two older children provide much more solid evidence of acquisition. Daisy produces one animate noun correctly marked as obviative in her earliest session, shown in (17). Her next 19 tokens are also correct, from age 3;09 to 4;10. Given her consistently high accuracy rating across time, Daisy acquired the inflectional pattern of marking obviative animate possessees as early as age 3;08.

(17) Upiipiimishh
u-piipii-m-ish-h
3-baby-POSS-DIM-OBV
'Her little baby' (Daisy, 3;08, B1.01, 581)

Billy correctly puts an obviative suffix on all nine of his animate possessees. These data begin at age 4;06, with (18) and (19). Given his accuracy rate, it is possible that Billy has acquired the pattern of marking animate nouns before 4;06.

(18) Ustaash
u-staas-h
3-older.brother-OBV
'Her older brother'

(19) Nimimaah aai ukaawiih
nimimaah aai u-kaawii-h
NEG HES 3-mother-OBV
'No, his mother.' (Billy, 4;06, B3.05, 66/97)

RQ5: How Do the Children Mark Their Inanimate Possessees?

Inanimate nouns with proximate possessors must not bear an overt obviative suffix. Only two of the 129 child possessives in this study involve obviative possessors. Table 6 tallies the children's inanimate possessees with proximate possessors.

At 2;07 Ani's two clearly off-target inanimate possessees lack the obligatory person prefix and possessive suffix, which indicates an omission of all inflectional material on possessees—not just obviative marking. However, at age 4;00 Ani produces five English tokens ('bed', 'chair' (three tokens), and 'purse') inflected with a person prefix and possessive suffix, and they are correctly missing an obviative

TABLE 6. Inanimate noun tokens correctly lacking overt obviative suffix

CHILD	ON-TARGET	OFF-TARGET/UNSURE	ACCURACY
Ani	5	3	62.5%
Daisy	22	1	95.7%
Billy	18	0	100.0%

suffix; see (20). Although she produces few tokens at this age, her accuracy indicates that Ani has likely acquired the pattern of marking obviative inanimate possessees by 4;00.

(20) Awaan uyaayiu upurseim
awaan u-yaayiu u-purse-im
who DEM.PXL-OBV 3-ENG-POSS
'Whose purse is this?' (Ani, 4;00, A1.35, 257)

Both of Daisy's inanimate tokens are on-target in her first recording session at 3;08, and at 3;09 all six of her tokens are also on-target. In (21), for example, she correctly inflects the possessee with a person prefix without an obviative suffix. Her verbal morphology also indicates that she is correctly navigating an obviative possessee argument.

(21) Chiih wiihminishikiniwiyiu uskaat
chiih-wiih-minish-ikiniwi-yiu uskaat
PST-want-remove.by.blade.TI-PASS-OBV 3-leg
'They wanted to cut off his leg.' (Daisy, 3;08, B1.01, 353)

With this high level of accuracy, Daisy demonstrates acquisition of the pattern of marking obviatives as early as 3;08.

Billy also shows clear mastery of this pattern, with all of his 18 noun tokens correctly lacking an obviative suffix. His first such construction in (22) comes in his first recording session at 4;06. This example also demonstrates Billy's command of differential marking patterns between demonstratives and nouns: The demonstrative modifying the noun needs an obviative suffix while the noun does not.

(22) Awaan aniyaah utoothbrushim

awaan	ani-yaah	u-toothbrush-im
who	DEM.DIST-OBV	3-ENG-POSS

'Whose toothbrush is that?' (Billy, 4;06, B3.05, 533)

RQ6: How Do the Children Mark Inanimate Nouns with Obviative Possessors?

Inanimate nouns with an obviative possessor should take an obviative suffix. Daisy and Billy each produce one construction with an obviative possessor. In Daisy's utterance the possessee is only a demonstrative pronoun, so this construction does not require her to apply obviative inflection to a noun with an obviative possessor. Billy, however, produces a noun with an obviative possessor in (23). Here he applies the proper suffix to the obviative possessor 'her little baby' as well as to the inanimate possessee ('bottle').

(23) Uchuuchuuyiu upiipiimishh

u-chuuchuu-*∅-yiu	u-piipii-m-ish-h
3-bottle-POSS-OBV	3-baby-POSS-DIM-OBV

'Her little baby's bottle' (Billy, 4;08, B3.07, 46)

Conclusions

This study has clear limitations stemming from its small sample size, especially because interchild variability is well established in language acquisition research and will have an even greater effect within small samples. Nonetheless, some circumscribed conclusions and implications may be drawn.

First, Ani's early productions of possessives follow cross-linguistic patterns in omitting obligatory marking for possession. In fact, until age 3;06 her common nouns as possessees lack all morphological encoding for possession. Only about six months later does Ani provide evidence that she has acquired her target language's inflectional system for encoding possession. The two older children do not produce bare possessees, but this is likely a consequence of the fact that their data begin at a later age.

Second, consistency in marking across categories does not have a clear impact on the acquisition of obviation in possessive constructions. Obviation manifests differently between demonstratives and nouns, where discrepancies in marking hinge upon grammatical animacy. The youngest child does not show obvious mastery of inflecting demonstratives, which take an obviative suffix regardless of the animacy of the referent. Animate nouns with third-person possessors always take an obviative suffix, but Ani produces so little evidence that no conclusion can be drawn there. Ani's inanimate nouns are correctly missing inflection at early ages, but this is a reflection of her global omission of possessive morphology.

Consistency also has a nonlinear relationship to Daisy's acquisition. Her mastery of demonstratives follows an unclear path, as she zigzags in accuracy until age 4;10. Perhaps this is less a function of inflectional consistency than of the multidimensionality of demonstrative elements, which involve more complex contextual considerations than common nouns. In other words, maybe her obviative marking on demonstratives lags because demonstratives are harder to master in general. Daisy shows high accuracy in her production of both animate and inanimate possessees from age 3;08, so the difference between animacy categories in inflectional marking does not seem to make a difference—unless it had some effect on her development before she appears in CCLAS data. The same can be said for Billy, who produces demonstratives and nouns of both genders with extreme accuracy, but whose data begin at age 4;05. This limitation on available data makes it difficult to see where the acquisition of NEC fits with cross-linguistic patterns regarding the impact of regularity on the acquisition of inflection.

Third, the development of obviative inflection for all three children generally supports the cross-linguistic rule of thumb that inflectional elements should be acquired by age 5;0. Although Ani's path is unclear regarding demonstratives and animate nouns, she demonstrates command of obviative inflection with inanimate nouns by 4;00. Daisy shows mastery of demonstrative inflection by 4;10, and her inflection of animate and inanimate nouns is highly accurate beginning at 3;08. Billy produces accurate demonstratives at 4;05 and accurate nouns of both genders at 4;06.

Finally, errors in the children's language production are relatively limited, and they tend to be errors of omission rather than comission. This also accords with cross-linguistic expectations.

Appendix

TABLE 7. Age ranges in the sample

	CHILD AGE						
	2;03	3;00	3;08	4;00	4;05	5;00	5;10
Ani	■	■	■				
Daisy			■	■	■	■	
Billy					■	■	■

TABLE 8. Tokens of possessive constructions with third-person possessors

CHILD	AGE	NUMBER OF CONSTRUCTIONS	TOTAL
Ani	2;03.24	1	23
	2;07.06	16	
	2;08.23	1	
	4;00.13	5	
Daisy	3;08.10	4	56
	3;09.22	10	
	4;01.20	8	
	4;06.27	10	
	4;10.03	15	
	5;04.12	1	
	5;07.03	5	
	5;10.02	3	
Billy	4;05.04	1	50
	4;06.08	2	
	4;06.23	4	
	4;07.27	1	
	4;08.21	6	
	4;10.08	6	
	5;00.13	8	
	5;03.22	8	
	5;05.23	1	
	5;06.27	4	
	5;10.06	8	
	5;10.20	1	
Total			*129*

TABLE 9. Coding scheme

VARIABLES	POSSIBLE VALUES FOR EACH VARIABLE				
Possessor status	Proximate	Obviative			
Possessee type	Cree noun	Cree demonstrative	Cree noun + Cree demonstrative	English noun	English noun + Cree demonstrative
Animacy of possessee	Animate	Inanimate	English noun	Unsure	
Does noun require obviative marking?	Yes	No	Unsure	N/A	
Noun correctly marked?	Yes	No	Unsure	N/A	
Does demonstrative require obviative marking?	Yes	No	Unsure	N/A	
Demonstrative correctly marked?	Yes	No	Unsure	N/A	

N/A, not applicable.

For example, the adult-level possessive construction in (7) would be coded as: *Proximate; Cree noun + Cree DEM; Inanimate; No; Yes; Yes; Yes.*

(7) Chichiih waapihtimwaan aa aniyaa uskaat
chi-chiih-waapihtim-w-aan aa ani-yaa u-skaat
2-PST-see.TI-REL-TH Q DEM-OBV 3-leg
'Did you see his leg?' (Adult, B1.01, 379)

NOTES

1. I gratefully acknowledge Dr. Julie Brittain of the CCLAS project at Memorial University of Newfoundland for sharing data and insight. I am also grateful for input from Dr. Andrea L. Berez-Kroeker and Dr. Kamil U. Deen at the University of Hawai'i at Mānoa, as well as to the audience at the 50th Algonquian Conference.
2. Children's ages are given using the standard format year;month.
3. Unless indicated otherwise, the first lines in all interlinear glosses are in NEC orthography. Double vowel graphemes such as <aa> indicate a phonemic long vowel. Hyphens represent morpheme breaks. Zero morphemes indicate obligatory inflectional

elements that are missing. Glossing follows Leipzig Glossing Rules. Exceptions used here are the following: 4 = animate obviative, DIM = diminutive, DIR = direct, EMPH = emphatic, ENG = English word, HES = hesitation, INV = inverse, N = name, OBV = obviative, POSS = possessive, PXL = proximal, REL = relational, REM = remote, SAP = speech act participant, TA = transitive verb with animate object, TI = transitive verb with inanimate object.

4. Example utterances from CCLAS cited here include the codename for the speaker of the utterance; the age of the child speaker; the corpus and recording session number; and the record number of that utterance. Non-CCLAS participant names are redacted for privacy.
5. Junker and MacKenzie (2003) explain that in nominal predications, 'Set One' demonstratives like *aniyaa* in (9) follow the noun, while demonstratives like 'Set Two' *maaniyaa* precede the noun.

REFERENCES

Allen, Shanley E. M. 2017. Polysynthesis in the Acquisition of Inuit Languages. *The Oxford Handbook of Polysynthesis*, ed. by Michael Fortescue, Marianne Mithun, and Nicholas Evans, pp. 449–472. Oxford: Oxford University Press.

Bloomfield, Leonard. 1946. Algonquian. *Linguistic Structures of Native America*, ed. by Cornelius Osgood and Harry Hoijer, pp. 85–129. Viking Fund Publications in Anthropology, vol. 6. New York.

Brittain, Julie, Carrie Dyck, Yvan Rose, and Marguerite MacKenzie. 2007. The Chisasibi Child Language Acquisition Study (CCLAS): A Progress Report. *Papers of the 38th Algonquian Conference*, ed. by H. Christoph Wolfart, pp. 1–17. Winnipeg: University of Manitoba.

Brown, Penelope. 1998. Children's First Verbs in Tzeltal: Evidence for an Early Verb Category. *Linguistics* 36(4):713–753.

Brown, Roger. 1973. *A First Language: The Early Stages*. Cambridge, MA: Harvard University Press.

Clancy, Patricia M. 1985. The Acquisition of Japanese. *The Crosslinguistic Study of Language Acquisition*, Volume 1: *The Data*, ed. by Dan Isaac Slobin, pp. 373–524. Hillsdale, NJ: Lawrence Erlbaum Associates.

Dahlstrom, Amy. 1996. Narrative Structure of a Fox Text. *Nikotwâsik Iskwâhtêm, Pâskihtêpayih! Studies in Honour of H. C. Wolfart*, ed. by John D. Nichols and Arden C. Ogg, pp. 113–162. Winnipeg: Algonquian and Iroquoian Linguistics.

Déchaine, Rose-Marie. 1997. Nominal Predication in Plains Cree. *Papers of the 28th Algonquian Conference*, ed. by David Pentland, pp. 105–135. Winnipeg: University of Manitoba.

Deen, Kamil Ud. 2012. The Morphosyntax Interface. *The Cambridge Handbook of Child Language*, ed. by Edith L. Bavin, pp. 259–280. Cambridge: Cambridge University Press.

Dyck, Carrie, Julie Brittain, and Marguerite MacKenzie. 2006. Northern East Cree Accent. *Proceedings of the 2006 Annual Conference of the Canadian Linguistic Association*, ed. by Claire Gurski and Milica Radišić. Toronto: York University.

Eisenbeiß, Sonja, Ayumi Matsuo, and Ingrid Sonnenstuhl. 2009. Learning to Encode Possession. *The Expression of Possession*, ed. by William B. McGregor, pp. 143–212. Berlin: Mouton de Gruyter.

Feurer, Hanny. 1980. Morphological Development in Mohawk. *Papers and Reports on Child Language Development* 18:25–42. Stanford, CA: Department of Linguistics, Stanford University.

Fortescue, Michael, Marianne Mithun, and Nicholas Evans (eds.). 2017. *The Oxford Handbook of Polysynthesis*. Oxford: Oxford University Press.

Goddard, Ives. 1990. Aspects of the Topic Structure of Fox Narratives: Proximate Shifts and the Use of Overt and Inflectional NPs. *International Journal of American Linguistics* 56(3):317–340.

Golinkoff, Roberta Michnick, and Joan Markessini. 1980. "Mommy Sock": The Child's Understanding of Possession as Expressed in Two-Noun Phrases. *Journal of Child Language* 7(1):119–135.

Hasler, Laurel Anne. 2002. Obviation in Two Innu-Aimun Atanukana. PhD Thesis, Memorial University of Newfoundland.

Hockett, Charles F. 1966. What Algonquian is Really Like. *International Journal of American Linguistics* 32(1):59–73.

Johansson, Sara. 2012. Learning Words Before Learning Grammar: A Case Study of Passives and Unaccusativity in Northern East Cree First Language Acquisition. MA thesis, Memorial University of Newfoundland.

Junker, Marie-Odile. 2002. La Grammaire des Relations: Constructions Possessives et Obviation en Cri de l'Est. *Actes du Congrès Annuel de l'Association Canadienne de Linguistique 2002*, ed. by Sophie Burelle and Stanca Somesfalean, pp. 145–155. Université du Québec à Montréal, Département de linguistique et de didactique des langues.

Junker, Marie-Odile. 2003. East Cree Relational Verbs. *International Journal of American Linguistics* 69(3):307–329.

Junker, Marie-Odile, and Louise Blacksmith. 2001. Obviation, Coreference, and Relational Verb Forms in East Cree. *Papers of the 32nd Algonquian Conference*, ed. by John D. Nichols, pp. 258–268. Winnipeg: University of Manitoba.

Junker, Marie-Odile, Marguerite MacKenzie, and Julie Brittain. 2012. Comparative Structures of East Cree and English. http://eastcree.org/pdf/Cree_English_Structure_2012.pdf.

Junker, Marie-Odile, Luci Salt, and Frances Visitor. 2013. East Cree Nouns (Northern Dialect). The Interactive East Cree Reference Grammar. https://www.eastcree.org/cree/en/grammar/northern-dialect/nouns/inflections-obviative/.

Kelly, Barbara, Gillian Wigglesworth, Rachel Nordlinger, and Joseph Blythe. 2014. The Acquisition of Polysynthetic Languages. *Language and Linguistics Compass* 8(2):51–64.

Leroy-Collombel, Marie, and Aliyah Morgenstern. 2012. Rising Grammatical Awareness in a French-Speaking Child from 18 to 36 Months: Uses and Misuses of Possession Markers. *Journal of French Language Studies* 22(1):57–75.

Marinis, Theo. 2016. Acquiring Possessives. *The Oxford Handbook of Developmental Linguistics*, ed. by Jeffrey L. Lidz, William Snyder, and Joe Pater. Oxford: Oxford University Press.

Mithun, Marianne. 1999. *The Languages of Native North America*. Cambridge: Cambridge University Press.

O'Neill, Katharine. 2013. A Phonetic Study of Word-Final Phenomena in Northern East Cree. MA thesis, Memorial University of Newfoundland.

Pedro, Pedro Mateo. 2015. The Acquisition of Inflection in Q'anjob'al Maya. Amsterdam: John Benjamins.

Pile, Stephanie C. 2018. Monolingual Language Acquisition in a Mixed Language Community: A Case Study of Northern East Cree. MA thesis, Memorial University of Newfoundland.

Pye, Clifton. 1979. The Acquisition of Quiche (Mayan). *Current Anthropology* 20(2):459–460.

Pye, Michael. 1992. The Acquisition of K'iche' Maya. *The Crosslinguistic Study of Language Acquisition*, Volume 3, ed. by Dan Isaac Slobin, pp. 221–308. Hillsdale, NJ: Lawrence Erlbaum Associates.

Rhodes, Richard A. 1990. Obviation, Inversion, and Topic Rank in Ojibwa. *Proceedings of the Sixteenth Annual Meeting of the Berkeley Linguistics Society: Special Session on General Topics in American Indian Linguistics*, 101–115. Berkeley, CA: Berkeley Linguistics Society.

Rose, Yvan, Julie Brittain, Carrie Dyck, and Erin Swain. 2010. The Acquisition of Metrical Opacity: A Longitudinal Case Study from Northern East Cree. *Proceedings of the 34th Annual Boston University Conference on Language Development*, ed. by K. Franich, K. M. Iserman, and L. L. Keil, pp. 339–350. Somerville, MA: Cascadilla Press.

Rose, Yvan, and Brian MacWhinney. 2014. The PhonBank Project: Data and Software-Assisted Methods for the Study of Phonology and Phonological Development. *The Oxford Handbook of Corpus Phonology*, ed. by J. Durand, U. Gut, and G. Kristoffersen, pp. 308–401. Oxford: Oxford University Press.

Rose, Yvan, Brian MacWhinney, Rodrigue Byrne, Gregory Hedlund, Keith Maddocks, Philip O'Brien, and Todd Wareham. 2006. Introducing Phon: A Software Solution for the Study of Phonological Acquisition. *Proceedings of the 30th Annual Boston University Conference on Language Development*, ed. by D. Bamman, T. Magnitskaia, and C. Zaller, pp. 489–500. Somerville, MA: Cascadilla Press.

Russell, Kevin. 1996. Does Obviation Mark Point of View? *Nikotwâsik Iskwâhtêm, Pâskihtêpayih! Studies in Honour of H. C. Wolfart*, ed. by John D. Nichols and Arden C. Ogg, pp. 368–382. Winnipeg: Algonquian and Iroquoian Linguistics.

Swain, Erin. 2008. The Acquisition of Stress in Northern East Cree: A Case Study. MA thesis, Memorial University of Newfoundland.

Terry, Kevin. 2010. The Emergence of Intransitive Verb Inflection in Northern East Cree: A Case Study. MA thesis, Memorial University of Newfoundland.

Tomasello, Michael. 1998. One Child's Early Talk about Possession. *The Linguistics of Giving*, ed. by John Newman, pp. 349–373. Amsterdam: John Benjamins.

Wolfart, H. Christoph. 1978. How Many Obviatives: Sense and Reference in a Cree Verb Paradigm. *Linguistic Studies of Native Canada*, ed. by Eung-Do Cook and Jonathan Kaye, pp. 255–272. Vancouver: University of British Columbia Press.

Derivational Functions of Theme Signs in Oji-Cree

Sarah Hoffman and Will Oxford

The THEME SIGN markers that appear on Algonquian transitive verbs are often described as part of the system of agreement inflection, but they also appear in certain derivational constructions, a role that has received relatively little study.[1] In order to investigate this issue, we worked with a speaker of Oji-Cree to examine the patterning of theme signs in various derivational processes that apply to transitive stems. In this paper we describe our findings and discuss their significance for the overall understanding of theme signs.

Background

This section provides some background information on theme signs and describes our research goals and methodology.[2]

Theme Signs

The theme sign (Bloomfield 1946: §48, 1962: §7.20–25, §7.34) is a morpheme that occupies a slot that lies between the stem and the inflectional suffixes of a transitive

FIGURE 1. Simplified Algonquian verb morphology template.

	STEM			INFLECTION	
Person prefix	Initial	Final	Theme sign	Central ending	Peripheral ending

inanimate (TI) or transitive animate (TA) verb, as illustrated by the simplified verb morphology template in figure 1 (for more complete templates, see, e.g., Nichols 1980:159; Dahlstrom 1986:25; Goddard 2004:104). The Proto-Algonquian morphemes that can appear in this slot include the TA direct theme sign *-a· ~ -e·, the TA inverse theme sign *-ekw, the TI Class 1 theme sign *-am ~ -e· ~ -a·, and the TI Class 2 theme sign *-aw ~ -o· ~ -a· (Goddard 1969:72–73, 82, 87; Pentland 1999:235, 252–254; cf. Bloomfield 1962:102–103). (Further theme signs exist but are not relevant to our study.) The question of whether theme signs are best characterized as derivational or inflectional is controversial, particularly for TI theme signs (Goddard 1969:§4.30; Piggott 1989; O'Meara 1990:110ff; Pentland 1999:236; Quinn 2006:211; Goddard 2007:240).

When a stem-forming derivational process applies to an existing transitive stem, two different patterns are possible. In the first pattern, illustrated in (1a), the derivational suffix, known as a SECONDARY FINAL in Algonquianist parlance (Goddard 1990), is added directly to the stem. In the second pattern, illustrated in (1b), the secondary final is added not to the bare stem, but to the combination of a stem plus a theme sign (Bloomfield 1962:243; Goddard 1990:472–477), a constituent known as a THEME (Bloomfield 1962:63). The second pattern is of interest as it contradicts the template in figure 1: In (1b) a theme sign (*-am* 'TII') appears to the left of a derivational final (*-mikat* 'IN.ACTOR.II'), an ordering that ought not to be possible if theme signs were purely inflectional elements. If the theme sign were inflectional, we would expect it to appear with the rest of the inflectional elements to the right of the derivational final.

(1) a. Stem + secondary final *-ikê*
pâskisikêw
pâskis -ikê -w
shoot.TI -DETRANS.AI -3
'she shoots' Plains Cree (Bloomfield 1946)

b. [Stem + **theme sign**] + secondary final *-mikat*

kehke·netamo·mikatwi

[kehke·net	-am]	-mikat	-w	-i
[know.TI	-TI1]	-IN.ACTOR.II	-3	-IN.SG

'it knows' Meskwaki (Anderson 1997)

The contrast in (1) raises two questions. First, what determines whether a particular derivational process applies to a transitive stem, as in (1a), or to a theme, as in (1b)? Second, are the theme signs that occur "inside" derivation (e.g., *-am* 'TI1' in (1b)) the same synchronic elements as the theme signs that occur "outside" derivation (e.g., *-am* 'TI1' in the inflection of a TI verb), or are the two kinds of theme signs synchronically distinct, with their homophony reflecting only a shared diachronic origin (cf. Macaulay and Salmons 2017)? Our goal in this paper is not to answer these questions; we aim only to contribute some new data that may help to advance the discussion.

Methodology

We conducted several elicitations with one Oji-Cree speaker. The elicitations primarily involved translation from English to Oji-Cree, with prompts designed to elicit derivational constructions of interest. We also created potential Oji-Cree word forms and asked our consultant whether it was possible to use these forms in a sentence (e.g., "Is there a way to say that using a word that sounds like *wanihtoowin*?"). We acknowledge that data elicited in this way are somewhat unnatural and may in many cases involve nonce formations. Nevertheless, our consultant had strikingly clear and consistent judgments regarding possible forms and their meanings. We believe that data collected in this way are valid as long as they are understood as representing one speaker's intuitions about their morphological system. The degree to which these intuitions are consistent across speakers is unknown, but, as we will show, most of our consultant's judgments do have antecedents in the existing literature.

Theme Signs in Derivation: Four Patterns

This section illustrates four patterns in which derivational suffixes can be added to a transitive theme rather than to a bare transitive stem: (1) patient nominalizations ('invite someone' → 'invitee'), (2) passive event nominalizations ('kill someone' → 'getting killed'), (3) active event nominalizations ('bring something' → 'bringing'), and (4) causatives of transitives ('see something' → 'make someone see something'). This is not an exhaustive list of the contexts in which theme signs appear within derivation, but these four patterns are sufficient to allow some interesting generalizations to be made.

Patient Nominalizations

In the existing literature, patient nominalizations ('invite someone' → 'invitee') are one of the best-documented examples of derivational morphology applying to a transitive theme (in particular, the TA direct theme) rather than to a bare transitive stem (Bloomfield 1946:§62; 1962:242; Goddard 2007:259; cf. Nichols 1980:80). This pattern did emerge in our elicitations, as illustrated in (2), where the nominalizer *-ikan* applies to the TA stem *natom-* 'invite someone' plus the TA direct theme sign *-aa*.[3]

(2) natomaakan
[natom -aa] -ikan
[invite.TA -DIR] -NOM
'invitee'

However, the pattern in (2) did not appear to be productive for our consultant, who more frequently added the nominalizer *-ikan* directly to the TA stem, as in (3).

(3) a. nihsikan
nihs -ikan
kill.TA -NOM
'killing victim'

b. waapamikan
waapam -ikan
see.TA -NOM
'the seen one'

In view of the limited distribution of the pattern in (2), it is debatable whether a synchronic morpheme boundary even exists between the putative direct theme sign *-aa* and the nominalizer *-ikan*, as discussed by Goddard (1990:473–474) for the equivalent pattern in Menominee. It may instead be the case that the *-aa-ikan* sequence has been lexicalized as a single nominalizing suffix *-aakan*, as indicated in (4).

(4) natomaakan
natom -aakan
invite.TA -NOM
'invitee'

The analysis in (4) is better suited to capturing the variation that exists between nominalizations in *-aakan* (e.g., ***natomaakan*** 'invitee') and *-ikan* (e.g., ***nihsikan*** 'killing victim'). Under the analysis in (4), the *-aakan/-ikan* variation is simply a matter of selectional properties: The *-aakan* and *ikan* nominalizers select different subsets of TA stems. Under the analysis in (2), in contrast, the nominalizer is always *-ikan*, and the variation lies in whether *-ikan* selects a TA stem (as in *nihs-ikan* 'killing victim') or a TA direct theme in *-aa* (as in [*natom-**aa***]*-ikan* 'invitee'). However, since direct themes in *-aa* exist for all TA stems but nominalizations in *-aa-ikan* exist only for certain TA stems, we would have to stipulate that the nominalizer *-ikan* combines with only those direct themes that are formed on a particular subset of TA stems (such as *natom-* 'invite' but not *nihs-* 'kill'). This leaves us in the awkward position of positing a selectional relationship that skips over an intervening element: In patient nominalizations such as [*natom-aa*]*-ikan* 'invitee', the nominalizer *-ikan* combines with a TA direct theme in *-aa* but selects for the TA stem *natom-* 'invite' that is contained within the TA direct theme. This problem does not arise under a synchronic analysis in which *-aakan* has been lexicalized as a single suffix that combines directly with the TA stem that it selects (Goddard 1990:473–474; see also O'Meara 1990:185, 218–219 for similar argumentation regarding a different pattern in Delaware). The analysis in (2) is likely valid as a representation of the historical origin of the *-aakan* nominalizer, but the analysis in (4) more accurately captures the synchronic patterning of patient nominalizations.[4]

Passive Event Nominalizations

Another well-documented pattern involves the creation of a lexical passive AI verb by adding an intransitive secondary final to a TA inverse theme (Bloomfield

1962:299; Wolfart 1973:47, 71; O'Meara 1990:213ff; Rhodes 1991:317–18; Drapeau 2012). Oji-Cree examples from our consultant are given in (5).

(5) a. waapamikosi

[waapam	**-ikw**]	-isi	-w
[see.TA	-INV]	-AI	-3

'she is seen'

b. kipihtinikosi

[kipihtin	**-ikw**]	-isi	-w
[stop.TA	-INV]	-AI	-3

'she is stopped'

A similar but less well reported pattern also exists. As an alternative to adding the AI final *-isi* to a TA inverse theme to create a passive verb stem as in (5), the abstract nominalizer *-win* may instead be added to create a passive event nominal, as in (6).

(6) a. waapamikowin

[waapam	**-ikw**]	-win
[see.TA	-INV]	-NOM

'being seen'

b. kipihtinikowin

[kipihtin	**-ikw**]	-win
[stop.TA	-INV]	-NOM

'getting stopped'

Like any noun, a passive event nominal can be possessed and pluralized. This is shown for *paaskisikowin* 'getting shot' in (7), with the possessor expressing the patient and the pluralization indicating the repetition of the event.

(7) nipaaskisikowinan

ni-	[paaskisw	**-ikw**]	-win	-an
1-	[shoot.TA	-INV]	-NOM	-IN.PL

'the times I got shot'

We are not aware of previous discussion of this construction in the literature, but we note that it is also attested in Plains Cree, as shown in (8) (Ahenakew and Wolfart 1998:102).

(8) kitasotamâkowininaw

ki-	[asotamaw	**-ikw**]	-win	-inaw
2-	[promise.TA	-INV]	-NOM	-21

'the promise made to us'

In the preceding section we argued that the apparent sequence of the TA direct theme sign *-aa* plus the nominalizer *-ikan* is better analyzed synchronically as a single nominalizing suffix *-aakan*. Can the same argument be made for the *-ikw-win* sequence in forms like (6) and (7)? Here we contend that the case for a synchronic morpheme boundary is stronger. The inverse theme sign *-ikw* occurs inside derivation not only in passive event nominals in *-ikw-win* such as (6) and (7) but also in lexical passive AI verbs in *-ikw-isi* such as (5). In both constructions, *-ikw* contributes the same passive meaning and the derivational suffix that follows *-ikw* contributes the same meaning that it expresses in other unrelated constructions (*-win* 'abstract nominalization', *-isi* 'stative AI verb'). The *ikw-win* sequence in forms like (6) and (7) is thus both segmentable and semantically compositional. We also found no indication of distributional restrictions on *-ikw-win* nominalizations, which, unlike the *-aakan* nominalizations discussed in the preceding section, were possible with all TA stems that we tested. We conclude, then, that the morpheme segmentation shown in (6) and (7), in which the inverse theme sign is followed by a derivational final, is accurate as a synchronic analysis of passive event nominalizations.[5]

Active Event Nominalizations

The existence of passive event nominalizations such as those in (6)–(8) raises the question of whether corresponding active event nominalizations also exist. In its inflectional use, the TA inverse theme sign *-ikw* can usually be exchanged with the direct theme sign *-aa* to create a form in which the subject and object are reversed. We might expect the same alternation to be possible in a derivational context. For example, the passive event nominalization *nihsikowin* 'getting killed' in (9a), with the inverse theme sign *-ikw*, might be expected to have an active counterpart with the direct *-aa*, as in (9b). However, as indicated, our consultant found such forms resoundingly ungrammatical.

(9) a. nihsikowin

[nihs	-**ikw**]	-win
[kill.TA	-INV]	-NOM

'getting killed' (passive)

b. *nihsaawin

[nihs	-aa]	-win
[kill.TA	-DIR]	-NOM

Intended: 'killing' (active)

Instead of starting with a TA theme, our consultant formed active event nominalizations by detransitivizing the TA stem and then nominalizing the resulting intransitive stem. In (10), for example, the nominalization *nihsiwewin* 'killing' is formed from the TA stem *nihs-* 'kill someone' via the intermediate stage of the detransitive AI stem *nihsiwe-* 'kill people in general'.

(10) nihsiwewin

nihs	-iwe	-win
kill.TA	-DETRANS.AI	-NOM

'killing'

The same passive–active asymmetry is attested in Plains Cree (Wolvengrey 2001): The passive event nominalization in (11a) is formed by nominalizing a TA inverse theme while the corresponding active event nominalization in (11b) is formed not by nominalizing a TA direct theme, but rather by nominalizing a detransitive AI stem.

(11) a. asotamâkowin

[asotamaw	**-ikw**]	-win
[promise.TA	**-INV**]	-NOM

'promise (made to one)'

b. asotamâkêwin

asotamaw	-ikê	-win
promise.TA	-DETRANS.AI	-NOM

'promise (that one makes)'

TI stems can also form active event nominalizations. The treatment of TI stems differs from that of TA stems in that two alternative nominalization strategies exist. The first strategy is to detransitivize the TI stem and then nominalize the resulting AI stem, parallel to the treatment of TA stems shown above. In (12), for example, the TI stem *kaat-* 'hide something' is first detransitivized to AI *kaacike-* 'hide things in general'; *-win* is then added to form the active event nominalization *kaacikewin* 'hiding (things)'.

(12) kaacikewin

kaat	-ike	-win
hide.TI	-DETRANS.AI	-NOM

'hiding (things)'

Where TI stems differ from TA stems is in the existence of a second strategy for forming active event nominalizations. Instead of adding the nominalizer to a detransitive AI stem (i.e., a TI stem plus an AI final), the nominalizer can instead be added to a TI *theme* (i.e., a TI stem plus a TI theme sign), as in the examples in (13).

(13) a. piitamowin

[piit	-am]	-win
[bring.TI	-TI1]	-NOM

'bringing'

b. wanihtoowin

[waniht	-oo]	-win
[lose.TI	-TI2]	-NOM

'loss'

The existence of this second strategy reveals an interesting difference between the patterning of TI and TA theme signs in derivation. TI and TA stems share the property that an active event nominalization cannot be formed by adding the nominalizer *-win* directly to the stem: Some other derivational suffix must first be added. For TI stems, there are two options: *-win* can follow either a detransitivizing AI final, as in (12), or a TI theme sign, as in (13). For TA stems, however, there is only one option: *-win* must follow a detransitivizing AI final, as in (10); it cannot follow a TA direct theme sign, as shown in (9). There is thus an asymmetry in the derivational patterning of theme signs: A TI theme can serve as a base for active event nominalization but a TA direct theme cannot.

Active event nominalizations formed from TI themes also provide insight into the relationship between "inflectional" and "derivational" theme signs. In inflectional formations, TI Class 2 stems invariably appear with the TI Class 2 theme sign *-oo*, as shown in (14) for the TI2 stems *waniht-* 'lose something' and *piit-* 'bring something'.

(14) a. niwanihtoon

ni-	waniht	-oo	-n
1-	lose.TI	-TI2	-1s

'I lose it'

b. nipiitoon

ni-	piit	-oo	-n
1-	bring.TI	-TI2	-1s

'I bring it'

When these same stems undergo derivation to form theme-based active event nominalizations, however, there is variation in which theme sign appears. As shown in (15), the TI2 stem *waniht-* takes the TI2 theme sign *-oo* in derivation, as expected, but the TI2 stem *piit-* instead consistently takes the TI1 theme sign *-am* in derivational constructions, in contrast to the TI2 theme sign *-oo* that it takes in inflection.

(15) a. wanihtoowin
[waniht **-oo**] -win
[lose.TI -TI2] -NOM
'loss'

b. piitamowin
[piit **-am**] -win
[bring.TI -TI1] -NOM
'bringing'

The existence of stems such as *piit-*, which take different theme signs in inflection and derivation, suggests an answer to one of the questions that we raised earlier: Do the inflectional and derivational uses of a particular theme sign such as *-oo* involve the same synchronic morpheme, or are we dealing with two homophonous morphemes that are related only diachronically? The ability of some TI2 stems to replace their theme sign with TI1 *-am* in derivation but not in inflection suggests that the derivational and inflectional theme signs may indeed be distinct morphemes. For the TI2 stem *piit-* in our consultant's speech, the inflectional theme sign is *-oo* but the derivational theme sign is *-am*. If we do not recognize a distinction between inflectional and derivational theme signs, this pattern becomes less straightforward to describe.

From a pan-Algonquian perspective, examples of the nominalization of a TI theme are also attested in Betsiamites Innu (Drapeau 1979:312–14), as shown in (16) (with TI1 theme sign *-em* and nominalizer *-un*, cognate with Oji-Cree *-am* and *-win*).[6]

(16) a. kusta·tsi·we·let**em**- 'fear something' → kusta·tsi·we·let**em**-un 'fear'
b. kune·let**em**- 'keep something' → kune·let**em**-un 'possession'
c. ta·pwe·let**em**- 'obey something' → ta·pwe·let**em**-un 'obedience'

We note that all of the numerous Innu examples in Drapeau 1979 are built from TI1 stems with final *-e·let* 'mental activity'. If this selection of examples is representative of the overall distribution of the construction in Innu, then it must be more restricted in Innu than it is for our Oji-Cree consultant, who freely adds the nominalizer *-win* to TI1 themes with various finals and TI2 themes, as shown above.

Causatives of Transitives

For intransitive verb stems, the existence of derivational causative morphology is well documented across Algonquian. In the most basic pattern, the TA final *-h is added directly to an AI stem: *ni·myi- AI 'dance' → *ni·myih- TA 'cause someone to dance' (Bloomfield 1946:112). For transitive verb stems, however, the literature contains very little discussion of causativization—possibly because transitive stems in many Algonquian languages simply cannot be morphologically causativized. Nichols (1980:247) explicitly states that this is the case in Southwestern Ojibwe: "Transitive stems do not form causative verbs, but appear as conjunct complements to the generalized transitive stems TA /iši-/ 'cause him' and TI-2 /išitt-/ 'cause it'." During our elicitation sessions, our consultant produced only one example of such a periphrastic causative, shown in (17) (causativizing an II stem, not a transitive stem), though we suspect that the construction may be more frequent in natural speech.

(17) nikii-ishihtoon waahkaahikan ci-pahkitek

ni-	kii-	ishiht	-oo	-n	[waahkaahikan	ci=	pahkite	-k]
1-	PAST-	make.TI	-TI2	-1s	[house	MOD=	explode	-0]

'I made the house explode'

In contrast to the situation in Southwestern Ojibwe, our Oji-Cree consultant freely produced derivational causatives of transitive stems. Two alternative strategies were used, parallel to the strategies used in the derivation of active event nominalizations. In one strategy, the TA causative final *-h* is added to a detransitive AI stem.[7] This "detransitivize, then causativize" strategy can be applied to both TA and TI stems, as shown in (18).

(18) a. nihsiweh-

nihs	-iwe	-h
kill.TA	-DETRANS.AI	-CAUS.TA

'make someone kill X'

b. piicikeh-

piit	-ike	-h
bring.TI	-DETRANS.AI	-CAUS.TA

'make someone bring X'

Looking at their derivational structure, we might expect the causative stems in (18) to take only two arguments, since the underlying transitive stem takes two arguments (agent and patient), the AI final removes one (patient), and the causative TA final adds one (causer). In reality, however, the stems in (18) can actually function as TA+O verbs taking three arguments: a causer subject, a causee primary object, and a patient secondary object, as shown by the examples in (19).

(19) a. nikii-nihsiwehaa naapen

ni-	kii-	nihs	-iwe	-h	-aa	naapew	-an
1-	PAST-	kill.TA	-DETRANS.AI	-CAUS.TA	-DIR	man	-AN.OBV

'I made him kill the man.'

b. nikii-piicikehaa mihsan

ni-	kii-	piit	-ike	-h	-aa	mihs	-an
1-	PAST-	bring.TI	-DETRANS.AI	-CAUS.TA	-DIR	wood	-IN.PL

'I made her bring the firewood.'

In the other strategy for producing derivational causatives of transitive stems, the TA causative final *-h* is added to a TI theme. In the existing literature, this strategy has been described for OBJECTLESS TI verbs, which are not syntactically transitive, such as Southwestern Ojibwe *osossot(am)-* OTI 'cough' in (20a) (Nichols 1980:247). A comparable example from our Oji-Cree consultant is given in (20b).

(20) a. osossotamoh-

[osossot	-am]	-h
[cough.TI	-TI1]	-CAUS.TA

'make someone cough'

b. wiihsakentamih-

[wiihsakent	-am]	-h
[feel.pain.TI	-TI1]	-CAUS.TA

'make someone feel pain'

Our consultant also freely applies this strategy to syntactically transitive TI stems such as *natoht-* TI 'listen to something' and *waapaht-* TI 'see something', as in (21).

(21) a. natohtamoh-

[natoht	-am]	-h
[listen.TI	-TI1]	-CAUS.TA

'make someone listen (to X)'

b. waapahtamoh-

[waapaht	-am]	-h
[see.TI	-TI1]	-CAUS.TA

'make someone see X, show someone X'

Causatives formed from TI themes can function as TA+O verbs with three arguments, as shown for *natohtamoh-* VTA(+O) 'make someone listen (to X)' in (22).

(22) nikii-natohtamohaa nikamowinini

ni-	kii-	[natoht	**-am**]	-h	-aa	nikamowin	-ini
1-	PAST-	[listen.TI	-TI1]	-CAUS.TA	-DIR	song	-IN.OBV.SG

'I made him listen to a song.'

For some transitive stems, our consultant is able to apply either of the derivational causative strategies. The TI stem *natoht-* 'listen to something', for example, can form both a theme-based causative, shown in (22) (*natohtamoh-* 'make someone listen to X'), and a detransitive-based causative, shown in (23) (*natohcikeh-* 'make someone listen to X'). Where such pairs exist, the detransitive version seems to imply a weaker, less direct form of causation, as indicated in (23) by our consultant's translation 'ordered a song request for him' rather than 'made him listen'.

(23) nikii-natohcikehaa nikamowinini

ni-	kii-	natoht	-ike	-h	-aa	nikamowin	-ini
1-	PAST-	listen.TI	-DETRANS.AI	-CAUS.TA	-DIR	song	-IN.OBV.SG

'I ordered a song request for him.'

Another similar pair is shown in (24): The TI2 stem *piit-* 'bring something' is causativized via a TI theme in (24a) (*piitamoh-* 'make someone bring X') and via a detransitive AI stem in (24b) (*piicikeh-* 'make someone bring X'). Our consultant commented that the theme-based version in (24a) sounds "more like an order" than the detransitive-based version in (24b).

(24) a. nikii-piitamohaa mihsan

ni-	kii-	[piit	**-am**]	-h	-aa	mihs	-an
1-	PAST-	[bring.TI	-TI1]	-CAUS.TA	-DIR	wood	-IN.PL

'I made her bring the firewood.'

b. nikii-piicikehaa mihsan

ni-	kii-	piit	-ike	-h	-aa	mihs	-an
1-	PAST-	bring.TI	-DETRANS.AI	-CAUS.TA	-DIR	wood	-IN.PL

'I made her bring the firewood.'

As observed for active event nominalizations in the preceding section, TI Class 2 stems show variation in which TI theme sign appears before the causative final.

For example, the TI2 stem *nipaht-* 'kill something' takes the TI2 theme sign *-oo* as expected (25a), but the TI2 stem *piit-* 'bring something' instead takes TI1 *-am* (25b).

(25) a. nikii-nipahtoohaak waapikwanini

ni-	kii-	[nipaht	**-oo**]	-h	-aa	-ak	waapikwan	-ini
1-	PAST-	[kill.TI	**-TI2**]	-CAUS.TA	-DIR	-AN.PL	flower	-IN.OBV.SG

'I made them kill the flower.'

b. nikii-piitamohaa mihsan

ni-	kii-	[piit	**-am**]	-h	-aa	mihs	-an
1-	PAST-	[bring.TI	**-TI1**]	-CAUS.TA	-DIR	wood	-IN.PL

'I made her carry the firewood.'

We conclude this section with a note on the morphosyntax of causatives derived from transitive stems. As shown above, such causatives can function as TA+O verbs, taking a causer subject, a causee primary object, and a patient secondary object. As with any TA+O verb, the primary object must be animate, but the secondary object—that is, the patient—can be of either gender (Bloomfield 1962:47; Rhodes 1990). For example, causative *nipahtooh-* 'make someone kill X', derived from TI2 *nipaht-* 'kill something', appears with an inanimate patient in (26a) but with an animate patient in (26b).

(26) a. nikii-nipahtoohaak waapikwanini

ni-	kii-	[nipaht	-oo]	-h	-aa	-ak	**waapikwan**	**-ini**
1-	PAST-	[kill.TI	-TI2]	-CAUS.TA	-DIR	-AN.PL	**flower**	**-IN.OBV.SG**

'I made them kill **the flower (INAN)**.'

b. nikii-nipahtoohaak pooshiihshan

ni-	kii-	[nipaht	-oo]	-h	-aa	-ak	**pooshiihsh**	**-an**
1-	PAST-	[kill.TI	-TI2]	-CAUS.TA	-DIR	-AN.PL	**cat**	**-AN.OBV**

'I made them kill **the cat (ANIM)**.'

A striking property of the causative TA+O stem nipahtooh- 'make X kill Y' in (26b) is that it contains a TI theme sign even though all three arguments are animate. This property is familiar from another better attested class of TA+O stems: applicatives derived from TI stems through the addition of *-amaw (Bloomfield

1946:115). In the Innu example in (27) (Brittain 1993:48), the applicative TA+O stem *nakuâtamu-* 'snare X for someone', derived from TI1 *nakuât-* 'snare something', contains the TI1 theme sign *-am* even though all three arguments are animate.

(27) ninakuâtamuâut uâpusha auâssat

ni-	[nakwât	**-am**]	-aw	-â	-w	-at	wâpush	-a	awâss	-at
1-	[snare.TI	-TI1]	-APPL.TA	-DIR	-1s	-AN.PL	rabbit	-AN.OBV	child	-AN.PL

'I snare a rabbit for the children.'

The occurrence of a TI theme sign in (26b) and (27) is problematic if we regard the TI theme sign as an inanimate object marker (as in Goddard 2007:240), since in these examples a TI theme sign occurs even though all arguments are animate. For applicative TA+O verbs the problem can be sidestepped by analyzing the *-amaw sequence as a single morpheme distinct from the TI1 theme sign *-am (as in Bloomfield 1946:115), but the recurrence of the same pattern in causative TA+O verbs casts doubt upon the validity of this move. Oji-Cree causative TA+O forms such as (26b) thus augment the existing evidence from applicatives that it is possible for a TA+O stem to contain a TI theme sign even if all arguments are animate. This conclusion entails that, at least in their derivational function, TI theme signs are not inanimate object markers.

Discussion

Certain derivational processes can productively apply to bare intransitive stems but cannot apply to bare transitive stems. In such cases there are two workarounds: Either (1) detransitivize the transitive stem and then apply the process, or (2) add a theme sign to the transitive stem and then apply the process. We observed the following theme signs playing this role in derivation: (1) TA direct *-aa* (in patient nominalizations; an unproductive historical relic that may not even be a separate morpheme synchronically), (2) TA inverse *-ikw* (in passive event nominalizations; productive), and (3) TI *-am* and *-oo* (in active event nominalizations and causatives of transitives; productive). The distribution of TI theme signs in derivation appears to be less restricted than that of TA theme signs, as active event nominalizations and causatives of transitives can both be built from TI themes but not TA themes.

Earlier in the paper we posed two general questions about the nature of theme signs. One question involved the distinction between derivational and inflectional theme signs: Is a given theme sign the same synchronic morpheme in both its derivational and inflectional functions? There are some indications that the answer may be no. First, the derivational direct theme sign *-aa* is susceptible to being reanalyzed as part of a larger suffix, as shown for *-aakan* in (4), whereas the inflectional direct theme sign *-aa* always retains its identity as a separate morpheme. Second, the inverse theme sign *-ikw* can be freely exchanged with the direct theme sign *-aa* in inflection but not in derivation, as shown for event nominalizations in (9). Third, there are some TI Class 2 stems that take the TI2 theme sign in inflection but the TI1 theme sign in derivation, as shown in (15) and (25). Fourth, the derivational TI theme signs can co-occur with an animate patient, as in (26b) and (27), but the inflectional TI theme signs cannot. We do not exclude the possibility that there may be ways to explain away some of these differences, but at least for descriptive purposes it seems necessary to recognize a distinction between derivational and inflectional theme signs.

The other question involved the distribution of theme signs in derivational processes: What determines whether a particular derivational process applies to a bare transitive stem (e.g., detransitivization) or a transitive theme (e.g., event nominalization)? We note that the processes that apply productively to transitive themes rather than bare transitive stems (i.e., event nominalization with *-win* and causativization with *-h*) also apply productively to intransitive stems. Their applicability to intransitive stems but not transitive stems suggests that these processes may be constrained to apply only to one-place predicates. Their applicability to transitive themes would then follow if we made the further assumption that the addition of a theme sign somehow saturates the object argument of a transitive stem, which leaves the transitive theme with only one open argument position and thus qualifies it for the same derivational processes that apply to intransitive stems. More research would be needed to validate this speculative line of analysis, but in any case, we are left with an interesting descriptive generalization: For the purposes of certain derivational processes, intransitive stems and transitive themes pattern as a natural class to the exclusion of transitive stems. The explanation of this generalization, whatever it may be, has the potential to deepen our understanding of the nature of Algonquian theme signs.

NOTES

1. We give special thanks to Samson Beardy for sharing his language with us. This paper would not have been possible without his patience, effort, and insight. We also thank David Pentland for providing us with carefully gathered examples of several obscure derivational constructions, as well as the audience of the 50th Algonquian Conference for many helpful comments, particularly from Rose-Marie Déchaine and Richard A. Rhodes. We are grateful for the constructive comments provided by two anonymous reviewers. Our research was supported by SSHRC (IDG 430–2016–00680, Structure and Change in Direct-Inverse Systems) and the University of Manitoba Undergraduate Research Award.
2. The following abbreviations are used in this paper: 0 = inanimate; 1, 2, 3 = first, second, third person; 1s = first person singular; 21 = inclusive first person plural; AI = animate intransitive; AN = animate; APPL = applicative; CAUS = causative; DETRANS = detransitive; DIR = direct; II = Inanimate Intransitive; IN = inanimate; INV = inverse; MOD = modal; NOM = nominalizer; OBV = obviative; PA = Proto-Algonquian; PL = plural; SG = singular; TA = transitive animate; TA+O = ditransitive TA; TI = transitive inanimate; TI1 = TI Class 1; TI2 = TI Class 2; X = argument that may be either animate or inanimate (in translations of stems).
3. Except where another language and/or source is noted, all data in this paper are from the authors' fieldwork on Oji-Cree.
4. We thank an anonymous reviewer for calling our attention to this point.
5. The conclusion that there is a synchronic morpheme boundary in the *-ikw-win* sequence does not entail that the inverse theme sign *-ikw* that occurs in such derivational constructions is the same synchronic morpheme as the inverse theme sign *-ikw* that occurs as an inflectional agreement marker. This is a separate question. It may be the case that the two *-ikw* morphemes are related only diachronically. We speculate that *-ikw* (PA *-ekw) may have originally been a passive marker, as proposed by McLean (2001). The passive meaning has been preserved in the lexical uses of *-ikw* but has been bleached in its inflectional uses.
6. We retain the orthography used in Drapeau 1979, which differs from the contemporary standard Innu orthography.
7. The TA final *-h* that appears in causatives, reflecting PA *-h, actually shows variation between *-h* and *-hiy* in our consultant's speech. For example, the AI stem *niimi-* 'dance' can be causativized as either *niimih-* or *niimihiy-* 'make ANIM dance'. In forms with the direct theme sign *-aa*, our consultant is able to use either of these stem shapes: 'I make her dance' can be pronounced as either *ni-niimih-aa* or *ni-niimihiy-aa*. In forms

with the inverse theme sign *-ikw*, however, our consultant uses only the longer *-hiy* stem shape: 'she makes me dance' can only be pronounced as *niniimihiik*, with long *ii* from the underlying *iyi* sequence in *ni-niimihiy-ikw*, not as *niniimihik*, with short *i* from the historically expected underlying sequence *-h-ikw*. We are not aware of other discussion of the *-hiy* variant in the literature and we do not know how widespread it is in Oji-Cree.

REFERENCES

Ahenakew, Freda, and H. C. Wolfart (eds). 1998. *The Counselling Speeches of Jim Kâ-Nîpitêhtêw.* Winnipeg: University of Manitoba Press.

Anderson, Gregory D. S. 1997. On "Animacy Maximization" in Fox (Mesquakie). *International Journal of American Linguistics* 63:227–247.

Bloomfield, Leonard. 1946. Algonquian. *Linguistic Structures of Native America*, ed. by Harry Hoijer et al., pp. 85–129. Viking Fund Publications in Anthropology 6. New York.

Bloomfield, Leonard. 1962. *The Menomini Language.* New Haven, CT: Yale University Press.

Brittain, Julie. 1993. Two Valency-Increasing Processes in Sheshatshit Innu-aimun: Applicative and Causative Formation. Master's thesis, Memorial University of Newfoundland.

Dahlstrom, Amy. 1986. Plains Cree Morphosyntax. PhD thesis, University of California, Berkeley. [Published 1991, Garland, New York.]

Drapeau, Lynn. 1979. Aspects de la morphologie du nom en montagnais. PhD thesis, Université de Montréal.

Drapeau, Lynn. 2012. Passives in Innu. *International Journal of American Linguistics* 78:175–201.

Goddard, Ives. 1969. Delaware Verbal Morphology: A Descriptive and Comparative Study. PhD thesis, Harvard University. [Published 1979, Garland, New York.]

Goddard, Ives. 1990. Primary and Secondary Stem Derivation in Algonquian. *International Journal of American Linguistics* 56:449–483.

Goddard, Ives. 2004. Meskwaki Verbal Affixes. *Papers of the 35th Algonquian Conference*, ed. by H. C. Wolfart, pp. 97–123. Winnipeg: University of Manitoba.

Goddard, Ives. 2007. Reconstruction and History of the Independent Indicative. *Papers of the 38th Algonquian Conference*, ed. by H. C. Wolfart, pp. 207–271. Winnipeg: University of Manitoba.

Macaulay, Monica, and Joseph Salmons. 2017. Synchrony and Diachrony in Menominee Derivational Morphology. *Morphology* 27:179–215.

McLean, Lisa Michelle. 2001. A Passive to Inverse Reanalysis in Cree. Master's thesis, University of Manitoba.

Nichols, John D. 1980. Ojibwe Morphology. PhD thesis, Harvard University.

O'Meara, John. 1990. Delaware Stem Morphology. PhD thesis, McGill University.

Pentland, David H. 1999. The Morphology of the Algonquian Independent Order. *Papers of the 30th Algonquian Conference*, ed. by David H. Pentland, pp. 222–266. Winnipeg: University of Manitoba.

Piggott, Glyne L. 1989. Argument Structure and the Morphology of the Ojibwa Verb. *Theoretical Perspectives on Native American Languages*, ed. by Donna B. Gerdts and Karin Michelson, pp. 176–208. Albany: SUNY Press.

Quinn, Conor. 2006. Referential-Access Dependency in Penobscot. PhD thesis, Harvard University.

Rhodes, Richard A. 1990. Ojibwa Secondary Objects. *Grammatical Relations: A Cross Theoretical Perspective*, ed. by Katarzyna Dziwirek, Patrick Farrell, and Errapel Meijas-Bikandi, pp. 401–414. Stanford, CA: CSLI.

Rhodes, Richard A. 1991. On the Passive in Ojibwa. *Papers of the 22nd Algonquian Conference*, ed. by William Cowan, pp. 307–319. Ottawa: Carleton University.

Wolfart, H. C. 1973. Plains Cree: A Grammatical Study. *Transactions of the American Philosophical Society* 63:part 5.

Wolvengrey, Arok. 2001. *Nēhiýawēwin: itwēwina/Cree: Words*. Regina: University of Regina Press.

Gatherings

The Transformation of Algonquin Settlement Patterns in the 19th Century

Leila Inksetter

The yearly mobility pattern observed among Northern Algonquians in the early twentieth century was marked by a winter dispersal alternating with a summer gathering.[1] This gathering would bring together a hundred or several hundred people, usually where the local trading post stood. There, the entire band would stay for a period of about two months. This period was one of trading, socializing, and ritual activity: Winter furs were exchanged at the post, young people would court and get married by the visiting missionary, band members would discuss and settle matters that needed to be addressed. Cemeteries at these sites marked the places where loved ones were buried. When fall came, people would disperse into small family groups, sometimes not reconvening until the following spring (Lips 1947:399; Rogers 1963:71–72, 1965:266, 1969:28–29).

So widespread was this pattern observed among Northern Algonquian peoples at that time that it came to be viewed as a timeless yearly settlement system. This model made its way into textbooks and general overview articles as the pre-European contact pattern generalized in the boreal and mixed forests of Canada (Leacock 1995; McMillan and Yellowhorn 2004:110, 117, 119; Rogers and Smith 1981:135–138). Taking a step further, several authors proposed that summer gathering places in use during the early 20th century preceded the trading post

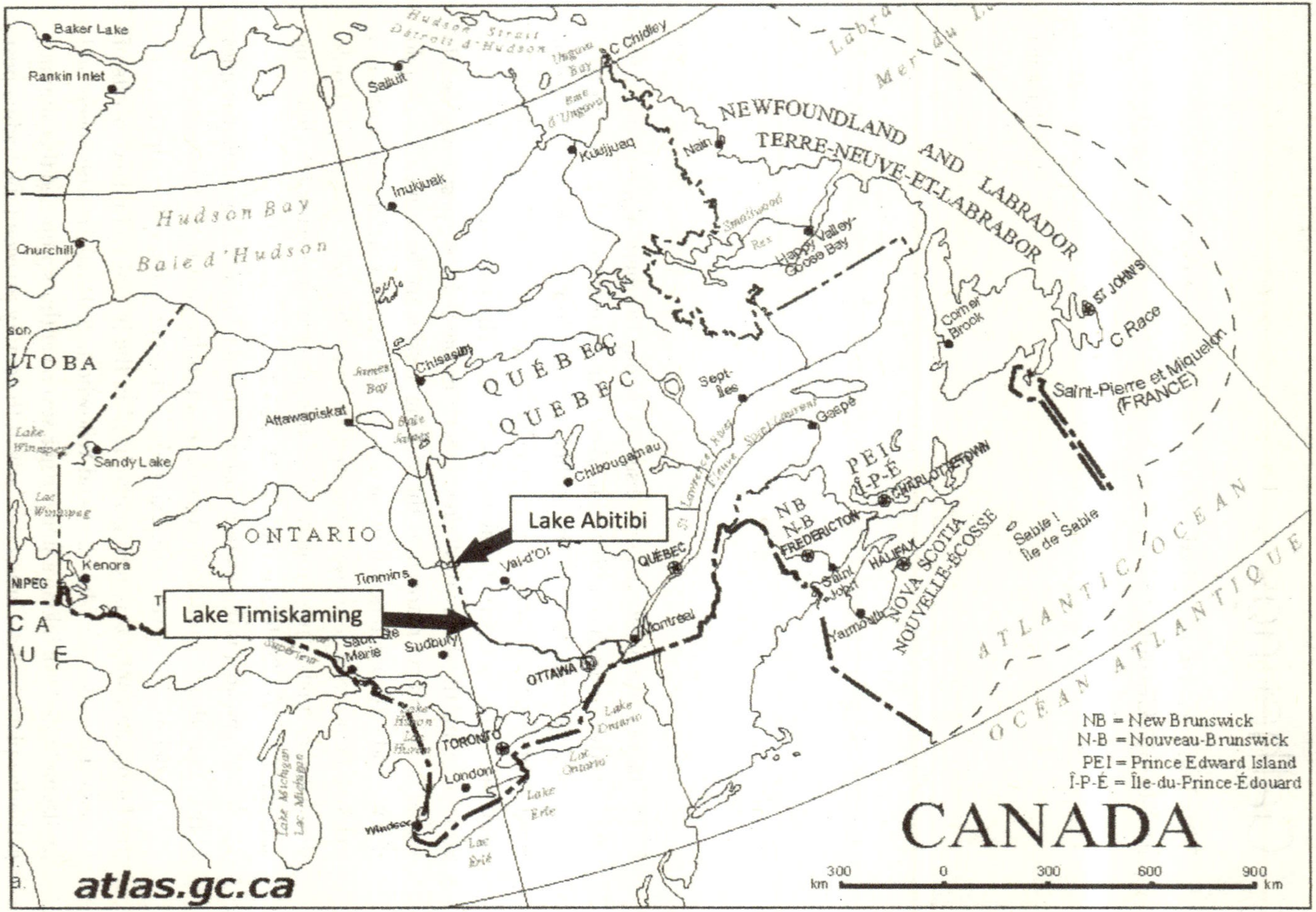

Lake Abitibi
Lake Timiskaming
NEWFOUNDLAND AND LABRADOR
TERRE-NEUVE-ET-LABRADOR
QUÉBEC
QUEBEC
ONTARIO
NB
N-B
PEI
Î-P-É
NOVA SCOTIA
NOUVELLE-ÉCOSSE
Hudson Bay
Baie d'Hudson
ATLANTIC OCEAN
OCÉAN ATLANTIQUE
Saint-Pierre et Miquelon (FRANCE)
Baker Lake
Rankin Inlet
Churchill
Salluit
Inukjuak
Kuujjuaq
Nain
Happy Valley-Goose Bay
Chisasibi
Attawapiskat
Sandy Lake
Kenora
Timmins
Val-d'Or
Chibougamau
Sept-Îles
Gaspé
Corner Brook
ST JOHN'S
C Race
C Chidley
QUÉBEC
Montréal
OTTAWA
TORONTO
London
Windsor
Sudbury
FREDERICTON
CHARLOTTETOWN
HALIFAX
Saint John
Yarmouth
Sable I
Île de Sable
NB = New Brunswick
N-B = Nouveau-Brunswick
PEI = Prince Edward Island
Î-P-É = Île-du-Prince-Édouard
CANADA
300 km 0 300 600 900 km
atlas.gc.ca

era, even conditioning the locations where trading posts were set up (Lawrence 2012:29; Scott 2018:102).

This article questions this ahistorical representation of summer gatherings and will show that this specific form of gathering is the result of several historical factors. This, in itself, is not new in the field of Northern Algonquian studies. Edward Rogers and John Honigmann have already shown that the presence of a trading post had the effect of coalescing a larger group of people than any social unit existing prior to the European fur trade (Honigmann 2005: 332; Rogers 1969: 46). Moreover, Rogers and others have argued that this artificial group gradually stayed for longer periods of time around the post in summer, and came to be interdependent with the goods and services obtained there, a historical process that Richard Preston has labeled "the posting process" (Bishop 1994:318; Preston 1975:328; Rogers 1994:318, 323–324).

The contribution this article makes is a detailed demonstration of the historical transformation that occurred for two Algonquin groups, one living around Lake Abitibi and the other around Lake Timiskaming, both located on the current Quebec-Ontario divide (figure 1). It will show that a series of 19th-century factors shaped the summer gatherings in that area. This article is ethnohistorical, reconstructing a historical process by drawing on archival sources, ethnological sources, archaeological sources, and direct testimony from the people concerned.

The People of Lake Abitibi and Lake Timiskaming and Their Summer Gathering Places

The people living around Lake Abitibi and Lake Timiskaming call themselves 'Anishnabe' or 'Algonquin'.[2] They are closely related to several communities in Ontario and in Quebec, along the Ottawa Valley and over the height of land, who use either one of those terms to refer to themselves. More generally, they share a lifestyle with Algonquian groups that I have loosely termed Northern Algonquian.

Archaeology has revealed a human presence in the Abitibi and Timiskaming lakes area for 6,000 years, and possibly longer, and has not revealed any major discontinuities, such as abandonment of the area (Côté 1993:21, 1998). Trading posts have existed on Lakes Abitibi and Timiskaming since the 17th century and

FIGURE 1 (*opposite*). Location of study area.

have operated almost uninterrupted until the 20th century, although posts were built and rebuilt, and changed ownership several times within that period.

Until the Algonquins moved to sedentary settlements over the course of the 20th century, they lived a mobile lifestyle based on hunting and fishing. Timiskaming First Nation band settled gradually on a reserve that was established at the head of Lake Timiskaming as early as 1853, but remained permanently unsettled for several decades. Until the transition to the reserve took place, the people living around the lake would converge in the summer further down, at a place where the lake narrows, and where the trading post and chapel stood. Two cemeteries also mark the site. In the early 20th century, the people of Lake Abitibi gathered for several weeks in the summer on a point of land at the eastern end of that lake, near the trading post, chapel, and adjacent cemetery. This group of people has since been split into two administrative bands: One of these contemporary bands, Wahgoshig First Nation, is now settled on the Abitibi Indian Reserve in Ontario, while the other, Abitibiwinni First Nation, is located on the Pikogan Reserve, in Quebec, 80 km east of the lake.

Although modern settlements have altered the pattern of summer gatherings, these are still remembered fondly by community members (Bousquet 1999:32–33; Larivière 2013:59–63, 158–168, 184–185; Mathias 1998:v, 34, 41, 85; Moore 1982:37–39, 82–83; Rankin and Tardif 2011:32–34). Elders remember how, as children, they would attempt to trick their parents into advancing the date of the departure toward the summer gathering place by secretly displacing the pin marking the current day on the family calendar, anxious to meet their age-mates. Community members return to these places and maintain the gravesites of loved ones, sometimes taking younger people with them to teach them about the place and the people who went there (Bousquet 1999:34, Mathias 1998:75). For these contemporary communities, the summer gathering places have become a strong symbol of tradition.[3]

This attachment to these former gathering sites has also led, on a more formal level, to the official recognition of these places as heritage sites by the Canadian government. Timiskaming First Nation is an official co-managing partner for the Obadjiwan–Fort Témiscamingue National Historic Site, which includes the place where the trading post stood at the narrows, the former gathering place, and adjacent cemeteries.[4] Abitibiwinni First Nation was a key actor in filing for and obtaining federal recognition of the general area where the summer gathering was held on Lake Abitibi, as a National Historic Site of Canada.[5] This area includes several pre-European contact archaeological sites, the place where the Hudson's Bay Company post and chapel stood, the gathering place, and the Catholic cemetery.[6]

Historical Depth

The important sense of tradition associated with these gathering places has led to a perception of great antiquity. This was recorded, for instance, by anthropologist Frank Speck. In 1913, Speck visited the Timiskaming reserve, where, by then, the local band had settled on a semipermanent basis and had stopped using the summer gathering place at the narrows. In the paper Speck wrote from this visit, he mentions the gathering place at the narrows as a former one. Speck's choice of wording shows he understood this gathering place as having predated the establishment of the trading post there (Speck 1915:3). Abitibiwinni community member Dominique Rankin stated in his recent autobiography that the summer gathering place on Lake Abitibi enticed the trading companies to establish their posts at that place, since "they knew they could find us there every year, assembled in great numbers" (Rankin and Tardif 2011:41, translation).

Anthropologist John MacPherson visited the people of Lake Abitibi in 1930 before they had moved to permanent settlements. In his report, he stated that at that time, people congregated at the gathering place between June and August (MacPherson 1930:7). Further on, MacPherson explains he understood this pattern as being an ancient one, albeit not necessarily at the exact place the post stood:

> Before the coming of the white man it was the custom of the band to congregate at a given rendezvous during the summer months. The underlying factor of the rendezvous was its social significance. The band got together for feasts, speech-making, dancing, etc. (MacPherson 1930:9)

Almost a century earlier, Father Poiré met with the Algonquins of Lake Timiskaming and recorded information on how they used to live. Although the information Poiré recorded is somewhat ambiguous on this point, it nonetheless gives the impression that summer gatherings were important, as people stated they gathered around their chief (Poiré 1841:17).

In an 18th-century collection of letters attributed to Father Antoine Silvy, one can read:

> The Aticamegues or Whitefish, Monsonis, Abitibis, Machtantibis or Teste de Boule and the Temiscamingues live from the Nemisco River to the end of Lake Superior; all these nations are in very small numbers and always wandering, [they] meet only in the summer for 15 days on a point of land or on a river, in 3 or 4 huts, then leave each other. (Silvy 1904:111, translation)[7]

Thus, oral history, ethnographies, and written documents all point to the social significance of Algonquin summer gatherings.

Abitibi and Timiskaming Gathering Places in Early Records

An examination of historical records made by in situ observers on Lake Abitibi and Lake Timiskaming leads to the startling observation that there did not appear to be any summer gathering at the place the trading posts stood, until the 19th century. I first proceed to present these historical records and the chronological transformation that can be observed through them, then discuss the significance of the discrepancies between the sources.

Post Journals Prior to the Hudson's Bay Company and North West Company Merger

Some of the earliest in situ observations on Algonquin settlement patterns that have survived in written form can be derived from post journals, starting in the late 18th century. At that time, the North West Company (NWC) operated a single post unhindered at the narrows on Lake Timiskaming. Over the height of land, on Lake Abitibi, the NWC and the Hudson's Bay Company (HBC) were rivals for a period of 18 years, between 1794 and 1812. The HBC then abandoned the area, leaving the NWC operating alone. After the 1821 merger between the two companies, the HBC became the single owner of the posts operating on both lakes.

Seventeen post journals dating between 1794 and 1821, held by post masters attached to one or the other company, have been studied for these two areas. These journals include daily entries about which hunters came to the post and when they left. This information was compiled from the journals, and from this, the total numbers of visits at the post were calculated for each month. The length of each visit was averaged per month (see examples, figures 2 and 3). From these entries, we can observe that until 1821, visits made to the posts by Algonquin hunters were unsynchronized and were spread throughout the year. The journals reveal that the hunters would arrive alone or in small groups of two or three, usually linked through kin. The post journals generally only mention male hunters; however, we can gather from information gleaned here and there that the hunters' families were also present at times, although it remains unclear whether this was always the case. When present, these family groups appear to have been small, made up of about 10 people. During those visits to the posts, the hunters and their families stayed, on average, only one night. As seen through the post journals, the visits to the trading post thus seem to have been linked exclusively to economic functions: Hunters would show up to buy or to sell something, and depart almost immediately.

There is one notable exception. This exception concerns the trading captains recognized at Abitibi by the rival trading companies. These trading captains received special treatment as a recognition of the greater amount of furs brought in to trade. The captains tended to arrive in large polygynous family groups and spent between three weeks and two months at the post.[8] They were provided with food during their stay and were presented with large quantities of alcohol by the post master. Ordinary hunters at Lake Abitibi did not receive such treatment, nor did they stay any significant length of time at the Abitibi posts. The presence of these trading captains has skewed the averages and thus explains the differences in lengths of stay observed at both posts, since there were no such captains at Timiskaming. The captain system disappeared at Abitibi with the merger of the trading companies.

We can conclude from the analysis of these post journals that the sum of the individual hunters who traded at each post did not congregate at a specific date around the post in the late 18th and early 19th century, and thus, we have no evidence of a summer gathering at the post at that time. Moreover, these post journals give no indication of a sizable gathering held elsewhere, away from the post.

The Hudson Bay Company and North West Company Merger and its Consequences for Settlement Patterns

The first change that can be observed through post journals occurred in the 1820s, after the merger of the HBC and NWC. One of the new administrative measures put in place concerned the way manufactured goods and furs were to be transported to and from the posts under study. In this area, the HBC decided that these would hence be sent to and from Moose Factory, on James Bay, rather than by the Ottawa

FIGURE 2. Number of visits to the post, by month.

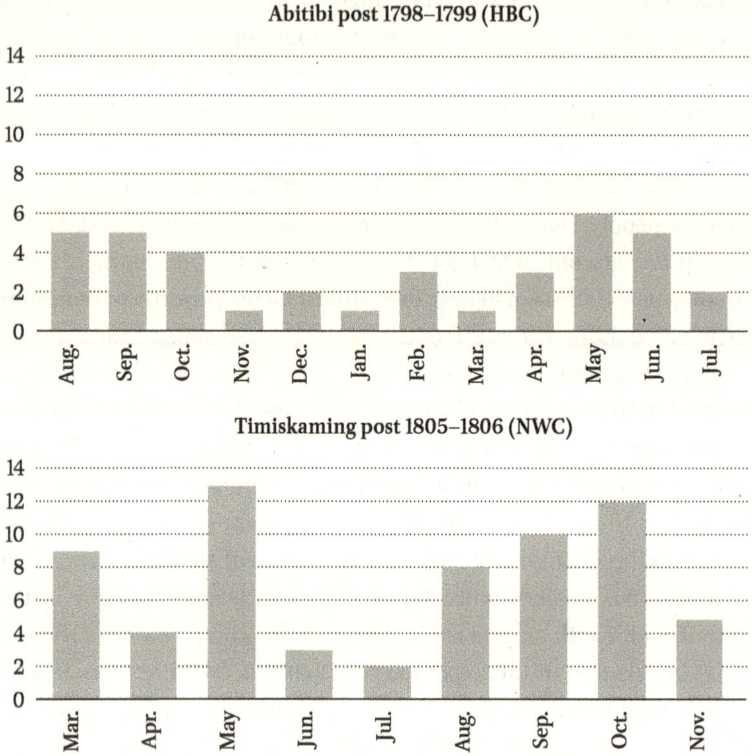

Note: The charts have been compiled according to the information provided by the journals, and therefore have kept the same time frame. These journals probably underestimate the total number of visitors, since only the main hunter was usually mentioned. Thus, each visit should be seen as possibly reflecting the presence of a family.

River system. More importantly, it was decided that local Algonquin men would be hired to do the freighting, instead of French Canadian and Iroquois men who had done much of this work under the NWC, the Company hoping to save money by offering lower wages to Algonquin men. There were a few test years, but as of the late 1820s, local Algonquin men were regular participants in the Moose brigades, as they were called, and this form of summer work continued until the early 20th century, especially in the Abitibi area.

This new form of employment for the local men had an immediate effect on the Algonquin families' annual movement around the posts. From then on, Algonquin men who had been hired for the fur brigade, along with their families, would converge at the trading post at a set time, usually in June. During a few days, the

FIGURE 3. Average time spent at each post per visit (as number of nights).

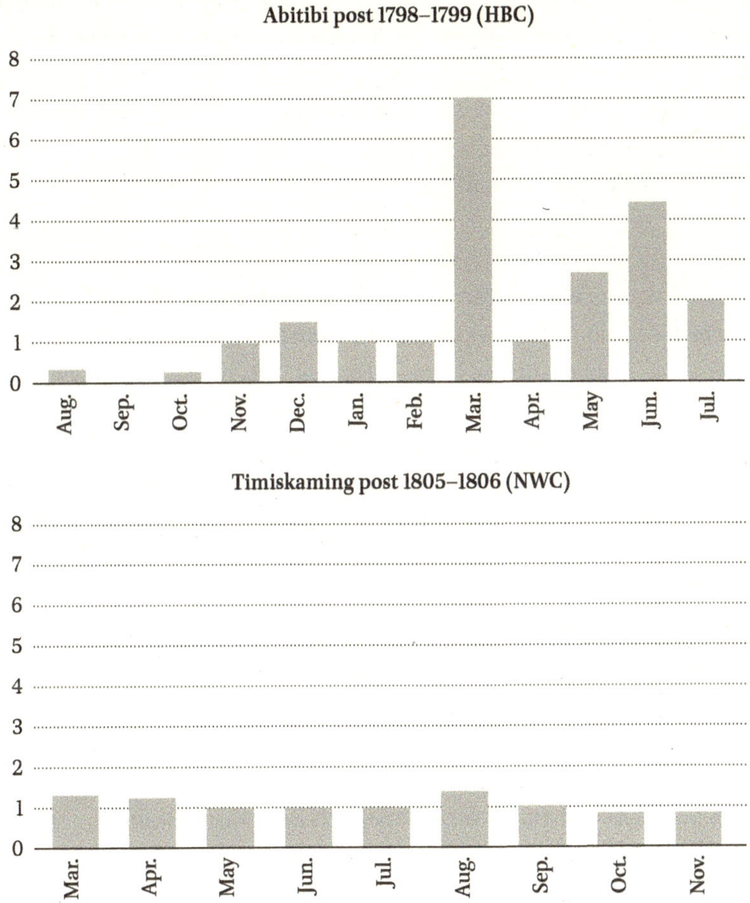

post would be in a bustle, and once ready, the brigade would set off toward Moose Factory, taking the year's crop of furs. When the men departed, the women and the children stayed behind. We can glimpse through historic records that some stayed in the immediate vicinity of the trading post, while others went and camped a little further away. They did not return to the family hunting ground.

When the Moose brigade was expected back one month later, the women and children would converge around the trading post. Once the brigade arrived, the post master would distribute the goods, and the families would return to their family hunting grounds within the next day:

> Monday 18th [July 1825]. [. . .] We have now all the Women & Children of the Indians that went to the Factory [Moose Factory] in the Large Canoe the 17 ultimo [June] about the House & will have till the arrival of the June Canoe from Moose. [. . .]
>
> Tuesday 19th July 1825. The Canoe that left this Place for Moose Factory the 17 of June last arrived this afternoon [. . .].
>
> Wednesday 20th. The Indians that arrived yesterday from Moose Factory departed.[9]

This involvement with the Moose brigades marks the beginning of a coordinated movement of Algonquin families toward and from the trading post. This movement was directly associated with the brigade. For instance, in 1828, the brigade was to arrive at Lake Abitibi in July, and that is when Algonquin families converged to the post, but in 1822 the incoming brigade made it back in October, and the families congregated at the post then.[10] The length of time spent at the post still remained quite short, limited to a few days, at the departure and the arrival of the brigade.

The Post and the Mission

The coordinated participation in the fur brigades had an unexpected consequence: It generalized encounters with Catholic missionaries. In the early 19th century, the Algonquins of Abitibi and Timiskaming areas had had no direct contact with Christian missionaries. In 1836, the Bishop of Montreal sent Catholic missionaries up the Ottawa River with the specific purpose of converting Indigenous populations of that area to Catholicism. Missions were then repeated every summer.

The reasons explaining the adoption of Catholicism by the Algonquins are well beyond the scope of this paper. However, on a very pragmatic level, it is noteworthy that the very first encounters between missionaries and Algonquins of Lakes Abitibi and Timiskaming were made possible by the fact that these initial missions were held when the men were busy with the fur brigades, and women and children were close to the post. Had the first missionaries arrived a decade or two earlier, they would probably have met just one or a few families at any given time—and perhaps none at all.

Few post journals dating from the mid 19th century have survived; however, missionary records are extensive. They reveal that as of the 1840s, the usual arrangement with the Catholic missionaries was the following. The missionaries would leave Montreal as early as they could in May, and would paddle up the Ottawa, stopping for a short mission at each trading post. At Abitibi; they would catch the Moose brigade and make their way to Moose and Fort Albany, then return, again stopping briefly at each trading post on their way back. They would reach Montreal in October, thus having completed close to 3,000 km in a canoe. Along this route, Indigenous families who wanted to attend the mission would make their way to the post and wait for the missionaries to arrive.

These missions were short and intense. They would last 10 to 14 days, after which the missionaries would continue on their way. During this short yearly mission, the missionaries would baptize, marry, and occasionally bless graves of the deceased. There would be processions and confessions, instructions, Mass, and prayers. The missionary records speak of intense praying and rites going from early morning to late at night (Dupuy 1839:41–42). The mission would end with a feast and speeches given by the chief.

Very early on, the missionaries set out to organize the physical surroundings for these missions. They built chapels adjacent to the trading posts, with the approval of the HBC managers. They also established cemeteries. With these yearly summer missions, the area surrounding the trading post took on a different ritual dimension. It was during these short yearly missions that the band would camp together around the post, pray, feast, and have other ritual activities on a scale that is unseen in earlier records. The scale of Catholic ritual intensity increased over the course of the 19th century, culminating in visits made by the bishop in the second half of that century (Proulx 1885, 1886).

Ecological Considerations

By the end of the 19th century, some Algonquin families were spending up to three months around the post and mission, a duration and form of summer gatherings similar to what anthropologist John MacPherson observed at Abitibi in 1930 (MacPherson 1930:7) and that current community members remember. A visiting geologist to Lake Abitibi made the following remark in his 1900 report:

> These Indians are in the habit of leaving the Hudson's Bay Company's posts about the beginning of September, to go to their different hunting grounds for the winter months. There they hunt all winter and return to the Hudson's Bay posts about the

> beginning of June with their furs, to pay for the PROVISIONS, etc., supplied them by the Hudson's Bay Company. They then idle about the posts all summer and set out in the fall again. [emphasis mine] (Baker 1901:26)

With Baker's statement about provisions and the length of stay next to the post, I would like to address an ecological consideration when thinking about the mere feasibility of gathering people in any given environment. In the early 19th century, the Algonquins of Lakes Abitibi and Temiskaming relied exclusively on food that was obtained by hunting, fishing, and some gathering. Imported food was not available for sale at the trading post then, because of the distance and difficulties involved in freighting. Even supplies for the post employees were limited: Employees were expected to hunt, trap, fish, garden, and buy game from their Algonquin customers to sustain themselves (Mitchell 1977:87–89). Algonquin families were thus completely self-reliant in terms of food for a portion of the 19th century.

Gathering a group of people in one place for any length of time requires either an abundant local food source, such as a good fishery, or stored food (acquired locally or imported). Summer fisheries and storage may well be an important adaptive feature for some Algonquian societies; however, they do not appear to have been feasible for the people of Lakes Abitibi and Timiskaming in the first half of the 19th century. Although local Algonquin families did dry some meat and fish, and the lakes provided some fish, the local environmental conditions were such that large and long gatherings appear practically impossible: Local Algonquin subsistence strategies seemed to have revolved around maintaining a very high level of mobility and dispersal. Some observers describe local families changing camp every few days, staying a maximum of five or six days in any given stop during this period (Du Ranquet, Ouellet, and Dionne 2000:219).[11] This strategy seemed well suited to the local environmental conditions, and even though occasional starvation did occur, it is noteworthy that early missionaries of the 1830s and the early 1840s remark on how healthy and well-off the local Algonquins appeared to be (Bellefeuille 1840:43–44; Laverlochère 1845:260).

As imported food was not available for sale at the post in the early 19th century, local fisheries were not adequate to support large groups of people, and dried food was only available in limited quantities, the pragmatic problem of feeding a group of people united in one place comes across very clearly in early missionary accounts. In fact, this factor is identified by the missionaries as an important obstacle to holding these missions (Dupuy 1839:46). The missionaries did bring provisions for themselves and their guides for their long summer journeys, but did not—and could not—bring along enough food to feed large groups of people for several weeks, when distances were covered in canoes and every parcel had to be carried over numerous portages. The missionaries stated that they shared what they could but finally resolved to end the mission early when there was not enough food available, so that people could disperse (Du Ranquet, Ouellet, and Dionne 2000:164–165; Laverlochère 1845:259–260; Moreau 1841:22, 1842:52).

A historical coincidence solved the missionaries' problem and led to prolonged summer gatherings. This coincidence is linked to the progression of the lumber industry up the Ottawa River system in the 19th century. This industry relied on a large workforce made up of seasonal workers who had to be fed imported food, such as flour, pork, and oatmeal. The first commercial lumbering operation in the area reached the foot of Lake Timiskaming in the late 1830s, but these first initiatives were on a limited scale, and lumbering only developed in full in the 1870s. The development of this industry was followed closely by the intrusion of a settler society.

The lumber industry did not reach the Abitibi area during the 19th century, since this lake is located in the Hudson Bay drainage and flows north, making it impossible to float logs to the mills located in southerly villages. Accordingly, the Lake Abitibi area had no intruding settler population until the construction of the railroad in the 20th century opened it up to logging and mining. I have described elsewhere the manner in which Algonquin families experienced the intrusion of a settler population (Inksetter 2017). The discussion will thus be limited here to the availability of imported food.

As the lumber industry appeared in the Timiskaming area, Algonquins began showing up at lumber camps, asking for flour and offering furs in exchange. The demand was such that the HBC, afraid of losing furs to these new competitors, began offering flour to its Algonquin customers as a trade item and opening new posts (Mitchell 1977:191). Over the course of the 19th century, new transportation methods, such as winter and summer roads, steamboats operating on segments of the Ottawa River, and, later still, railroads, made freighting cheaper. Large quantities of flour could henceforth be brought to HBC posts where it had been difficult to bring before. Flour thus became an accessible commodity for Indigenous peoples in the Abitibi and Timiskaming area in the second half of the 19th century.

Although it is tempting to assume that flour was adopted by Algonquin families out of necessity due to environmental degradation in the wake of the progressing lumber industry, this does not appear to be historically correct, at least as far as the initial introduction of flour goes. The initial interest in flour appears to have predated any detectable consequence on hunting in the Timiskaming area. More convincingly, Algonquin interest in flour is apparent in the Abitibi area, at a time when there was no lumber industry and no intruding settler population, and hunting conditions were excellent. In 1888, the Abitibi post master wrote in his yearly report: "The Indians are very well off; furs and food are plentiful and easy to obtain."[12] Accounting from that same year reveals nonetheless that large quantities of flour were bought by Algonquin hunters of that post.[13] In fact, in the Abitibi area, demand for flour by the Algonquins was such that the HBC had to resort to special orders so that Abitibi families would not purchase this item from petty traders operating further south along the Ottawa Valley. In the initial period at least, flour thus appears to have been deemed an interesting food item by Algonquin families, complementary to country foods. Moreover, it was easily accessible and appeared affordable.

At the same time, Algonquin families in the area started gardening small potato patches, sometimes cultivating other root vegetables as well. These patches were located at the gathering site, but could also be located on the family hunting ground (Baker 1901:37; Proulx 1892:206). Potatoes, like flour, appear to have been deemed an interesting food that could supplement other country foods. Their cultivation mirrors the initial introduction of flour into the local diet: Potato cultivation first appears in the Timiskaming area at a moment preceding extensive lumbering in that sector, then appears in the Abitibi area, at a time when game was abundant by all accounts and lumbering had not started yet.

The availability of stored foods, such as flour and potatoes, and long summer gatherings are closely linked in the area under study: Only when the former are present is the latter possible. Accordingly, only once flour and potatoes were available did the Algonquins stay for several weeks or months gathered around the post in the summer, and Catholic missionaries cease to lament about the difficulties in maintaining their converts united for the duration of the mission. This complaint disappears completely from yearly missionary reports dating from the second half of the 19th century. The actual extent of time spent at the post during the summer appeared to be a matter of choice. In the early 20th century, the summer became a period of semisettlement for certain families. For those families, children were sent to school and parents tended their crops, especially in the Timiskaming area. Others departed after the summer mission ended.

Discussion

It appears that the long summer gathering of several hundred people observed near the trading post and mission in the early 20th century did not exist in this exact format prior to the late 19th century on Lake Abitibi and Lake Timiskaming. Only when certain specific historical events and conditions were met, such as a reason for uniting at a specific time at the post, and the means to stay there for several weeks, such as the availability of stored food, did the Algonquins of Lake Abitibi and Lake Timiskaming gather near their posts for several weeks in the summer. This form of gathering is the one that is remembered by current community members.

This interpretation is supported by archaeological research done around the trading posts on Lake Timiskaming and Lake Abitibi. Archaeological research around the HBC post on Lake Timiskaming revealed a limited quantity of pre-European contact artifacts at that place. These were consistent with traces left by multiple reoccupations of the same space by many small groups over a long length of time. These finds were similar to many other finds in the general area and were not interpreted by archaeologists as a gathering place (Côté 2006). The area adjoining the historic HBC trading post on Lake Abitibi did not reveal any concentration of pre-European artifacts. The area surrounding the trading post is, in fact, rather poor as far as pre-European contact artifacts are concerned (Côté, Inksetter, and Roy 2002).

How, then, can we explain the importance of gatherings as remembered by living community members, and reported to visiting anthropologists and missionaries? The notion of great antiquity associated with the specific sites near the posts on Lake Abitibi and Lake Timiskaming may be a recent perception. This, in itself, does not indicate that the Algonquins did not have summer gatherings at all. We can only conclude that there do not appear to have been summer gatherings at the trading post before the mid 19th century and that large and long gatherings are the product of that century.

I suggest the answer to this discrepancy lies in a question of scale. Large and prolonged gatherings are not mentioned in early historical records because they did not have that format prior to the mid 19th century. Summer gatherings did exist nonetheless, but were much smaller groupings, involving fewer people and for shorter periods, scattered on several lake shores. When reading early-19th-century records, one comes across glimpses of such summer groupings. Missionaries met them, for example, on their long journeys (Du Ranquet, Ouellet, and Dionne

2000:220). These groups appear to be slightly larger than the winter group composed of two or three hunters and their families but did not include the total population of a few hundred people associated with each post. One of these small summer groups, for example, filled seven canoes (Poiré 1841:7–8); another was composed of 12 families (Laverlochère 1849:65).

These fleeting mentions of small summer groups could well be missed in historical records; they would also be poorly visible in the archaeological record. Nonetheless, I suggest this is the format Algonquin summer gatherings took prior to the mid 19th century. It is possible these are the forms of summer gatherings Father Silvy was referring to, when he spoke of groups filling three or four huts, united for 15 days. These gatherings were socially significant and thus remembered to have existed. The confusion therefore lies in the definition one gives of an Algonquin summer gathering.

Conclusion

Algonquin people of Lake Abitibi and Lake Timiskaming have developed a strong sense of belonging to the areas adjoining the historic trading posts. These important places have become symbols of a way of life that existed prior to settlements on reserves, and are remembered for the summer gatherings that were held there. They have also become markers of a collective identity. On an individual level, they are remembered for weddings and christenings that were held in those places, and the graves of loved ones that also rest there.

The importance of these places cannot be underestimated. However, by assuming these gatherings existed unchanged in ancient times, I believe the ethnographic present has been transposed into the past. Summer gatherings such as those shared by many Northern Algonquian peoples and observed by anthropologists in the early 20th century were not the same in the past for peoples of Lake Abitibi and Lake Timiskaming. In fact, for these specific groups, these long summer gatherings at the post appeared only in the 19th century: First, with the coordinated movement of families towards the post due to men's participation in the fur brigades, second, with the participation in Catholic summer missions, and third, by the introduction of imported food—flour and potatoes—which allowed a group of several hundred people to remain in one place for an extended period of time if they so wished.

Prior to these combined factors, gatherings existed, but were small and short, scattered on lakeshores during the summer time. It seems likely that this format was linked to resource distribution: Algonquin adaptive strategies relied mainly on maintaining a high level of mobility and dispersion. Nonetheless, the social importance of these gatherings explains the reason they are remembered so vividly. The transformation of their format explains their near invisibility in early historic records.

NOTES

1. I use the term Northern Algonquians as a general grouping for those Algonquian speakers living in the mixed and boreal forest of the interior, as opposed to the Algonquians living around the Great Lakes area or those living in maritime environments. This article concerns more specifically a group of people known as the Algonquins, living in the Ottawa Valley and slightly further north, over the height of land.
2. Although both agree on their cultural and linguistic closeness, Timiskaming First Nation tends to prefer the term Algonquin when referring to itself, whereas the two administrative bands derived from people congregating on Lake Abitibi (Abitibiwinni First Nation and Wahgoshig First Nation) tend to refer to themselves either as 'Anishnabe' or 'Algonquin'. When a collective term is required to designate these communities, I have used either a generic wording such as 'people of Lake Abitibi and Lake Timiskaming', or 'Algonquin', as the latter term appears to be more widely in use.
3. See, for example, how Abitibiwinni First Nation presents its history, on pikogan.com.
4. See Site Management at www.pc.gc.ca.
5. See the Register of Canada's Historic Places at www.historicplaces.ca.
6. The following abbreviations have been used: HBC for Hudson's Bay Company, NWC for North West Company, and HBCA for Hudson's Bay Company Archives.
7. There is some uncertainty on whether Silvy was the actual author of these letters. At the very least, it seems likely he was the informant to the author, having traveled to James Bay in the late 17th century.
8. Hudson's Bay Company Archives (HBCA), B.1/a/9, fo. 3d.
9. HBCA, B.1/a/19, fo. 4 and 4d.
10. HBCA, B.1/a/17, fo. 1 ; HBCA, B.1/a/21, fo. 1d.
11. See also Archives administratives OMI, 2D4, 1.2: Coup d'œil sur la mission de Témiskamingue et d'Abittibbi.
12. HBCA, B.1/e/10, fo. 6.
13. HBCA, B.1/e/10, fo. 16.

REFERENCES

Baker, Marcus B. 1901. Geologist's Report of Exploration Survey Party No. 1. *Report of the Survey and Exploration of Northern Ontario, 1900*, ed. by The Legislative Assembly of Ontario, pp. 21–37. Toronto: L. K. Cameron.

Bellefeuille, Louis Charles Lefebvre de. 1840. Relation d'une mission faite en l'été de 1837, le long de la Rivière de l'Outawa jusqu'au lac de Témiskaming, et au delà jusqu' au Lac d'Abbítibbi dans le District de Monseigneur de Juliopolis. *Rapport de l'Association de la propagation de la foi, établie à Montréal* (2):17–72.

Bishop, Charles. 1994. Northern Algonquians and the Hudson's Bay Company, 1821–1890. *Aboriginal Ontario. Historical Perspectives on the First Nations*, ed. by E. S. Rogers and D. B. Smith, pp. 307–343. Toronto: Dundurn Press.

Bousquet, Marie-Pierre. 1999. Sites ancestraux et territoire chez les amérindiens du Québec. *Études canadiennes/Canadian Studies* 47:29–40.

Côté, Marc. 1993. Préhistoire de l'Abitibi-Témiscamingue. *Recherches amérindiennes au Québec* 23(2–3):5–24.

Côté, Marc. 1998. Le site Ramsay. Un témoignage furtif des premiers occupants de l'Abitibi-Témiscamingue. *L'éveilleur et l'ambassadeur. Essais archéologiques et ethnohistorique en hommage à Charles A. Martijn*, ed. by R. Tremblay, pp. 127–139. Montréal: Recherches amérindiennes au Québec.

Côté, Marc. 2006. L'occupation amérindienne au Témiscamingue: l'exemple du Lieu historique national du Canada du Fort-Témiscamingue (Obadjiwan), une présence multi-millénaire. *Recherches amérindiennes au Québec* 36 (1):7–22.

Côté, Marc, Leila Inksetter, and Christian Roy. 2002. *Lieu historique national du Canada de Apitipik. Inventaire archéologique 2001.* Québec: rapport remis à Parcs Canada.

Du Ranquet, Dominique, Fernand Ouellet, and René Dionne. 2000. *Journal du père Dominique du Ranquet, missionnaire jésuite en Ontario de 1843 à 1900, de la mission qu'il fit en 1843 dans l'Outaouais supérieur sous la direction de l'abbé Hippolyte Moreau. Tensions socioculturelles en dehors des peuplements majoritaires blancs au milieu du XIXe siècle. Texte annoté et édité par Fernand Ouellet et René Dionne, Documents historiques n° 96.* Sudbury: Société historique du Nouvel-Ontario.

Dupuy, Jean-Baptiste. 1839. Journal d'un voyage fait à Temiskaming en 1836. *Rapport de l'Association de la propagation de la foi, établie à Montréal* (1):24–53.

Honigmann, John H. 2005. Indians of Nouveau-Québec. *Du Nouveau-Québec au Nunavik. 1964–2004. Une fragile autonomie*, ed. by J. Malaurie and J. Rousseau, pp. 315–373. Paris: Ed. Economica.

Inksetter, Leila. 2017. *Initiatives et adaptations algonquines au XIXe siècle*. Québec: Septentrion.

Larivière, Roger. 2013. *Les richesses d'un peuple. Les Abitibiwinnik de Pikogan*. Rouyn-Noranda: L'ABC de l'édition.

Laverlochère, Jean-Nicolas. 1845. Extrait d'une lettre du R.P. Laverlochère, Oblat de Marie immaculée, au R. P. Guigues, Visiteur général des Missions du Canada. *Annales de la propagation de la foi. Recueil périodique des lettres des évêques et des missionnaires des missions des deux mondes, et de tous les documents relatifs aux missions et à l'Oeuvre de la propagation de la foi* (17):257–264.

Laverlochère, Jean-Nicolas. 1849. Mission de la baie d'Hudson. Lettre du Père Laverlochère, O.M.J. à Monseigneur l'Archevêque de Québec. *Rapport sur les missions du Diocèse de Québec et autres qui en ont fait ci-devant partie* (8):34–68.

Lawrence, Bonita. 2012. *Fractured Homeland. Federal Recognition and Algonquin Identity in Ontario*. Vancouver and Toronto: UBC Press.

Leacock, Eleanor. 1995. The Montagnais-Naskapi of the Labrador Peninsula. *Native Peoples: The Canadian Experience*, ed. by B. Morrison and R. Wilson, pp. 150–180. Toronto: McClelland & Stewart.

Lips, Julius. 1947. Naskapi Law (Lake St. John and Lake Mistassini Bands). Law and Order in a Hunting Society. *Transactions of the American Philosophical Society* 37(4):379–492.

MacPherson, John. 1930. *An Ethnological Study of the Abitibi Indians*. Ottawa: National Museums of Canada.

Mathias, Joseph "Josie." 1998. *The Man from Neawigak . . . and Other Algonquin Stories*. Self published.

McMillan, Alan, and Eldon Yellowhorn. 2004. *First Peoples in Canada*. Vancouver and Toronto: Douglas & McIntyre.

Mitchell, Elaine Allan. 1977. *Fort Timiskaming and the Fur Trade*. Toronto: University of Toronto Press.

Moore, Kermot. 1982. *Kipawa: Portrait of a People*. Cobalt, ON: Highway Book Shop.

Moreau, Hippolyte. 1841. Lettre de M. Moreau à Mgr. L'Évêque de Montréal, sur la mission du lac Abbitibbi, etc. faite en l'été de 1839. *Rapport de l'Association de la propagation de la foi, établie à Montréal* (3):19–26.

Moreau, Hippolyte. 1842. Mission du lac Temiskaming. Lettre de M. Moreau à Mgr de Montréal. *Rapport de l'Association de la propagation de la foi, établie à Montréal* (4):45–55.

Poiré, Charles Édouard. 1841. Relation d'une mission faite en l'été de 1839, le long de la rivière de l'Ottawa, jusqu'au lac de Témiskaming, &c. *Rapport de l'Association de la propagation de la foi, établie à Montréal* (3):3–18.

Preston, Richard. 1975. Eastern Cree Community in Relation to the Fur Trade Post in the 1830's: The Background of the "Posting" Process. *Papers of the Sixth Algonquian Conference*, ed.

by William Cowan, pp. 324–335. Ottawa: Carleton University.

Proulx, Jean-Baptiste. 1885. *Au lac Abbitibi. Visite pastorale de Mgr. J. Thomas Duhamel dans le Haut de l'Ottawa.* Montréal: Librairie Saint-Joseph.

Proulx, Jean-Baptiste. 1886. *À la baie d'Hudson ou récit de la première visite pastorale de Mgr N. Z. Lorrain, Evêque de Cythère et Vicaire apostolique de Pontiac, dans ses missions sauvages de Témiscamingue, d'Abbitibi, de New-Port, de Moose et d'Albany.* Montréal: Librairie Saint-Joseph, Cadieux & Derome.

Proulx, Jean-Baptiste. 1892. Douze cents milles en canot d'écorce ou Première visite pastorale de Mgr N. Z. Lorrain, Évêque de Cythère, Vicaire apostolique de Pontiac, dans ses missions sauvages du haut des rivières Ottawa et Saint-Maurice, de Waswanipi et de Mékiskan (suite et fin). *Annales de la propagation de la foi pour les provinces de Québec et de Montréal* 48:193–253.

Rankin, Dominique, and Marie-Josée Tardif. 2011. *On nous appelait des Sauvages. Souvernirs et espoirs d'un chef héréditaire algonquin.* Montréal: Le Jour éditeur.

Rogers, Edward. 1963. Changing Settlement Patterns of the Cree-Ojibwa of Northern Ontario. *Southwestern Journal of Anthropology* 19(1):64–88.

Rogers, Edward. 1965. Leadership among the Indians of Eastern Subarctic Canada. *Anthropologica* 7(2):263–284.

Rogers, Edward. 1969. Band Organization Among the Indians of Eastern Subarctic Canada. *Contributions to Anthropology: Band Societies*, ed. by D. Damas, pp. 21–50. Ottawa: National Museum of Man.

Rogers, Edward. 1994. Northern Algonquians and the Hudson's Bay Company, 1821–1890. *Aboriginal Ontario. Historical Perspectives on the First Nations*, ed. by E. S. Rogers and D. B. Smith, pp. 307–343. Toronto: Dundurn Press.

Rogers, Edward, and James Smith. 1981. Environment and Culture in the Shield and Mackenzie Borderlands. *Subarctic*, ed. by J. Helm, pp. 130–145. Washington, DC: Smithsonian Institution.

Scott, Colin. 2018. Family Territories, Community Territories: Balancing Rights and Responsibilities through Time. *Anthropologica* 60(1):90–105.

Silvy, Antoine. 1904. *Relation par lettres de l'Amérique septentrionalle (années 1709 et 1710), édité et annoté par Camille de Rochmonteix.* Paris: Letourzey et Ané, éditeurs.

Speck, Frank. 1915. *Family Hunting Territories and Social Life of Various Algonkian Bands of the Ottawa Valley, Memoir n° 70, Anthropological Series n° 8.* Ottawa: Canadian Dept. of Mines, Geological Survey.

The Bible in "Plain" Cree

A Look at the Language of the 1862 Translation

Bill Jancewicz

In 1891, the Smithsonian Bureau of Ethnology Bulletin (Pilling 1891) listed only TWO "whole Bibles" in its *Bibliography of Algonquian Languages:* the Bible in the Massachusetts language by J. Eliot, and the Bible in Cree by W. Mason.[1] The "Eliot Bible" was published in Cambridge, Massachusetts, in 1663, and it is the first Bible of ANY language to be printed in North America, and the first Native American language Bible. Nearly 200 years later, the Bible in Cree was published in London by the British and Foreign Bible Society, and thus was the second Native American (First Nations) language Bible.

This Bible translation has had wide distribution and influence across several languages and dialects of Cree, Ojibwe and Oji-Cree. Its broad acceptance over many years is unprecedented. Even though in recent decades there has been a growing movement among Cree speakers toward producing contemporary, localized translations of portions of the Bible, this early Cree translation is still regularly used and to date remains the only complete Bible in Cree.

This article outlines the history of this translation, examines the variety of the Cree language found in the most widely read edition of this translation, and provides a brief interlinear lexical and morphological analysis that compares lexical inventory and grammatical structures found therein with contemporary Plains Cree translations of these passages.

"The Bible in Plain Cree" in the title of this article is a reference to the English subtitle that is printed on the overleaf of the title page of the 1904 edition of the New Testament, "THE NEW TESTAMENT IN PLAIN CREE," which very likely was meant to specify the variety of Cree spoken "on the plain": that is, the language that has come to be referred to as "Plains Cree" (y-dialect), following Wolfart (1973) and others.

As it happened, when the first edition was published in 1861–62,[2] only one person's name was on the title page, that of William Mason. This Cree Bible is thus often referred to as the "Mason" Cree Bible.

As is often the case, these early translations are identified with the name of the nonindigenous European missionaries who were involved in various ways (often extensively), as William Mason was. But in fact there was considerable contribution from indigenous speakers of these languages. Besides the legendary stories of the Cree elders who were given the syllabic characters that were used by James Evans (Dusenberry 1962:267–269, cited in Nichols 1996), there are several other indigenous persons who were deeply involved in the preparation of this first Cree translation of the Bible.

Translators and Revisers

Evans and Mason were both born in England and came to North America as Wesleyan Methodist missionaries. However, Sophia Thomas was a mother-tongue Cree speaker from Red River, Sowengisik (Henry Bird Steinhauer) was Anishinaabe from the Rama First Nation community, John Sinclair was Cree from Oxford House, and John Alexander Mackay was Cree from Mistassini, Quebec. The timeline of interactions of these individuals is a fascinating story; see figure 1.

FIGURE 1 (*opposite*). Timeline of the 19th century into the first two decades of the 20th century.

Credit: Timeline by the author for this submission. Banks 1983, Peel 1976, Peel 1987, Peel 2003, Sieciechowicz 1982, Still 2013, Van Kirk 1983, Waiser 2005.

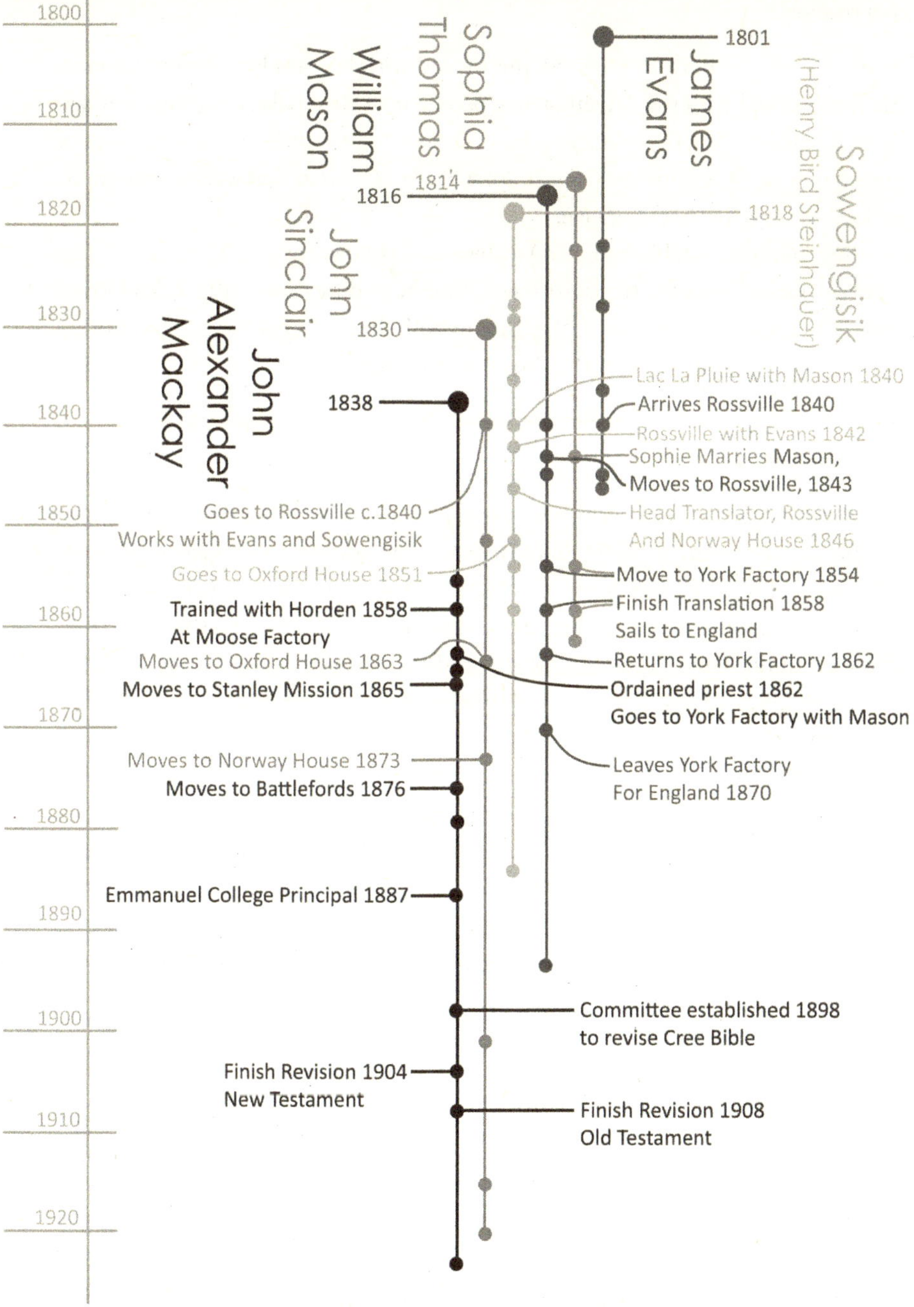

James Evans

James Evans was born in England and moved with his family to Upper Canada. He first worked with the Anishinaabeg people near Rice Lake, and there devised Ojibwe syllabics, but the writing system was rejected by the Bible Society. He then took a new posting with the Cree at Rossville in 1840, and that winter revised his syllabic system for that language.

Rossville was established as a Wesleyan Methodist mission community just outside Norway House, a Hudson's Bay Company trading post on the Nelson River. This is an important location with regard to both the spread of the syllabic writing system and the translation of the Cree Bible; see figure 2.

Sophia Thomas

Sophia Thomas was born c1815, and was baptized 10 November 1822 at Red River. Sophia was the youngest daughter of Hudson's Bay Company Chief Factor Thomas Thomas and his Cree wife Sarah (Peel 1987). When she was still a young girl she was placed in the care of the Church of England missionaries. It was reported that she was studious and "a good pious girl" and that she grew up a devout Christian (Van Kirk 1983). In 1843, she married the Reverend William Mason and, with her knowledge of Cree and her sincere interest in the welfare of her people, was a great help to her husband's ministry at Rossville. Although she had a delicate constitution, Sophia was reputed to have devoted herself unceasingly to the operation of the day school, visiting the sick, and translating hymns and scripture. After her marriage to William Mason, Sophia spent most of the rest of her life at Rossville. Her lasting legacy was her work on the translation of the Cree Bible. She traveled to England with her husband in 1858 and died there just as the Bible was going to press (Peel 1976).

William Mason

William Mason was born in England in 1816. He went to Canada as a missionary with the Wesleyan Methodists, and took his first assignment at Lac La Pluie in 1840. He married Sophia Thomas in 1843 and the two went together to Rossville. When Evans left the mission he took charge of the ministry at Rossville beginning in 1845, when the first commercial printing press arrived there. When the Wesleyan Methodists

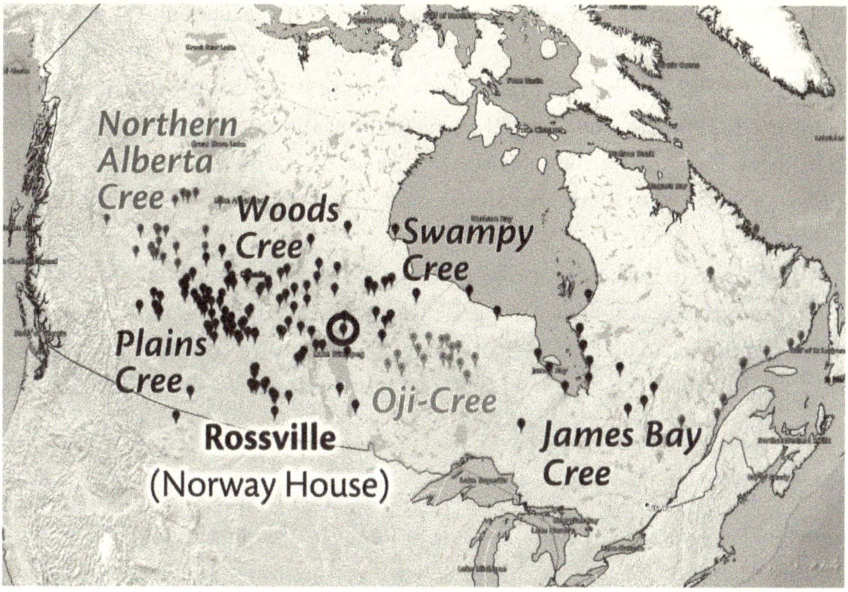

Credit: Image by the author for this submission.

FIGURE 2. Location of Rossville in relation to Algonquian language communities.

left Rossville in 1854, he took his priest's orders with the Church of England and remained at Rossville. He continued coordinating the translation work until 1858 when he and Sophia traveled to England to oversee the typesetting and publication. In 1862 he returned to Canada with approximately 1000 copies of the Bible and 2000 copies of the New Testament (Banks 1983). He established himself at York Factory, where for the next eight years he served with the Church Missionary Society and in distribution of the Bibles. He returned to England permanently in 1870.

Sowengisik (Henry Bird Steinhauer)

The Anishinabe who became Henry Bird Steinhauer in 1828 was originally named Sowengisik. He was born in 1818, but he took his new name after a Methodist missionary found an American patron who agreed to fund his education. He attended Cazenovia Seminary in Cazenovia, New York, from 1832 to 1835. He was sent to teach at the Credit River mission on Lake Ontario in 1835 by the Wesleyan Methodist Church, and the next year he enrolled at Upper Canada Academy in Cobourg. He graduated at the head of his class from Upper Canada Academy in 1839.

In 1840 he went to Lac La Pluie, where he worked as a teacher, and also assisted William Mason as translator and interpreter. James Evans asked him to come to Rossville in 1842. He learned Cree quickly because he spoke Anishinaabemowin as his mother tongue, and assisted Evans in translating the Bible and hymns. By 1846 he was the chief translator at Norway House. In 1851 he was asked to establish a Methodist mission at Oxford House, 200 miles northeast of Norway House (Sieciechowicz 1982).

He traveled to England in the fall of 1854 to promote the indigenous missionary work, returning the following spring. He was ordained a minister in the Wesleyan Methodist Church in June 1855, and that same month received news of his posting to Lac La Biche, Alberta, but soon moved to establish his own work at Whitefish Lake.

John Sinclair

John Sinclair was born in Oxford House in 1830. He was sent to Rossville around 1840 for his education and worked closely with James Evans and Sowengisik, and later with William and Sophia Mason on the Bible translation. He married Betsy Omand from York Factory in 1851, and moved to Oxford House in 1863. He returned to Norway House 10 years later and worked as a clerk for the Hudson's Bay Company, but afterward set up a trading company of his own to compete with Hudson's Bay (Still 2013).

It was recorded that John Sinclair translated the first draft of the Old Testament from the Psalms to Malachi, and the New Testament from the book of Romans to Revelation, while Sowengisik translated the first draft of the Old Testament from Genesis to the book of Job, and the Gospels and Acts in the New Testament (Pilling 1891).

John Alexander Mackay

John Alexander Mackay was born in 1838 in Mistassini, Quebec. He was the son and grandson of men who worked for Hudson's Bay Company, but he himself chose a life of religious ministry. Even though he was baptized in the Methodist church, he associated himself with the Church Missionary Society (CMS, Church of England) early on, going to serve under E. A. Watkins at Fort George in Quebec in 1855. He then went to Moose Factory, Ontario, to receive catechist training under John Horden. He enrolled in St. John's College in Red River, Manitoba, at the end of the 1850s.

His ordination as a priest on 29 May 1862 was part of the mid-19th-century attempt by the Church Missionary Society to create an indigenous native clergy in Rupert's Land (Waiser 2005). Mackay next went to York Factory, where he worked with William Mason, who had just returned to Canada from England with the supply of newly printed Cree Bibles. Many of these new Cree Bibles went with him as he continued his service to his people.

He moved to The Pas, Manitoba, where he served during 1864–65, and then transferred to Stanley Mission, Saskatchewan, where he worked for another 10 years. There he was also involved in Cree language translation of scripture and church-related materials.

He was transferred to the Battleford area of Saskatchewan, where he founded an indigenous church. In 1879 he was one of the founding staff members at Emmanuel College in Prince Albert, Saskatchewan, where he taught Cree grammar and composition to Cree speakers—a remarkable achievement in its time.

In 1887 Mackay was appointed principal at Emmanuel, which had achieved university status in 1883. He continued to serve as a Cree tutor, and worked on translation of the Bible, the Book of Common Prayer, and the hymn book into Cree, as well as working on revisions of other translators' works. In 1898 a committee was formed under Robert Machray to revise the Cree Bible. Eventually Mackay became responsible for the final form of the work. He used a Yost typewriter fitted with the Cree syllabic symbols to prepare his revised copy (Peel 2003). Over the course of about 10 years Mackay completed this work and made three trips to England to see the revised publication through typesetting and printing, which were completed in 1908.

Interactions between Translators and Revisers over Time

The first phase of interactions, in 1840–50, set the stage, bringing most of the participants together at Rossville, just outside Norway House. This is when the first draft was produced, which was mainly the work of Sowengisik and John Sinclair.

The second phase began about 1850, as Sowengisik and then Sinclair left Rossville, leaving William Mason and Sophia to complete the checking and proofreading, and to bring the work to publication in England.

The third phase was printing and distribution, from about 1858 to 1870. Importantly, Mason and Mackay worked together at York Factory during this time. Then after Mason returns to England the fourth phase began.

During this phase the three remaining indigenous participants, Sowengisik, Sinclair, and Mackay, continued to use and teach the Cree Bible to their own people within their own spheres of influence. Thus, by the turn of the century, J. A. Mackay was ideally prepared and positioned to perform the revision of the text into its current version.

I believe that one important reason that this translation had so much influence and has continued to be used by thousands of Cree speakers across Canada for the past century and a half is that from the earliest days of the translation process it was a task accomplished certainly FOR but also to a large degree BY indigenous people. Today this text is highly valued by Cree speakers as part of their history and is an extensive written resource in their language (Aldred-Shull 2013).

An Examination of the Language

To perform the lexical and morphological interlinear analysis described in this section of the paper, the original syllabic text was transcribed and digitized (in Unicode syllabics) and then converted to Standard Roman Orthography. Next, a software program with interlinearizing capabilities was used to analyze and gloss each line of text. This interlinearization is provided in the online appendix. The interlinear display is divided into two columns: the analysis of the legacy (Mason) Cree text is on the left, with a corresponding interlinear analysis of the contemporary Cree translation that was recently published by the Canadian Bible Society (2018).

The text passage examined is a portion of the Gospel of Luke, chapter 10, the parable of the Good Samaritan, verses 25–37. Also provided with the interlinear analysis is the English source text for each translation: the King James Version (KJV) for the legacy Cree text, and the Good News Bible (GNB) as the usual source text for the contemporary Cree translation.

I have used the convention of marking the person participants with numerals: [1] is first person, [2] is second person, and so on. Further third person is marked with the numeral [4], rather than [3′] (three-prime) as is also sometimes found in Algonquian studies.

The portion of the text I have focused on is verses 33 and 34, in which the

FIGURE 3 (*opposite*). Similar lexical items.

Legacy Cree: Wm. Mason 1862; Revised J.A. Mackay 1904

Gospel of Luke

nātikot māka , ē ki takopitamiyit o
/nāt/ -ikot /takopit/ -amiyit
come [4>3] bind [4]
come but , [conj] [past] tie up his

miswākanikātikowina , ē tominamiyit , mina ē
/miswākanikātikowin/ -a /tomin/ -amiyit
wound [pl] anoint [4]
wounds , [conj] anoint , and [conj]

sikinamākot sominājpo ; mina ē ki tētapiikot
/sikinam/ -ākot /sominājpo/ /tētapi/ -ikot
pour [4>3] wine sit [4>3]
pour wine ; and [conj] [past] sit

kēhciwāk o pisiskimiyiwa , ē ki pēsikot
/kēhciwāk/ /pisisk/ -im -iyiwa /pēs/ -ikot
on beast [poss] [obv] bring [4>3]
on his beast , [conj] [past] bring

kapēsiwikamikok mina ē ki kanawēyimikot . [v35] ēkosi
/kapēsiwikamik/ -ok /kanawēyim/ -ikot
inn [loc] care [4>3]
inn and [conj] [past] be cared for . so

wiyāpaniyik , niso soniyāsa ki otinēyiwa , ē
/wāpan/ -iyik /niso/ /soniyās/ -a /otin/ -ēyiwa
morning [obv] two coin [pl] take [4]
morning , two coins [past] take , [conj]

miyāyit kā kanawēyitamiyit kapēsiwikamik , ē ki
/miy/ -āyit /kanawēyit/ -amiyit /kapēsiwikamik/
give [4] care for it [4] inn
give [rel] keeper inn , [conj] [past]

itayit , kanawēyim ; ēkosi piko iyikohk awasimē kē
/it/ -ayit /kanawēyim/ /piko/ /iyikohk/ /awasimē/
say [4] care for him but as much as more
say , care for him ; so but as much as more [fut]

mēstinamowanē : ispi mina pē itohtēyāni , ki ka
/mēstinam/ -owanē /itohtē/ -yāni
use up [if you] go [when I]
use up : when and come go , [2] shall

Contemporary Cree: Stan Cuthand 1991; Revised Dolores Sand 2018

Gospel of Luke

nātāt , kī - kāsīyāpāwahēw pimiy mīna sōminapoy
/nāt/ -āt kī- /kāsīyāpāwah/ -ēw /pimiy/ /mīna/ /sōminapoy/
come [3>4] past wash [3>4] oil and wine
come , [past] - wash oil and wine

ē - āpacihtāt ita kā - kī-pakamahomiht , ēkosi ē -
/āpacihtā/ -t /ita/ kā- kī- /pakamahw/ -imiht
use [3] where [rel] [past] beat [X>4]
[conj] - use where [rel] - beat , so [conj] -

kī-wēwēkahpitāt kī - tēhtapihēw otēmihk , mīna kī
/kī-/ /wēwēkahpit/ -āt kī- /tēhtapih/ -ēw o- /atēm/ -ihk /mīna/ kī-
— wrap, bind [3] past sit on, mount [3>4] his horse [loc] mīna past
— [past] - sit on, mount horse , mīna [past]

- itohtahēw kapēsiwikamikohk mīna kī - pamihēw . [v35]
/itohtah/ -ēw /kapēsiwikamik/ -ihk /mīna/ kī- /pamih/ -ēw
take [3>4] inn [loc] mīna past tend [3>4]
- took inn mīna [past] - tend .

ē - wāpaniyik kī - miyēw nīso wāpiski-sōniyāsa
/wāpan/ -iyik kī- /miy/ -ēw /nīso/ /wāpiski/ -sōniyās -a
morning [obv] past give [3>4] two white coin [pl]
[conj] - morning [past] - gave two silver coins

anihi kā - paminamiyit kapēsiwikamik , ē - itāt , ' pamih
kā- /pamin/ -amiyit /kapēsiwikamik/ /it/ -āt /pamih/
[past] attend [4] inn say [3] tend
who [rel] - tender hotel , [conj] - say , ' tend

awa , ēkwa awasimē mēstinikēhiski itāp
/mēstinikē/ -hiski /itāp/
spend [if you] afterwards
this , and more spend afterwards

kika-tipahamātin pē - kīwēyāni ."
kika- /tipaham/ -ātin /kīwē/ -yāni
[fut] pay [1>2] back [when I]
will pay come - back ."

Credit: Illustration by the author for this submission.

Samaritan meets the injured traveler and has pity on him, goes to him, treats his injuries, and brings him to an inn to be cared for. This section appears starting toward the bottom of the third sheet of the appendix. If possible, the reader should listen to these two verses read in the two different translations.[3] The legacy Cree Bible is read by the Rev. Fred Evans of Swan River, Manitoba; the contemporary Cree translation is read by Dolores Sand of Saskatoon, Saskatchewan.

Consider first the lexical items that are nearly identical in the two translations: *sominaapo/soominaapoy* 'wine' and *kaapeesisikamikohk* 'inn'. The only differences are a few phonological or orthographical inconsistencies. These words indicate very little change between the early and the contemporary translation; see figure 3.

Turn now to examine some items that are completely different: The legacy Cree translation uses the verb *tominam* 'anoint (with oil)', whereas the contemporary Cree translation uses the noun *pimiy* 'oil', as the compound subject with 'wine' for the verb *e-aapichihtaat* 'he uses it'.

Further, the legacy Cree uses the word *pisiskiw* 'beast, domestic animal' with the obviative suffix, while the contemporary Cree has *otem* 'his horse' with the locative suffix; see figure 4.

Finally, consider the obviative marking of the participants. In the legacy Cree Bible, we have the inverse marking for *naatikot* 'he [4] comes to him [3]'. The contemporary Cree renders this word with the direct marking *naataat* 'he [3] comes to him [4]'. For the legacy Cree, this entire segment indicates that the Samaritan is obviative, whereas in the contemporary Cree it is the wounded man who is obviative, and the Samaritan is proximate. This can also be observed throughout with other noun and verb inflections, such as *e-ki-tetapihikot* 'mount, sit on' in the legacy Cree and *ki-tetapihew* 'mount, sit on' in the contemporary Cree, and *e-ki-kanaweyimikot* 'he was cared for' in the legacy Cree and *ki-pamihew* 'tended him' in the contemporary Cree; see figure 5.

The marking or identification of a participant as proximate or obviative in Algonquian narrative discourse has been observed and discussed by scholars for decades. Goddard (1984), Wolfart (1973), and others point out that the spotlighting or foregrounding of participants is often handled by this linguistic feature. In a translation, the translator is challenged with determining the relative foregrounding of participants that was intended by the original storyteller. In the older translation,

FIGURE 4 (*opposite*). Different lexical items.

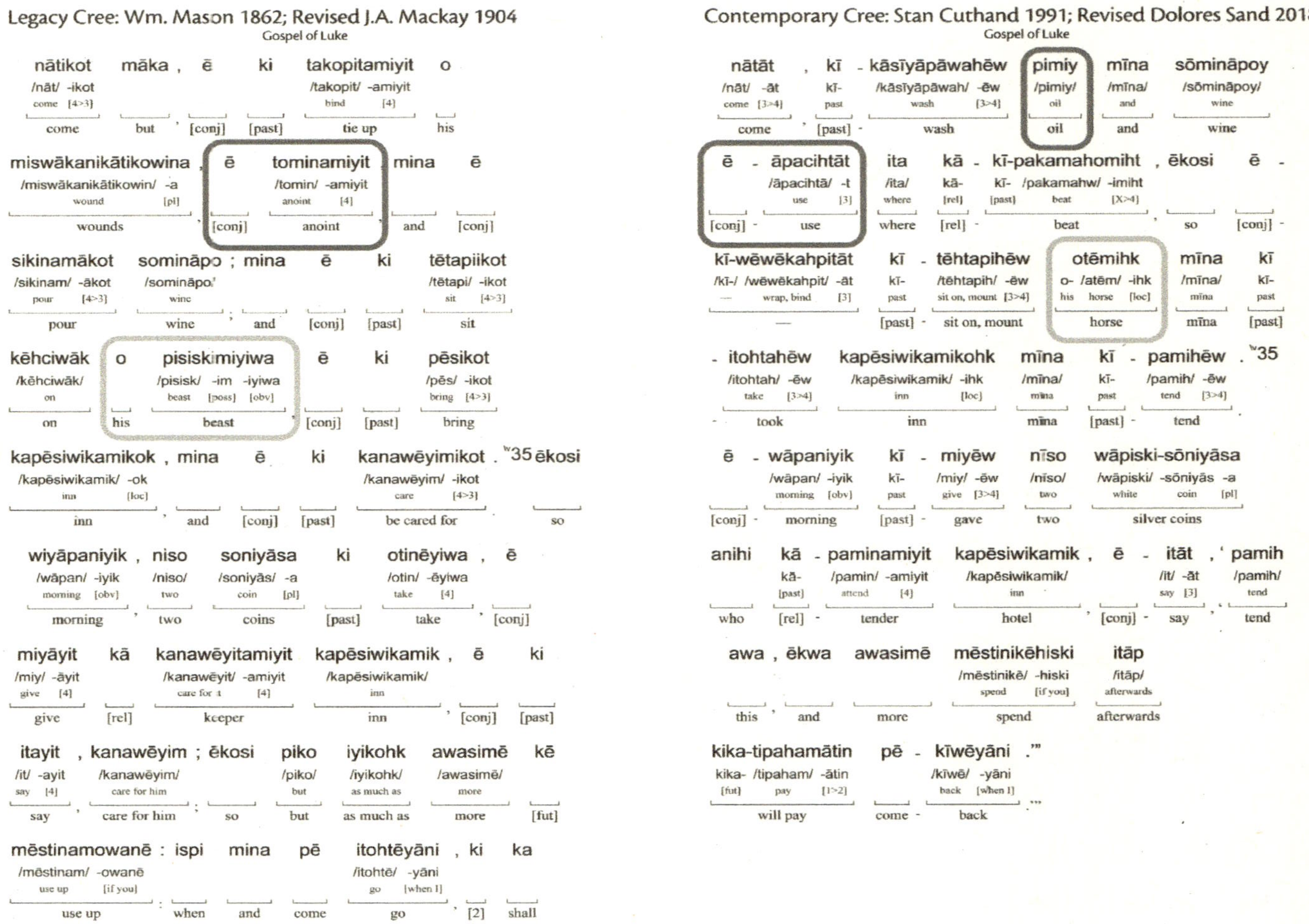

Credit: Illustration by the author for this submission.

Legacy Cree: Wm. Mason 1862; Revised J.A. Mackay 1904

Gospel of Luke

nātikot māka , ē ki takopitamiyit o
/nāt/ -ikot · /takopit/ -amiyit
come [4>3] · bind [4]
come but , [conj] [past] tie up his

miswākanikātikowina , ē tominamiyit , mina ē
/miswākanikātikowin/ -a · /tomin/ -amiyit
wound [pl] · anoint [4]
wounds , [conj] anoint , and [conj]

sikinamākot somināpo ; mina ē ki tētapiikot
/sikinam/ -ākot · /somināpo/ · /tētapi/ -ikot
pour [4>3] · wine · sit [4>3]
pour wine ; and [conj] [past] sit

kēhciwāk o pisiskimiyiwa , ē ki pēsikot
/kēhciwāk/ · /pisisk/ -im -iyiwa · /pēs/ -ikot
on · beast [poss] [obv] · bring [4>3]
on his beast , [conj] [past] bring

kapēsiwikamikok , mina ē ki kanawēyimikot "35 ēkosi
/kapēsiwikamik/ -ok · /kanawēyim/ -ikot
inn [loc] · care [4>3]
inn , and [conj] [past] be cared for so

wiyāpaniyik , niso soniyāsa ki otinēyiwa , ē
/wāpan/ -iyik · /niso/ · /soniyās/ -a · /otin/ -ēyiwa
morning [obv] · two · coin [pl] · take [4]
morning , two coins [past] take , [conj]

miyāyit kā kanawēyitamiyit kapēsiwikamik , ē ki
/miy/ -āyit · /kanawēyit/ -amiyit · /kapēsiwikamik/
give [4] · care for it [4] · inn
give [rel] keeper inn , [conj] [past]

itayit , kanawēyim ; ēkosi piko iyikohk awasimē kē
/it/ -ayit · /kanawēyim/ · /piko/ · /iyikohk/ · /awasimē/
say [4] · care for him · but · as much as · more
say , care for him ; so but as much as more [fut]

mēstinamowanē : ispi mina pē itohtēyāni , ki ka
/mēstinam/ -owanē · /itohtē/ -yāni
use up [if you] · go [when I]
use up : when and come go , [2] shall

Contemporary Cree: Stan Cuthand 1991; Revised Dolores Sand 2018

Gospel of Luke

nātāt , kī - kāsīyāpāwahēw pimiy mīna sōmināpoy
/nāt/ -āt · kī- · /kāsīyāpāwah/ -ēw · /pimiy/ · /mīna/ · /sōmināpoy/
come [3>4] · past · wash [3>4] · oil · and · wine
come , [past] - wash oil and wine

ē - āpacihtāt ita kā - kī-pakamahomiht , ēkosi ē -
/āpacihtā/ -t · /ita/ · kā- · kī- /pakamahw/ -imiht
use [3] · where · [rel] · [past] beat X>4]
[conj] - use where [rel] - beat , so [conj] -

kī-wēwēkahpitāt kī - tēhtapihēw otēmihk , mīna kī
/kī-/ /wēwēkahpit/ -āt · kī- · /tēhtapih/ -ēw · o- /atēm/ -ihk · /mīna/ · kī-
— wrap, bind [3] · past · sit on, mount [3>4] · his horse [loc] · mīna · past
— [past] - sit on, mount horse , mīna [past]

- itohtahēw kapēsiwikamikohk mīna kī - pamihēw . "35
/itohtah/ -ēw · /kapēsiwikamik/ -ihk · /mīna/ · kī- · /pamih/ -ēw
take [3>4] · inn [loc] · mīna · past · tend [3>4]
- took inn mīna [past] - tend

ē - wāpaniyik kī - miyēw nīso wāpiski-sōniyāsa
/wāpan/ -iyik · kī- · /miy/ -ēw · /nīso/ · /wāpiski/ -sōniyās -a
morning [obv] · past · give [3>4] · two · white coin [pl]
[conj] - morning [past] - gave two silver coins

anihi kā - paminamiyit kapēsiwikamik , ē - itāt , ' pamih
kā- · /pamin/ -amiyit · /kapēsiwikamik/ · /it/ -āt · /pamih/
[past] · attend [4] · inn · say [3] · tend
who [rel] - tender hotel , [conj] - say , ' tend

awa , ēkwa awasimē mēstinikēhiski itāp
/mēstinikē/ -hiski · /itāp/
spend [if you] · afterwards
this , and more spend afterwards

kika-tipahamātin pē - kīwēyāni ."'
kika- /tipaham/ -ātin · /kīwē/ -yāni
[fut] pay [1>2] · back [when I]
will pay come - back .'"

Credit: Illustration by the author for this submission.

the traveler who is attacked (and becomes the wounded man) starts out in the story as proximate and thus the participant in focus. Each other person who passes by (a priest, a Levite, and the Samaritan) is inflected as the obviative participant, keeping the wounded man in the foreground throughout the story.

In the contemporary Cree translation, as in the older translation, the wounded man is introduced in the story as proximate, as one would expect. But once he is encountered by each person who passes by (priest, Levite, and the Samaritan), the proximate marking shifts from the wounded man to the newly introduced participant, with the wounded man then being marked as obviative through the end of the story.

This seems to indicate that while the translators of the legacy Cree Bible were capable and fluent speakers of Cree, they crafted their translation without a shift in focus with regard to proximate and obviative inflection. On the other hand, the translators of the contemporary Cree text began with a different understanding of the story's purpose and the relative importance of the central figure in this story (that is, the Samaritan) who is being presented to the hearers as an example to follow, crafting their translation to reflect this by the shift in focus.

The comparison serves to illustrate one of the challenges associated with translating English texts into Cree that would likely occur in many other Algonquian languages. This challenge is the need for the translator to determine which of two third-person participants in different roles was foregrounded from the perspective of the original storyteller, and whether the original storyteller intended to keep that same participant in focus throughout. In showing how the translator of the contemporary text shifted the focus after initially having placed it on the wounded man, we have demonstrated how the understanding of a story's purpose must be understood so that it will be expressed through a translator's use of obviation.

This short analysis also raises a number of other translation questions. For example, is shifting the focus of the narrative reflected in the contemporary translation because of a more Cree-centric worldview of the concepts in the Bible, resulting in a more dynamic translation? Or does it represent the development of the language and a deeper understanding of Biblical concepts over time? Does this reflect a change in Cree understanding of the world around them? In considering

FIGURE 5 (*opposite*). Different proximate participant.

these questions, it is important to keep in mind that mother-tongue speakers of Cree crafted both of the Cree translations that were examined here.

It must be admitted that this is a very short passage that has been examined in this way, and far more analysis of longer portions of the text is still required, along with discovering the perspectives of a wider range of mother-tongue Cree readers and indigenous theologians. When more of the Biblical text is examined, and more Cree speakers provide their own views on the subject, the tentative conclusions that have been drawn here may be confirmed or challenged, and more be said about the language of the legacy Cree Bible translation relative to contemporary Cree.

NOTES

1. The author would like to gratefully acknowledge the assistance and support of the Canadian Bible Society and the Naskapi Development Corporation. He also expresses his deep respect and gratitude to Cree speakers the Rev. Fred Evans (reader of the Western Cree Bible text) and Dolores Sand (reader of the contemporary Cree translation text) for their collaboration, encouragement, and support. The author also expresses his heartfelt thanks to David Pentland for his generosity in sharing access to the rare books in his collection that contributed to the author's understanding of the various editions of the legacy Cree text.
2. The reason that the publication date is sometimes listed as 1861 and sometimes as 1862 is because the Old Testament was published in 1861 and the New Testament in 1862, and these are the dates listed on the title pages of the respective sections. However, these two publications were almost always bound together in one volume.
3. The recorded audio files for these passages are provided as supplementary material on the Algonquian Conference website, along with the interlinear text display from the appendix (Filenames: PAC_50_Appendix_interlinear text display.pdf, Legacy_Cree_Syllabic_Text_and_Audio, Legacy_Cree_Roman_Text_and_Audio, Contemporary_Cree_Syllabic_Text_and_Audio, Contemporary_Cree_Roman_Text_and_Audio: https://algonquianconference.atlas-ling.ca/eng/supplementary-materials/).

REFERENCES

Aldred-Shull, Catherine. 2013. Rhetoric, Discourse and the Surplus of Meaning. MA thesis, McGill University. https://mcgill.academia.edu/CatherineAldredShull.

Banks, Joyce M. 1983. The Printing of the Cree Bible. *Papers of the Bibliographical Society of*

Canada XXII, pp. 14–24. Toronto: The Bibliographical Society of Canada. https://jps.library.utoronto.ca.

Dusenberry, Verne. 1962. The Montana Cree: A Study in Religious Persistence. *Acta Universitatis Stockholmiensis* 3. Stockholm: Almqvist and Wiksell.

Goddard, Ives. 1984. The Obviative in Fox Narrative Discourse. *Papers of the Fifteenth Algonquian Conference*, ed. by William Cowan, pp. 273–286. Ottawa: Carleton University Press.

Nichols, John. 1996. The Cree Syllabary. *The World's Writing Systems*, ed. by Peter Daniels, pp. 599–611. New York: Oxford University Press.

Peel, Bruce B. 1976. Thomas, Sophia (Mason). *Dictionary of Canadian Biography*, vol. 9. University of Toronto/Université Laval, 2003. http://www.biographi.ca/en.

Peel, Bruce B. 1987. Thomas, Thomas. *Dictionary of Canadian Biography*, vol. 6. University of Toronto/Université Laval, 2003. http://www.biographi.ca/en.

Peel, Bruce B. 2003. Catalogue ID Peel 3194. *Peel's Bibliography of the Canadian Prairies to 1953*. [3rd ed.], rev. and enlarged, compiled by Bruce B. Peel (1916–1998) (compiler), and ed. and compiled by Ernest Boyce Ingles and N. Merrill (Norman Merrill) Distad (1946–). Toronto: University of Toronto Press.

Pilling, James C. 1891. Bibliography of the Algonquian Languages. *Bureau of [American] Ethnology Bulletin*, vol. 13. Washington, DC: Government Printing Office.

Sieciechowicz, Krystyna Z. 1982. Steinhauer, Henry Bird. *Dictionary of Canadian Biography*, vol. 11. University of Toronto/Université Laval, 2003. http://www.biographi.ca/en.

Still, Gary N. 2013. John Colfield Sinclair (1830–1920). https://www.redriverancestry.ca.

Van Kirk, Sylvia. 1983. *Many Tender Ties: Women in Fur-Trade Society, 1670–1870*. Norman: University of Oklahoma Press.

Waiser, W. A. 2005. Mackay, John Alexander. *Dictionary of Canadian Biography*, vol. 15. University of Toronto/Université Laval, 2003. http://www.biographi.ca/en.

Wolfart, H. Christoph. 1973. Plains Cree: A Grammatical Study. *Transactions of the American Philosophical Society* 63:part 5.

Denominative and Quantitative Verbs of Possession in Plains Cree

H. C. Wolfart

In the study of Cree word formation, the various roles played by nominal and verbal elements have attracted the attention of grammarians from the outset. Beyond the practical concerns of missionaries and fur-traders, linguists have been fascinated above all by the appearance of patient nominals within the inflectional prefix-and-suffix structures surrounding the verb stem. Concentrating on the morphological and semantic aspects of NOUN INCORPORATION (e.g., Wolfart 1968) and on the stylistic and cultural salience of incorporative verbs based on highly transitive roots or stems (e.g., Wolfart 1997), they have largely ignored (with the notable exception of Dean Mellow) the syntactic links these nominal morphemes may display even while incorporated into an intransitive verb stem.

As Mellow has argued as long ago as 1989 (in a paper presented to the Algonquian Conference at St. John's, Newfoundland),[1] a verb stem based on the underlying stem *nôcih–* VTA 'pursue s.o.' and incorporating the medial constituent *-acaskw-* 'muskrat' (followed by the VAI stem final *-ê-*) may be construed with an external noun phrase made up of the demonstrative *ôhi*, inflected for the obviative third person, and the numeral *nîso* 'two'[2]:

(1) a. nôcihacaskwîw ôhi nîso.
nôcihacaskwî-w ôhi nîso
hunt.muskrat-VAI(-T)3IND this.3' NUM
'He hunts these two muskrats.' (Mellow 1990:256)

While the additional context may render his English illustration, *We will baby-sit the twins next weekend* (Mellow 1989:65), more idiomatic, Mellow's example (obtained by elicitation) corresponds in all relevant respects to sentences offered by Freda Ahenakew, for example,

(1) b. ê-mêk**iskwêw**êt mêrîwa.
ê=mêkiskwêwê-t mêrîw-a
CP=give.woman.away-VAI(-T)3CJ mêrîw--NA3'
'He gave Mary away.'

Most important, it is confirmed by the evidence of spontaneously produced sentences found in running text:

(1) c. . . . , êtikwê êkot êkwa awa nipâpâ kâ-mêk**iskwêw**êt niya.
êtikwê êkotê êkwa awa ni-pâpâ
presumably there then this.3 1PS-dad.NDA3

kâ=mêkiskwêwê-t niya
CP=give.woman.away-VAI(-T)3IND I/me
'. . . , it must have been there that my dad arranged to marry me off.' (MT)

The incorporative verb in both cases, (1b) and (1c), consists of the root *mêk-* 'release, give up' and the medial *-iskwêw-* 'woman' (followed by the VAI stem final *-ê-*); the personal name *mêriy* is inflected for the obviative third person, while the personal pronoun *niya* 'I, me' is indeclinable. Consider (1d):

(1) d. . . . ê-nitawi-nitom**iskwêw**êcik ôh ôskinîkiskwêwa., . . .
ê=nitawi=nitomiskwêwê-cik ôhi oskinîkiskwêw-a
CP=go.and=ask.for.woman's.hand-VAI(-T)3CJ this.3' young.woman-NA3'
'. . . they went to ask for the young woman's hand, . . .' (MT)

Here, the nominal morpheme *-iskwêw-* appears both in the incorporative verb 'seek a wife; sue for a woman', which is derived from the underlying VTA stem *nitom–* 'call s.o., invite s.o.', and in the full patient noun *oskinîkiskwêw–* 'young woman'.

Though mostly based on highly transitive stems, incorporative verbs are formally intransitive, belonging to the VAI stem class and inflected in accordance with the VAI paradigm. At the same time, their potential to be construed with a full patient noun phrase indicates a degree of ambivalence with respect to transitivity.

The present essay explores analogous patterns in a distinct part of Cree grammar: the syntactic properties of the nominal morphemes that figure in verbs of possession.[3] DENOMINATIVE VERBS OF POSSESSION, which are derived from dependent noun stems by the prefix *o(t)-* (or *w-* in the case of vowel-initial nouns) and the VAI suffix *-i-* , are mostly based on kin terms (and a few other dependent nouns, generally denoting intimate possessions). QUANTITATIVE VERBS OF POSSESSION show no overt sign of their derivation beyond the ordinary VAI final *-ê-*. With an initial constituent like *nîsw-* 'two' or *mihcêtw-* 'many' (but also less prototypical ones like *osk-* 'young, new' or *takahk-* 'beautiful') modifying a nominal medial, they are rather less common than their denominative counterpart. Stems of both types are prominently construed with quantity expressions.

At the same time, Cree relies heavily on quantity predicates. While grammatical number manifests itself in distinct suffixes for singular and plural shown by both nouns and verbs, the obviative endings are number-indifferent. Where precision is required, therefore, obviative noun forms like *nôtokwêsiwa* (3') 'old woman/women', *otêma* (3') 'his dog/dogs; his horse/horses' or *ôsisima* (3') 'her grandchild/grandchildren' may be supplemented by cardinal numbers or by quantifiers like *mihcêt* 'many' (or its diminutive *mihcêcis* 'quite a few'), as in (2):

(2) a. nawasonêw êh-mîhkawikiyit **nîso** otêmah.

nawasonêw	ê=mîhkawiki-yit	nîso	o-têm-a
choose.s.o.-VTA3-(3')IND	CP=be.fleet-VAI3'CJ	NUM	3PS-horse-NDA3'

'He picked out two of his swiftest horses.' (ET)

b. nôhkom ê-kî-otinât **mihcêt**

n-ôhkom-	ê=kî=otin-ât	mihcêt
1PS-grandmother-NDA3	CP=ASP=take.s.o.-VTA3-(3')CJ	many

ôsisima . . .
-ôsisim-a
3PS-grandchild-NDA3'

'My grandmother took in many of her grandchildren . . . ' (MT)

Cardinal numbers and quantifiers alike, both indeclinable, are matched by verb stems expressing their values; participial constructions employing these quantity predicates are also common in disambiguating obviative noun phrases:

(3) a. – ayis **nîsiyiwa** otânis[a] âwa –

ayis	nîsi-yiwa	o-tânis-a	awa
for	be.two-VAI3'IND	3PS-daughter-NDA3'	this.3

'– for he had two daughters –' (MT)

b. . . . , kâ-wâpamât oskinîkiskwêwa **ê-mihcêtiyit.**

kâ=wâpam-ât	oskinîkiskwêw-a	ê=mihcêti-yit
CP=see.s.o.-VTA3-(3')CJ	young.woman-NA3'	CP=be.numerous-VAI3'CJ

'. . . , there he saw a great many young women.' (ET)

Denominative Verbs of Possession and Their Syntactic Ambivalence

The vast majority of VAI verbs are intransitive (e.g., *nipâ–* 'sleep, be asleep' or *pimohtê–* 'walk along'), but some are transitive (e.g., *mêki–* 'give (it/him) away, release (it/him); give (her) in marriage') without showing overt morphological differentiation. Denominative verbs of possession are syntactically ambivalent.

Denoting elementary social relationships, denominative stems like *onâpêmi–* 'have a husband, be married (woman speaking); have (him/them) as one's husband/husbands' (cf. *-nâpêm–* NDA 'husband') and its counterpart *wîwi–* 'have a wife, be married (man speaking); have (her/them) as one's wife/wives' (cf. *-îw–* NDA 'wife') may be construed with or without a patient noun, as in the following:

(4) a. **kônâpêmin cî?**

k-onâpêmi-n cî

1-have(him/it as)husband-VAI(-T)1/2IND INTERROG

'Do you have a husband?' (ET)

b. nipê-wîwin.

ni-pê=wîwi-n

1-CISLC=have(her/it as)wife-VAI(-T)1/2IND

'I have come to take a wife.' (ET)

c. **êwakôw ana** kônâpêmin **kisêyiniw.**

êwako	ana	k-onâpêmi-n	kisêyiniw-
the.very.RES3	that.3	have(him/it as)husband-VAI(-T)1/2IND	old.man-NA3

'That old man you now have for your husband.' (ET)

d. wâpahkih ka-ntaw-wîwin

wâpan-kih	ka=nitawi=wîwi-n
be.dawn-VII0SUBJ	ASP=go.and=have(her/it as)wife-VAI(-T)1/2IND

nisîmak.

ni-sîm-ak

1PS-younger.sibling-NDA3p

'Tomorrow you will come to take my sisters to wife.' (ET)

The Early Texts also provide copious instances of two more of the denominative stems based on elementary kin terms. The most common is *ocawâsimisi–* 'have a child/children; give birth; have (him/them) as one's child/children; give birth to one's child/children' (cf. *-awâsimis–* NDA 'child'):

(5) a. êkwah ocawâsimisiw awa iskwêw.

êkwa	ocawâsimisi-w	awa	iskwêw-
then	give.birth(to.him/her/it)-VAI(-T)3IND	this.3	woman-NA3

'Then that woman gave birth.' (ET)

b. . . . , ocawâsimisiw **misacimosisah.**

ocawâsimisi-w misacimosis-a

give.birth(to.him/her/it)-VAI(-T)3 foal.DIM-NA3'

'. . . , she gave birth to a foal.' (ET)

The inherent polysemy of this stem is often resolved by an adverbial such as *âsay* 'already' or a temporal phrase, as shown in (5d):

(5) c. **âsay** ocawâsimisiwak nâpêsisah;

âsay ocawâsimisi-wak nâpêsis-a

already have(him/her/it as)child-VAI(-T)3pIND boy-NA3'

tahkopisoyiwa.

tahkopiso-yiwa

be.swaddled-VAI3'CJ

'By this time they had a little boy; he was still in the mossbag.' (ET)

d. kêkâc êsah êh-wâpaniyik, ocawâsimisiw

kêkâc êsa ê=wâpan-iyik ocawâsimisi-w

almost reportedly CP=be.dawn-VII0'CJ give.birth(to.him/her/it)-VAI(-T)3

aw oskinîkiskwêw.

awa oskinîkiskwêw-

this.3 young.woman-NA3

'When dawn had almost come, the young woman bore her child.' (ET)

Another common verb of this type is *osîmi–* 'have a younger sibling; have (him/them) as a/one's younger sibling/siblings' (cf. *-sîm–* NDA 'younger sibling') along with the corresponding diminutive *osîmisi–*:

(6) a. miywêyihtam
miywêyiht-amw
be.glad(about.it)-VTI3-0/0p IND

êh-osîmisit.
ê=osîmisi-t
CP=have(him/her/it as)younger.sibling.DIM-VAI(-T)3 CJ
'He was glad that he had a little brother.' (ET)

b. **ôhi nâpêwa** osîmiw
ôhi nâpêw-a osîmi-w
this.3' man-NA3' have(him/her/it as)younger.sibling-VAI(-T)3IND

aw îskwêw.
awa iskwêw-
this.3 woman-NA3
'The men were the younger brothers of the woman.'
[lit., 'the woman had the men as her younger brothers'] (ET)

Remarkably, however, other elementary kinship terms do not appear at all in the Early Texts, notably such pairs as *otânisi–* 'have a daughter/daughters; have (her/them) as a/one's daughter/daughters' and *okosisi–* 'have a son/sons; have (him/them) as a/one's son/sons' or the corresponding grandmother/grandfather terms *oyôhkomi–* and *omosômi–*. Even the parental terms *oyokâwi–* and *oyohtawî–* are extremely rare.

Beyond kin terms, the same derivational pattern is used for intimate possessions, for example, *otêmi–* 'have a dog or horse; have (him/them) as a/one's dog/dogs or horse/horses' (cf. *-têm–* NDA 'dog; horse') or *otihkomi–* 'have a louse/lice; have (him/them) as a/one's louse/lice' (cf. *ihkw–* NA 'louse' and the corresponding possessive *-ihkom–* 'one's louse'), as in the following:

(7) a. **wâkayôs-ah** otêmiw iskwêw.
wâkayôs-a otêmi-w iskwêw-
bear-NA3' have(him/her/it as)beast.of.burden-VAI(-T)3IND woman-NA3
'The woman had a bear as her beast of burden.' (ET)

b. . . . , nanâtohk maci-pisiskiwak, . . . , **êyakonih**

nanâtohk	maci=pisiskiw-ak	êwakoni
various	evil=animal-NA3p	the.very.RES3'

êh-otihkomit	awa.
ê=otihkomi-t	awa
CP=have(him/her/it as)louse-VAI(-T)3 CJ	this.3

'. . . , all the different evil animals, . . . , these he had as lice.' (ET)

Quantitative Verbs of Possession

As roots, numerals and quantifiers like *nîsw-* 'two' or *mihcêtw-* 'many' are restricted to serving as the initial constituent of a stem. With a nominal medial, such as *-iskwêw-* 'woman' or *-astimw-* 'dog; horse', and the ordinary VAI final *-ê-*, such quantity-initial stems display the constructional meaning of verbs of possession, as in *nîsôskwêwê–* 'have two women, have two wives' or *mihcêtastimwê–* 'have many horses'.

Whether viewed as roots or as initial constituents, numerals and quantifiers like *nîsw-* 'two' or *mihcêtw-* 'many' could not be considered transitive or agentive by any definition, and the verbs in which they appear do not show any overt sign of their formation as verbs of possession; however, their sense is clearly transitive, as in the following:

(8) a. wîwa nayêstaw nistiwak,

w-îw-a	nayêstaw	nisti-wak
3PS-wife-NDA3'	only	be.three-VAI3pIND

êh-**nîsôskwêwêt.**
ê=nîsôskwêwê-t
CP=have.two.wives-VAI3CJ
'With his wives, there were only three, for he had two wives.'
[lit., 'they were three, he and his wives, him having two wives'] (ET)

b. "ninôhtê-**nîsôskwêwân**, -**nistôskwêwân** ahpô,"

ni-nôhtê=nîsôskwêwâ-n [anacolouthon]=nistôskwêwâ-n ahpô
1-DESID=have.two.wives-VAI1/2IND =have.three.wives-VAI1/2 IND even

nititâwak, . . .
nit-it-âwak
say.thus.to.s.o.-VTA1-3p IND
'"I want to have two wives, or even three wives," I said to them, . . . ' (MT)

These quantitative stems are prototypical of nondenominative verbs of possession, but the same construction also appears in parallel stems (perhaps to be called QUALITATIVE VERBS OF POSSESSION) built on other common roots such as *osk-* 'young, new' or *takahk-* 'nice, beautiful', for example, *oskiskwêwê–* VAI 'have a new wife, be newly married' or *takahkôskwêwê–* VAI 'have a beautiful wife'.

In none of the preceding instances is the verb construed with an external patient nominal. It must be kept in mind, however, that we lack detailed phonetic–phonological studies of Cree phrase structure that might allow us to discriminate between patient nouns and supplementary nouns belonging to a subsequent clause. Even then, of course, indeterminacy may remain, classically illustrated in sentences structured by repeated quotative phrases. In the following example, the segmentation by quotative *nititâw* 'I said to him' (contextually rendered as 'I said to them') suggests that the obviative noun form *oskinîkiskwêwa* 'a young woman', which otherwise might well have been interpreted as a patient noun, may be nothing more than an afterthought:

(8) c. || . . . , mitoni awa kisêyiniw, <u>nititâw</u>,

mitoni awa kisêyiniw- nititâw
very this.3 old.man-NA3 say.thus.to.s.o.-VTA1-3IND

|| ê-**oskiskwêwêt**, <u>nititâw</u>,
ê=oskiskwêwê-t nititâw,
CP=have(her/it as)new.wife-VAI(-T)3CJ say.thus.to.s.o.-VTA1-3IND

|| mitoni **oskinîkiskwêwa**, nititâw.
mitoni   oskinîkiskwêw-a   nititâw
very   young.woman-NA3'   say.thus.to.s.o.-VTA1-3IND
|| '. . . , this very old man, I said to them,
|| he had a new wife, I said to them,
|| a very young woman, I said to them.' (MT)

Another prominent set of stems illustrating this type is that built on the medial *-ôs-* 'offspring; have offspring' (and always with the VAI final *-ê-*), which is not restricted to female referents, as shown next:

(9) a. êkwa ê-kî-**mihcêtôsêt** miton âna niciwâmiskwêw.
êkwa   ê=kî=mihcêtôsê-t   miton   âna   ni-ciwâmiskwêw-
then   CP=ASP=have.many.children-VAI3CJ   very   that.3   1PS-sister.in.law-NDA3
'And that sister-in-law of mine really had many children.' (MT)

b. wîst êkwa **mihcêtôsêw** nikosis,
wîsta   êkwa   mihcêtôsê-w   ni-kosis-
he.too.EMPH   then   have.many.children-VAI3IND   1PS-son-NDA3

âh-oyôsisimiw, . . .
âh-oyôsisimi-w
RED-have(him/her/it as)grandchild-VAI(-T)3IND
'Now that son of mine, too, has many children, he is having grandchildren, . . .' (MT)

The next example illustrates the common pattern of verbs of possession appearing in parallel clauses, with the second amplifying the first:

(9) c. . . . , êkwa ê-**pêyakôsêcik** êsa, môy
êkwa   ê=pêyakôsê-cik   êsa   namôya
then   CP=have.one.child-VAI3pCJ   reportedly   NEG

ê-misikitiyit nâpêsisa ê-ayâwâcik, . . .
ê=misikiti-yit   nâpêsis-a   ê=ayâw-âcik
CP=be.big-VAI3'CJ   boy-NA3'   CP=have.s.o.-VTA3p-(3')CJ
'. . . , and they reportedly had an only child, they had a little boy who was not very old, . . .' (MT)

Again, while quantity expressions seem to be most common, verbs of this type are not limited to numerals and quantifiers; a stem like *takahkôsê–* VAI 'have a beautiful child, have beautiful children', for example, leaves the number of children open.

It needs to be emphasized that these stems, called QUANTITATIVE VERBS OF POSSESSION mainly for ease of reference, are entirely distinct—despite their "transitive sense"—from the canonical type of incorporative stems with their explicitly transitive initial constituent.

The case is most clearcut in stems built on fully transitive primary stems, for example, *kanawêyimiskwêwê–* VAI 'look after one's wife, guard one's (young) women', cf. *kanawêyim–* VTA 'keep s.o., look after s.o., take care of s.o.; guard s.o. closely'; *kîwêhtahiskwêwê–* VAI 'take a woman/women home, bring a wife back', cf. *kîwêhtah–* VTA 'take s.o. back, take s.o. home'; *wîcêwiskwêwê–* VAI 'have a woman/women along, be accompanied by one's wife', cf. *wîcêw–* VTA 'join s.o., get along with s.o., live with s.o.'; or *wanihastimwê–* VAI 'lose one's horse/horses', cf. *wanih–* VTA 'lose s.o.'; and *pamihastimwê–* VAI 'drive the horses, drive the team', cf. *pamih–* VTA 'tend to s.o., look after s.o.; guide s.o.'

In root-initial stems, the transitive quality may be less striking but still unmistakeable; the root *nôt-* 'hunt, seek to obtain', for example, appears beside the VTA stem *nôcih–* in *nôtiskwêwê–/nôcihiskwêwê–* VAI 'pursue a woman/women, court a woman' and in *nôtacaskwê–/nôcihacaskwê–* VAI 'hunts muskrats' or *nôcikinosêwê–* VAI 'get fish, be engaged in fishing'; and the root *mêk-* 'give away, release' is found not only in *mêkiskwêwê–* VAI 'give a woman in marriage; give (her) in marriage' or *mêkastimwê–* VAI 'give away a horse/horses' but also in the stem *mêki–* VAI 'give (it/him) away, release (it/him); give (her) in marriage', which is freely construed with patient noun phrases.

External Quantification with Incorporative Stems

The classic case of incorporative verbs, their transitivity attenuated and ambivalent, being construed with external noun phrases provides the analytical context for a close-grained study of verbs of possession and their syntactic links. To the illustrations given in the introduction of nouns and personal pronouns let us now add the quantifier *misahkamik* 'a great many, in great number':

(10) a. **misahkamik pêtastimwêw.**
misahkamik pêtastimwê-w
in.great.numbers bring.horse-VAI3IND
'She brought a great troop of horses.' (ET)

The incorporative stem combines the initial *pêt-* 'bring hither' with the medial constituent *-astimw-* 'dog, horse' and the VAI final *-ê-*: *pêtastimwê–* VAI 'bring one's horse/horses'.

The incorporated nominal may also be linked, in weak cross-reference, to the agent or patient of another verb:

(10) b. kî-nipahik ê-kakwê-wâpamâwasot.
kî=nipah-ik ê=kakwê=wâpamâwaso-t
ASP=kill.s.o.-VTA(3')-3IND CP=CONAT=be.delivered.of.one's.child-VAI3CJ
'As she was trying to give birth, the child killed her.' (MT)

In *wâpamâwaso–* VAI 'give birth to one's child' the underlying stem *wâpam–* VTA 'see s.o.' is combined with the medial-final constituent *-âwaso-* 'child/children'; the preverb is *kakwê* 'try to'. The proximate agent (3) of the inflected form *ê-kakwê-wâpamâwasot* agrees with the proximate patient (3) of the verb form *kî-nipahik* 'she/he (3') killed her (3)', while the obviative agent (3') of the transitive verb is cross-referenced with the incorporated nominal *-âwaso-* 'child/children'. Such complex sentences are rare but sufficient to establish the pattern of covert cross-reference.

The presence of external quantifiers with incorporative stems is characteristic of the rhetorical figure of CONTRASTIVE PARALLELISM, with the contrast expressed either in the quantifiers or in the patient nominals of the two clauses:

(11) a. || ê-pê-kitimâkisit êwakw âna

ê=pê=kitimâkisi-t êwako ana

CP=CISLC=be.pitiable-VAI3IND the.very.RES3 that.3

nisîmis,

ni-sîmis-

1PS-younger.sibling.DIM-NDA3

|| **iyikohk** ê-pê-oh-~-**ohpikinâwasot,**

iyikohk ê=pê=oh-~-ohpikinâwaso-t

QUANT CP=CISLC=raise.child-VAI3CJ

|| êkwa âsamîn ôma, **ôsisima iyikohk**

êkwa âsamîna ôma -ôsisim-a iyikohk

then once.again FACT 3PS-grandchild-NDA3' QUANT

kâ-~ kâ=pamihât wîsta.

kâ-~ kâ=pamihât wîsta

CP=take.care.of.s.o.-VTA3-(3')CJ she.too.EMPH

|| 'She has had a rough life, that younger sister of mine,

|| having raised so many children all along,

|| and now once again she looks after so many of her grandchildren.' (MT)

The repetition of *iyikohk* 'so much, to such a degree, to such an extent' highlights the contrast between *ôsisima* 'her grandchild/grandchildren' in the second clause and the incorporated nominal *-âwaso-* 'child/children' in the first. The initial of the incorporative stem *ohpikinâwaso–* VAI 'raise one's child/children' is highly transitive (though only sparsely attested as an independent stem, *ohpikin–* VTA 'raise s.o. by hand'), as is *pamih–* VTA 'tend to s.o., look after s.o.'

The same contrastive pattern is implemented by the verb *tahkonâwaso–* VAI 'hold one's child/children, carry one's child/children' as matched against *sipwêhtah–* VTA 'take s.o. away, leave with s.o.' but without either the nominal or the full noun being repeated:

(11) b. || . . . **ê-pimitisahoskik kicawâsimisak,**
ê=pimitisahw-iskik kic-awâsimis-ak
CP=follow.behind.s.o.-VTA3p-2CJ 2PS-child-NDA3p

|| **âtiht** ê-tahkon**âwaso**yan;
âtiht ê=tahkonâwasoyan
QUANT CP=carry.child.on.arm-VAI(-T)2CJ

|| **kahkiyaw** ê-sipwêhtahacik.
kahkiyaw ê=sipwêhtah-acik
QUANT CP=depart.taking.s.o.along-VTA2-3pCJ
|| '. . . your little children followed behind you,
|| while you carried some of them in your arms;
|| you took all of them with you.' (MT)

Instead, the sentence is dominated by the preceding full noun *kicawâsimisak* 'your children' (with the plural ending *-ak*), resumed in its incorporated synonym *-âwaso-* 'child/children' in the first clause and in the second singular-on-third plural ending *-acik* in the second. The contrast thus resides in the contraposed quantifiers *âtiht* 'some' and *kahkiyaw* 'all'.

External Quantification with Verbs of Possession

Denominative verbs of possession are by preference construed with numeral adverbs, as in:

(12) a. **nistwâw êh-onahâhkisîmit, . . .**
nistwâw ê=onahâhkisîmi-t
NUM.ADV CP=have(him/it as)son.in.law-VAI(-T)3CJ
'Three sons-in-law he has had, . . . '
[lit., 'three times he has had a son-in-law'] (ET)

b. . . . , âta wiya namôy **mihcêtwâw**

âta wiya namôya mihcêtwâw

although.EMPH NEG NUM.ADV

nôh-pê-taw-~ nôh-pê-**otawâsimisin**, . . .

n-ôh=pê=taw-~ n-ôh=pê=otawâsimisi-n

1-ASP=CISLC=have(him/her/it as)child-VAI(-T)1/2 IND

'. . . , although I did not bear many children, . . . '

[lit., 'although I have not given birth to a child many times'] (MT)

In fact, this is the only type of syntactic elaboration to be documented in the Early Texts for denominative verbs. In particular, they do not appear with such common quantifiers as *âtiht* 'some' or *mihcêt* 'many'.[4]

The Modern Texts show external quantification by ordinals and the corresponding quantifiers freely occurring with possessive verbs, for example:

(13) a. êkwa **nîso** mîna kî-**otânisiwak**.

êkwa nîso mîna kî=otânisi-wak

then NUM also ASP=have(her/it as)daughter-VAI(-T)3pIND

'They also had two daughters.' (MT)

b. **mihcêcis** ôma mitoni kî-**otawâsimisiwak**,

mihcêcis ôma mitoni kî=otawâsimisiwak

QUANT.DIM FACT very ASP=have(him/her/it as)child-VAI(-T)3pIND

cî?

cî?

INTERROG

'They really had quite a few children, eh?' (MT)

This less restricted pattern even extends to independent (and inanimate) stems like *wîhowin–* 'name' as the underlying noun:

(13) c. . . . , **êkwa aya nîso kî-owîhowiniw**, . . .

êkwa aya nîso kî=owîhowini-w

then HES NUM ASP=have(it as)name-VAI(-T)3IND

'. . . , and he had two names, . . . ' (MT)

A denominative verb of possession with external quantification is often paralleled by another construed with a full noun phrase:

(13) d. || – **pêyak kî-omisiwak**. [. . .]

pêyak kî=omisiwak

NUM ASP=have(her/it as)older.sister-VAI(-T)3pIND

|| **êkoni anihi** ê-kî-**omisicik**, . . .

êkoni anihi ê=kî=omisi-cik

the.very.RES3' that.3' CP=ASP=have(her/it as)older.sister-VAI(-T)3pCJ

|| '– they had one older sister. [. . .]

|| She was their older sister, . . . '

[lit., 'they had that one as their older sister'] (MT)

With quantitative verbs of possession, it is the initial constituent that is subject to modification, including further quantification:

(14) a. . . . , êkonik mîna ê-kî-**pêyakôsêcik** aniki **piko**.

êkonik mîna ê=kî=pêyakôsê-cik aniki piko

the.very.RES3p also CP=ASP=have.one.child -VAI3pCJ that.3p only

'. . . , they also had only one child.' (MT)

Although postpositional *piko* 'only' usually modifies the immediately preceding constituent, the discontinuous *êkonik aniki* 'these, they' clearly is not affected by it; instead, *piko* has scope either over the numeral morpheme *pêyakw-* 'one' as the initial constituent of the complex stem, or over the entire possessive stem *pêyakôsê–* VAI 'have one child'.

The parallelism between the two parts of a sentence need not be contrastive; in the next example, the first instance of *ayiwâk* 'more' modifies the stem *kitimâkêyim–* VTA 'feel pity toward s.o., be kind to s.o., love s.o.', while the scope of the second one is indeterminate, as in the previous example:

(14) b. . . . , **ayiwâk** êwako ê-kî-kitimâkêyimit, mîn
ayiwâk êwako ê=kî=kitimâkêyim-it mîna
QUANT the.very.RES3 CP=ASP=tenderly.love.s.o.-VTA3-1CJ also

âyiwâk êwako ê-kî-**mihcêtôsêt**.
ayiwâk êwako ê=kî=mihcêtôsê-t
QUANT the.very.RES3 CP=ASP=have.many.children-VAI3CJ
'. . . , she especially used to love me, and she also had more children [than her sister].' (MT)

Since *ayiwâk* 'more' most often occurs alone rather than as a modifier, this sentence is remarkable in showing it in construction with *mihcêtôsê–* VAI 'have many children'.

In the case of *iyikohk* 'so much, to such a degree, to such an extent', too, we find the same indeterminacy with respect to the initial constituent *takahk-* 'beautiful' or the stem as a whole, *takahkôskwêwê–* VAI 'have a beautiful wife':

(14) c. â, takahkêyihtamâsow **iyikohk**
â takahkêyihtamâso-w iyikohk
well be.pleased.with.oneself-VAI3 IND QUANT

ê-**takahkôskwêwêt**.
ê=takahkôskwêwê-t
CP=have.beautiful.wife-VAI3 CJ
'Well, he was pleased with himself to have such a beautiful wife.' (MT)

As these illustrations show, denominative and quantitative verbs of possession alike are subject to external restriction, amplification, or emphasis.

Quantity of the Agent, Quantity of the Patient

Quantitative verbs of possession, though both inflectionally and derivationally part of the (prototypically intransitive) VAI class, predicate the quantity of the patient. The opposite holds for the vast majority of other intransitive verb types based on quantitative roots; such verbs, which are typically stative, specify the quantity of the agent, for example:

(15) a. *nîswatwêmo–* VAI 'cry as two':

…, mâtow mâka wîsta, ni**nîswatwêmo**nân êkwa, …

mâto-w	mâka	wîsta	ni-nîswatwêmo-nân	êkwa
cry-VAI3.IND	but	he.too.EMPH	cry.as.two-VAI1pIND	then

'…, but he cried, too, now we both cried together, …' (MT)

b. *nîswastê–* VII 'lie as two, lie side by side':

nîswastêwa anihi mâna miyawa, …

nîswastê-wa	anihi	mâna	miyaw-a
lie.as.two-VII0pIND	that.0p	habitually	body-NI0p

'The two bodies lie buried next to each other, …' (MT)

The most common stems of this type, such as *nîswapi–* VAI 'sit as two', *nîsôhkwâmi–* VAI 'sleep as two, sleep side by side', or *nîsopayi–* VAI 'ride as two', are built on simple intransitive finals like *-api-* 'sit' and *-hkwâmi-* 'sleep' or on freely recurring secondary finals like *-payi-* 'move, ride'.[5]

Verb stems built on quantitative roots and transitive finals, by contrast, for the most part specify the quantity of the patient, as in the following:

(16) a. *nîswaskinah–* VTA 'fit in two of s.o., carry two of s.o. (e.g., pieces of bannock); carry twins':

ê-**nîswaskinah**ât maskimotihk

ê=nîswaskinah-ât	maskimot-ihk
CP=carry.two.of.s.o.-VTA3-(3')CJ	bag-NI LOC

'She carried two [bannocks] in a bag'(MT)

b. *nîswakwât–* VTA 'snare s.o. as two':

…, niwî-nipahi-koskwêyihtên

ni-wî=nipahi=koskwêyiht-ên

1-ASP=to.death=be.surprised(about it)-VTI1-0/0pIND

ê-**nîswakwât**akik.

ê=nîswakwât-akik

CP=snare.two.of.s.o.-VTA1-3pCJ

'…, I'd be absolutely shocked to snare two of them [weasels] together.' (MT)

c. *nîsokwât–* VTI 'sew two of s.t. together':

. . . , êkwa êkoni ê-nâh-**nîsokwât**ahk,

êkwa	êkoni	ê=nâh-nîsokwât-ahk
then	the.very.RES0p	CP=RED-sew.together.two.of.s.t.-VTI3-0/0pCJ

ê-nâh-napokwâtahk anihi, . . .

ê=nâh-napokwât-ahk	anihi
CP=RED-sew.s.t.in.pairs-VTI3-0/0pCJ	that.0p

'. . . , and she sewed two of these together, sewing them in pairs, . . . ' (MT)

As in many other sections of the derivational system, it is not uncommon to find VTA and VTI stems paired:

(17) a. *pêyakwahpit–* VTA 'tie s.o. in as one, harness s.o. (horse) singly':

wa tâpwê êkwa ê-**pêyakwahpit**ak misatim, . . .

wa	tâpwê	êkwa	ê=pêyakwahpit-ak	misatimw-
now	truly	then	CP=harness.one.of.s.o.-VTA1-3 CJ	horse-NA3

'So then sure enough I hitched up a horse, . . . ' (MT)

b. *nîswahpit–* VTI 'tie two of s.t. together':

ê-kî-**nîswahpit**ahkik mân ôhi oskana, . . .

ê=kî=nîswahpit-ahkik	mâna	ôhi	oskan-a
CP=ASP=tie.together.two.of.s.t.-VTI3p-0/0pCJ	habitually	this0p	bone-NI0p

'They used to tie the bones together in pairs, . . .' (MT)

(18) a. *pêyakwaskat–* VTA 'leave one of s.o. behind, leave s.o. behind alone':

êkota êkwa, iyinitw êkw

êkota	êkwa	iyinito	êkwa
at.that.point	then	simply	then

ê-ati-**pêyakwaskat**iht nikâwiy, . . .

ê=ati=pêyakwaskat-iht	ni-kâwiy
CP=TRANSLC=leave.behind.one.of.s.o.-VTA INDF-3CJ	1PS-mother-NDA3

'At that point now my mother was simply left there by herself, . . . ' (MT)

b. *pêyakwaskat–* VTI 'leave one of s.t. behind, leave s.t. behind alone':

. . . , kîspin kâ-wî-**pêyakwaskat**amâhk anima

kîspin	kâ=wî=pêyakwaskat-amâhk	anima
if	CP=ASP=leave.behind.one.of.s.t.-VTI1p-0/0PCJ	that(0)

nayahcikan, . . .

nayahcikan
sacred.bundle-NI0

'. . . , if we were going to leave that sacred bundle unattended, . . . ' (MT)

While these examples all illustrate concrete meanings, the same pattern also holds for more abstract transitive finals, as shown here:

(19) a. *nîsonikê–* VAI-T 'use two at a time; use two pails':

êkwa, kwâpikêtân, nâh-**nîsonikê**tân, . . .

êkwa	kwâpikê-tân	nâh-nîsonikê-tân
then	fetch.water-VAI21IMVE	RED-use.two-VAI21IMVE

'Now then, let us fetch water, let us each get two pails of water, . . . ,' (MT)

The intransitive stem *nîsonikê–* is secondarily derived by the detransitive VAI final *-ikê-* (action on a general patient) from the stem *nîson–* VTA 'hold s.o. (e.g., pail) by hand', which is based on the transitive final *-n-* 'by hand'; like other abstract finals, *-n-* is often used in an attenuated sense, for example, *nitonito–* VAI 'dance in pairs'.

In modern usage, the primary stem *pêyakoh–* VTA 'treat s.o. as the only one, deal exclusively with s.o.' also has the extended meaning 'be faithful to s.o.':

(19) b. . . . , ê-**pêyakoh**itân ôma, . . .

ê=pêyakoh-itân	ôma
CP=have.s.o.uniquely-VTA1-2CJ	FACT

'. . . , in fact I am being faithful to you, . . . ' (MT)

While the transitive final *-h-* often shows causative force, especially in secondary derivation, its function in primary word formation often appears to be little more than to define the stem class.

Supported by frequencies in the texts and in the lexicon alike, these examples suggest an ergative pattern: In general, the quantity root is construed to identify the agent in intransitive and the patient in transitive stems.

In transitive stems, however, the quantity root is not in fact restricted to identifying the patient. A small set of verbs combining a quantity root with the VTA final *-hkaw-* 'engage with s.o.; tackle s.o., attack s.o.' constitutes a prominent exception to the general pattern:

(20) a. *nîsôhkaw–* VTA 'be two in attacking s.o.'

(20) b. *pêyakôhkaw–* VTA 'attack s.o. single-handedly'

The semantic scope of this VTA final is broad and by no means limited to confrontation; cf. Lacombe's entry <nisokkawew> 'he comes to his assistance' (1874). For the most part, however, stems showing this final with numeral and quantifier roots seem to refer to combat; note also, for example, *mâmawôhkaw–* VTA 'attack s.o. as a group, go at s.o. in full numbers' with the root *mâmawi-* 'as a group, in full numbers'. The best illustration of the agent-specified set has two (parallel) cousins fighting for their lives with a *pâkahkos* or Bony Specter:

(20) c. **nîsôhkawêwak**, êh-mâsîhâcik.

nîsôhkawê-wak	ê=mâsîh-âcik
be.two.in.attacking.s.o.-VTA3p-(3')IND	CP=wrestle.with.s.o.-VTA3p-(3')CJ

'The two attacked it and wrestled with it.'
[lit., 'the two attacked him, wrestling with him'] (ET)

With the VTA final *-yaw-* 'win over s.o.; shoot s.o.', by contrast, the quantity verbs specify the patient:

(21) a. *nîsoyaw–* VTA 'shoot two of s.o.'
b. *mihcêtoyaw–* VTA 'shoot many of s.o.'

The context of choice for the patient-quantified set is the proverbial wish of Plains Cree hunters to bring down two or more game birds with a single shot, but the same verb may also refer to a warrior firing at two of his enemies:

(21) c. . . . , êwakoni pâskiswêw, ê-sâkowêt.

êwakoni	pâskisw-êw	ê=sâkowê-t
the.very.RES3'	shoot.at.s.o.-VTA3-(3')IND	CP=whoop-VAI3CJ

nîsoyaw-êw.
nîsoyawêw
shoot.two.of.s.o.-VTA3-(3')IND
'. . . , he shot at those and gave a whoop. He hit two of them.' (ET)

d. êkotah ninîsoyawâwak.

êkota	ni-nîsoyaw-âwak
at.that.point	1-shoot.two.of.s.o.-VTA1-3pIND

'That was when I shot two of them.'
[lit., 'at that point I shot two of them'] (ET)

It seems remarkable that the contrasting sets of agent-quantity *-hkaw-* and patient-quantity *-yaw-* stems represent a single semantic field, of combat. (Until analogous verbs from other domains can be identified, the present pairs also stand out for the high transitivity typical of verbs of striking, prominently used to illustrate voice paradigms in the earliest grammars of Greek and Arabic.)

If such pairs are rare in Cree, the syntactic and semantic properties of the exemplary *-hkaw-* : *-yaw-* pair are strikingly echoed by its cognates in Ojibwe and Meskwaki (graciously provided from their unpublished collections by John D. Nichols and Lucy Thomason, respectively).

(22) a. Ojibwe *niizhookaw–* VTA 'go at s.o. as a pair'
b. Ojibwe *niizhoonaw–* VTA 'shoot two of s.o.'

(23) a. Meskwaki *ni·šo·hkaw–* VTA 'deal with s.o. as a pair'
b. Meskwaki *ni·šo·če·naw–* VTA 'deal with s.o. as a pair'
(with *-eče·-* here as if 'lumped together')

Note also the parallel pair:

(24) a. Meskwaki *ča·ko·hkaw–* VTA 'all assail s.o.'
b. Meskwaki *ča·katenaw–* VTA 'shoot all of s.o. to pieces' (with *-at-* 'violently')

The corresponding agent-quantity form is also documented for Menominee:

(25) Menominee *ni·so·hkawɛwak* 'they both go at him' (Bloomfield 1975)

Most important, the lexical evidence of Meskwaki in (21a) and (21b) is splendidly corroborated by a sentential pair (also from Lucy Thomason's corpus):

(26) a. e·h=**ni·šo·hkawa**·wa·ci·='nini mahkwani. (Jim Peters)
'The pair of them tackled that bear.' (Lucy Thomason)

b. peno·ci=meko e·h=a·yahkwahte·ci e·h=na·**ni·šo·ce·nawa**·ci nenoso·hi. (Sam Peters)
'He kept shooting into the far distance, shooting two buffalos at once each time.' (Lucy Thomason)

The comparative evidence, in sum, demonstrates beyond any doubt that these pairs are neither accidental nor recent.

Style

This is not the place to discuss such thorny issues as the definition of quantity roots or the quantity interpretation of heavy reduplication. Let us at least note, however, that the stem *mâmawôhkaw–* VTA 'attack s.o. as a group, go at s.o. in full numbers' may well be taken as evidence that the root *mâmawi-* 'as a group, in full numbers' does indeed belong, however marginally, among the quantity roots (and that an analogous argument might perhaps be made for Meskwaki *ča·k-*). At the same time, the heavy reduplication in *pâh-pimw–* VTA 'shoot at s.o. distributively in time or space' also shows quantity being ascribed to the agent: The children will be shooting their arrows repeatedly and severally.

(27) atimwak ka-**mâmawôhkâkwak**; mîn awâsisak

atimw-ak	ka=mâmawôhkaw-ikwak	mîna	awâsis-ak
dog-NA3p	ASP=as.a.group.attack.s.o.-VTA3p-2IND	also	child-NA3p

ka-**pâh**-pimokwak.
ka=**pâh**-pimw-ikwak
ASP=RED-shoot.arrows.at.s.o.-VTA3p-2IND
'The dogs [as a pack] will set upon you; and the children will shoot at you.' (ET)

To have them appear in two parallel clauses, contrasting the collectivity of the dogs and the individuality of the children, splendidly illustrates the canons of Plains Cree rhetoric.

NOTES

1. Having challenged the validity of his experimental data at the conference, I was stunned, within a matter of days, to encounter textual examples in the course of my work with Freda Ahenakew. I welcome the opportunity, however belated, to repeat in print the retraction (and apologies) first offered in my Belcourt Lecture of 1997.
2. Unless otherwise indicated (mainly by square brackets), all sentential illustrations are cited from spoken texts, identified as ET for Early Texts (dictated to Bloomfield in 1925; cf. Bloomfield 1930, 1934) and MT for Modern Texts (published over the past three decades by Wolfart and Ahenakew; cf. F. Ahenakew ed. 1986; Vandall and Douquette 1987; Bear et al. 1992; Whitecalf 1993; Minde 1997; kâ-pimwêwêhahk/Kâ-Nîpitêhtêw 1998; A. Ahenakew 2000; kêkêk/Masuskapoe 2010; kâ-mimikwatowêt/Greyeyes 2014).

   Abbreviations are as follows: NA = animate noun, NDA = dependent animate noun, NDI = dependent inanimate noun, NI = inanimate noun, s.o. = someone, s.t. = something, VAI = animate intransitive verb, VAI-T = syntactically transitive verb of the VAI class, VII = inanimate intransitive verb, VTA = transitive animate verb, VTI = transitive inanimate verb; person-number-obviation categories: 3, 3p, 3', 2, 2p, 21, 1, 1p; stems are marked with a trailing en-dash, and compounds with an internal hyphen.

   The interlinear representation (line 2) of the text shows stems and affixes rather than individual morphemes. Matters of stem formation are discussed in the prose preceding and following the illustrations.

   In the interlinear definitions (line 3), the trailing hyphen of noun stems indicates their lexical status; the stem-final *-w-* of *misatimw-* 'horse', for instance, does not appear in the actually occurring form *misatim* (example 17a). A leading hyphen is employed in a form like *-ôsisim-a* 'her/his grandchild/grandchildren' (examples 2b, 11a), where the personal prefix *o-* coalesces with the stem-initial *-ô-*.

The compound boundary that defines preverbs and prenouns (cf. Wolfart 1973:sec. 6.5) is marked with the symbol =. For the morphophonological rules that govern the combination of morphemes within a stem cf. appendix A in Wolfart 1973.

The verb stems are identified as to their paradigmatic class quâ their syntactic and semantic potential rather than showing their actual manifestation in each case. Transitive stems of the VTA and VTI classes are glossed with 's.o.' and 's.t.', respectively, while those of the VAI-T class have the patient, which may be of either gender or number, indicated by 'her/him/it'.

The following additional abbreviations are used to elaborate on verb, noun, pronominal, and numeral forms; except for the latter, all particles are simply glossed. Boldface is used to highlight items being discussed; the symbol || indicates parallel clauses.

Verbal: ASP = aspectual preverb, CISLC = cislocative preverb, CJ = (changed) conjunct, CP = complementizer, CONAT = conative preverb, IMVE = imperative, IND = independent, INDF = indefinite agent, SUBJ = subjunctive conjunct, TRANSLC = translocative preverb.

Nominal and pronominal: LOC = locative, PS = possessor, RES = resumptive.

Elsewhere/passim: DIM = diminutive, EVID = evidential, FACT = factive particle, HES = hesitation particle, INTERROG = interrogative, NEG = negator, NUM = numeral, NUM.ADV = numeral adverb, QUANT = quantifier, QUANT.DIM = quantifier diminutive, RED = reduplication.

3. Thanks are due first and always to the generations of Cree speakers whose texts and comments constitute the empirical foundation of all linguistic analysis. This essay is part of a larger set, variously presented (and critically responded to, for which I am grateful) at the UBC Cree Linguistics Workshop (2008), the Centre d'Etudes des Langues Indigènes d'Amérique (CELIA-CNRS), Paris (2008), the Sixth International Conference on Construction Grammar, Prague (2010), the University of Lethbridge (2011) and the 50th Algonquian Conference, Edmonton (2018).
4. The internal syntax of stems, unfortunately, is not always transparent, and an analysis that depends heavily on translation is inherently problematic. Though the morphemes *-pipon(w)-* 'winter' and *-kât-* 'leg', for instance, are well documented, the constituency of *nîsopipon(w)ê–* VAI 'be two years old' and *nîsokâtê–* VAI 'be two-legged; walk upright on two legs' has not been reliably established. In the case of *nîsoyîhkâso–* VAI 'have two

names [lit., 'be doubly named']', phrases like *nîswayak isiyîhkâtêw* 'it has two names [lit., 'is doubly named']' may be taken as evidence that the relationship between the medial *-iyîhkâso-* (even without the usual *is*-initial) and the numeral root *nîsw-* is one of manner.

5. The record shows variation in the length of the preceding vowel: Besides *nîsôhkwâmi–* we also find *nîsohkwâmi-*. While this may simply be a case of surface variation before pre-aspirated stops, which is found widely in Plains Cree, the fact that the internal sandhi boundary also yields a long *-ô-* in *nîsôskwêwê–* VAI 'have two women, have two wives', *nistôskwêwê–* VAI 'have three women, have three wives', *takahkôskwêwê–* VAI 'have a beautiful wife', etc. might instead suggest a prefinal accretion involving *-w-*.

REFERENCES

Ahenakew, Alice. 2000. *âh-âyitaw isi ê-kî-kiskêyihtahkik maskihkiy/They Knew Both Sides of Medicine: Cree Tales of Curing and Cursing Told by Alice Ahenakew*, ed., trans., and with a glossary by H. C. Wolfart and Freda Ahenakew. Publications of the Algonquian Text Society. Winnipeg: University of Manitoba Press.

Ahenakew, Freda, ed. 1986. *kiskinahamawâkan-âcimowinisa/Student Stories*, written by Cree-speaking students, ed., trans., and with a glossary by Freda Ahenakew. Algonquian and Iroquoian Linguistics Memoir 2. Winnipeg.

Bear, Glecia, Irene Calliou, Janet Feitz, Minnie Fraser, Alpha Lafond, Rosa Longneck, and Mary Wells. 1992. *kôhkominawak otâcimowiniwâwa/Our Grandmothers' Lives as Told in Their Own Words*, told by Glecia Bear et al., ed. and trans. by Freda Ahenakew and H. C. Wolfart. Saskatoon: Fifth House Publishers.

Bloomfield, Leonard. 1930. *Sacred Stories of the Sweet Grass Cree*. National Museum of Canada Bulletin 60. Ottawa.

Bloomfield, Leonard. 1934. *Plains Cree Texts*. American Ethnological Society Publication 16. New York.

Bloomfield, Leonard. 1975. *Menomini Lexicon*, ed. by Charles F. Hockett. Milwaukee Public Museum Publications in Anthropology and History, 3. Milwaukee.

kâ-mimikwatowêt/William Greyeyes. 2014. The Travelling Companion, told by kâ-mimikwatowêt/William Greyeyes, ed. and trans. by H. C. Wolfart and Freda Ahenakew. H.C. Wolfart, Two Plains Cree Performances of a pre-Victorian Kunstmärchen, Appendix, pp. 177–215. *Anthropological Linguistics* 56(2):159–218.

kâ-pimwêwêhahk/Jim Kâ-Nîpitêhtêw. 1998. *ana kâ-pimwêwêhahk okakêskihkêmowina/The Counselling Speeches of Jim Kâ-Nîpitêhtêw*, ed., trans., and with a glossary by Freda Ahenakew and H. C. Wolfart. Publications of the Algonquian Text Society. Winnipeg:

University of Manitoba Press.

kêkêk/Cecilia Masuskapoe. 2010. *piko kîkway ê-nakacihtât: kêkêk otâcimowina ê-nêhiyawastêki* [There's Nothing She Can't Do: Kêkêk's Autobiography Published in Cree]. mitoni ê-âh-itwêt mâna Cecilia Masuskapoe, itasinahamiyiwa ôhi nîso, H.C. Wolfart êkwa Freda Ahenakew [Exactly as told by Cecilia Masuskapoe, in a critical edition by H.C. Wolfart and Freda Ahenakew]. Algonquian and Iroquoian Linguistics Memoir 21. Winnipeg.

Lacombe, Albert. 1874. *Dictionnaire de la langue des Cris*. Montréal: C.O. Beauchemin et Valois.

Mellow, Dean. 1989. A Syntactic Analysis of Noun Incorporation in Cree. MA thesis, McGill University.

Mellow, Dean. 1990. Asymmetries between Compounding and Noun Incorporation in Plains Cree. *Papers of the Twenty-first Algonquian Conference*, ed. by William Cowan, pp. 247–257. Ottawa: Carleton University.

Minde, Emma. 1997. *kwayask ê-kî-pê-kiskinowâpahtihicik/Their Example Showed Me the Way: A Cree Woman's Life Shaped by Two Cultures*, told by Emma Minde, ed., trans., and with a glossary by F. Ahenakew and H.C. Wolfart. Edmonton: University of Alberta Press.

Vandall, Peter, and Joe Douquette. 1987. *wâskahikaniwiyiniw-âcimowina/Stories of the House People*, told by Peter Vandall and Joe Douquette, ed., trans., and with a glossary by Freda Ahenakew. Publications of the Algonquian Text Society. Winnipeg: University of Manitoba Press.

Whitecalf, Sarah. 1993. *kinêhiyâwiwininaw nêhiyawêwin/The Cree Language is Our Identity: The La Ronge Lectures of Sarah Whitecalf*, ed., trans. and with a glossary by H. C. Wolfart and Freda Ahenakew. Publications of the Algonquian Text Society. Winnipeg: University of Manitoba Press.

Wolfart, H. C. 1968. Plains Cree Internal Syntax and the Problem of Noun Incorporation. Paper read at the 38th Internationaler Amerikanistenkongress, Stuttgart. [Subsequently published as Wolfart, H. C. 1971. Plains Cree Internal Syntax and the Problem of Noun Incorporation. *Verhandlungen des 38. Internationalen Amerikanistenkongresses* 3:511–518.]

Wolfart, H. C. 1973. *Plains Cree: A Grammatical Study*. Transactions of the American Philosophical Society, n.s., vol. 63, part 5. Philadelphia.

Wolfart, H. C. 1997. On Syntax and Style in Cree Noun Incorporation. The Belcourt Lecture, University of Manitoba.

CONTRIBUTORS

Irene Appelbaum is a professor of linguistics at the University of Montana in Missoula. Her research focuses on Ktunaxa language documentation and linguistics.

Amy Dianne Bergseth received her PhD in American Indian history at the University of Oklahoma in 2018. She focused on intertribal interactions and nation-building among the small Native American nations in northeastern Oklahoma. She obtained her master's in history from the University of Oklahoma and her bachelor's in history and American studies from Miami University, Oxford, Ohio.

Amy Dahlstrom is associate professor of linguistics at the University of Chicago. Her research deals with issues of morphology, syntax, and information structure in Meskwaki and Plains Cree.

Rose-Marie Déchaine is a faculty member in the Department of Linguistics at the University of British Columbia. Her research areas include Algonquian, Na-Dene, and Niger-Congo languages, with a focus on how syntax interfaces with other parts of the grammar. Her work on Algonquian covers topics such as nominal predication, verbal agreement, morpheme ordering, the morphosemantics of gender, the morphosyntax of pronouns, and the root lexicon.

Yvonne Denny lives in Eskasoni, Cape Breton, Nova Scotia, where she is a language mentor and home care worker.

Monique Dufresne is an associate professor at Queen's University, Kingston, Canada. A specialist in historical linguistics and the theory of change, she conducts research on the syntax and morphology of medieval French (based on corpus data) and has authored numerous articles on prepositions, particles, and aspect. Her current work on Algonquian and Iroquoian languages focuses on using her expertise in theoretical and corpus linguistics.

Dianne Friesen lives in Sydney, Cape Breton, Nova Scotia, where she studies the Mi'kmaq language and grammar. She is a PhD student in linguistics at the University of Victoria.

Lex Giesbrecht is a graduate student at the University of Alberta in the Department of Linguistics. Lex has been involved in linguistic research in North American Indigenous languages since 2014, and is dedicated to Indigenous language sustainability.

Ryan E. Henke is a PhD student at the University of Hawai'i at Mānoa and contributor to the Chisasibi Child Language Acquisition Study (CCLAS). He studies language acquisition, documentation, and revitalization. His in-progress dissertation focuses on the acquisition of nominal inflection in Northern East Cree by three children between the ages of two and six.

Sarah Hoffman graduated from the University of Manitoba in 2019 with an advanced bachelor's degree in Linguistics and is currently pursuing her master's in communication sciences and disorders. She was active in research and Algonquian studies during her undergraduate years and received an undergraduate research award in 2018.

Leila Inksetter worked as an archaeologist before undertaking a PhD in ethnohistory. She is interested in the dynamics of Algonquian cultural change in a colonial setting, including both historical aspects and contemporary outcomes.

She published *Initiatives et adaptations algonquines au XIXe siècle* in 2017. She is a professor with the Department of Sociology at Université du Québec à Montréal.

Bill Jancewicz is a member of SIL International and Wycliffe Bible Translators, and has served the Naskapi community in language development with his wife Norma Jean since 1988. He has worked with the Naskapi Development Corporation as a linguistics resource person since 1992, providing linguistic and technical support for Naskapi language development and training and facilitation in translation and literature production in the Naskapi community. He is co-editor of the *Naskapi Lexicon* (1994) and the *East Cree Lexicon: Eastern James Bay Dialects* (2004), and project coordinator for the Naskapi Legends and Stories series.

Jordan Lachler is the director of the Canadian Indigenous Languages and Literacy Development Institute (CILLDI) at the University of Alberta and an assistant professor in the Department of Linguistics. His work focuses on the documentation, revitalization, and long-term sustainability of Indigenous languages.

Mary Ann Naokwegijig-Corbiere has taught Nishnaabemwin, her mother tongue from growing up in Wikwemikong, Ontario, in the University of Sudbury's Indigenous Studies Department since 1989. Her research focuses on Nishnaabemwin curriculum and translation issues, as well as lexicography as applied to her language.

Will Oxford is an associate professor of Linguistics at the University of Manitoba. His research focuses on the morphosyntax of the Algonquian languages from comparative and theoretical perspectives.

Elizabeth Paul lives in Eskasoni, Cape Breton, Nova Scotia, where she works as a translator, orthography expert, and Mi'kmaw language curriculum builder for the Essissoqnikewey Siawa'sik-l'nuey Kina'matnewo'kuo'm (Eskasoni Immersion School).

Richard Preston has focused on James Bay Cree since 1963. See richardpreston.ca for further details.

Arlene Stevens lives in Eskasoni, Cape Breton, Nova Scotia, where she works as a translator and Mi'kmaw language curriculum builder for the Essissoqnikewey

Siawa'sik-l'nuey Kina'matnewo'kuo'm (Eskasoni Immersion School) and in the Mi'kmaw choir at church.

Barbara Sylliboy lives in Eskasoni, Cape Breton, Nova Scotia, where she works as a translator, language teacher, and Mi'kmaw language curriculum builder for the Essissoqnikewey Siawa'sik-l'nuey Kina'matnewo'kuo'm (Eskasoni Immersion School).

H. C. Wolfart is a professor emeritus of linguistics at Manitoba. He has long concentrated on the analysis of spoken texts. For Plains Cree, the results of this work include a variety of grammatical, lexical, historical, and literary studies, and, most importantly, a series of text editions prepared jointly with Freda Ahenakew.